CRUDE GENIUS

THE MAKING OF AN INTERNATIONAL OIL BARON

CRUDE GENIUS

THE MAKING OF AN INTERNATIONAL OIL BARON

 mosaicPRESS

Library and Archives Canada Cataloguing in Publication

Title: Crude genius: the making of an international oil baron : William H.McGarvey /
Gary May.

Names: May, Gary, 1951- author.

Identifiers: Canadiana (print) 20220173206 |
Canadiana (ebook) 20220174245 |

ISBN 9781771616409 (softcover) | ISBN 9781771616416 (PDF) |
ISBN 9781771616423 (EPUB) | ISBN 9781771616430 (Kindle)

Subjects: LCSH: McGarvey, William H. | LCSH: Businessmen—Canada—Biography. |
LCSH: Petroleum industry and trade. | LCGFT: Biographies.

Classification: LCC HD9560.5 .M39 2022 | DDC 338.7/6655092—dc23

Published by Mosaic Press, Oakville, Ontario, Canada, 2022.

MOSAIC PRESS, Publishers
www.Mosaic-Press.com
Copyright © Gary May 2022

Printed and bound in Canada.

ONTARIO ARTS COUNCIL
CONSEIL DES ARTS DE L'ONTARIO
an Ontario government agency
un organisme du gouvernement de l'Ontario

Funded by the Government of Canada
Financé par le gouvernement du Canada

Canadä

ONTARIO CREATES

MOSAIC PRESS
1252 Speers Road, Units 1 & 2, Oakville, Ontario, L6L 5N9
(905) 825-2130 • info@mosaic-press.com • www.mosaic-press.com

DEDICATION

For Charles Oliver Fairbank III, whose encouragement and assistance started me down this uncharted road.

CONTENTS

THE MCGARVEYS: A FOUR-

Edward McGarvey   m.   Sarah Gamble
1819-1900   1816-1892

Mary Augustus	William Henry	James	Ellen
1842-1912	1843-1914	1846-1911	1848-1917

Mary Augustus

m. Sydney
Vanalstyne
(1841-1930)

Children:
Edward
(1868-1953)

Ella Helena
(1875-??)

William Henry

m. Helena Idwega
Wesolowski
(1845-1898)
m. Eleanor Hamilton
(1877-??)

Children:
Nellie Edith
(1869-1882)

William Edward
(1871-1872)

Frederick James*
(1873-1963)
m. Margaret Bergheim (1877-1952)

Mary Helena "Mamie"
(1875-1961)
m. Eberhard Von Zeppelin (1869-1926)

Sarah Katie "Kate"
(1883-1934)
m. Erik Jurie Von Lavandal (1879-1917)

*Fred's Children:
-Leila Helena
(1902-1963)
-Molly
(1906-2002)

James

m. Julia Williams
(1857-1950)

Children:
Helena Mary
(1880-1959)

Ellen

m. George
Westland
(1834-1908)

Children:
Frank E.
(1874-1910)

William S.
(1875-1939)

Mabel Claire
(1877-1911)

GENERATION TALE

Albert	Edward Wesley	Thomas
1851-1925	1854-1896	1856-1893
m. Lucinda Jane	m. Annie McLeod	m. Louisa Taylor
Taylor	(1860-1908)	(1868-??
(1853-1923)		
	Children:	Children:
	Edward Allen	Nellie Louisa
	(1885-1953)	(1889-??)
	Albert Hugh	
	(1889-1924)	

William Henry McGarvey, 1910

INTRODUCTION

The development of the petroleum industry today provides the means for the satisfaction of the desire, which has existed among mankind from time immemorial, for more light, greater power, and accelerated motion.

William Henry McGarvey,
Vienna, 1910

When William McGarvey wrote the above words for a book on oil resources in the British Empire, he was reflecting on the preceding half century, on his own career, and on the remarkable creation of what had become the world's premier industry: petroleum. Much of the story of that creation had been written by McGarvey himself. Starting off as a shopkeeper and then a small-time oil driller in Ontario's Lambton County, he became a leader in the evolution of procuring oil, raising it up from a primitive act to a modern industry. It had all happened in just five decades.

When circumstances aligned, McGarvey left the Canadian oil fields and took his skills to Europe, one of a band of a few hundred Canadians who left their homeland over the course of about seventy years and became known as the Foreign Drillers. These skilled technicians of oil had learned their expertise the hard way, by trial and error, and then shared it in the great fields of the world: in Russia and Eastern Europe, Africa, the Middle East, Asia, Latin America and the United States.

William McGarvey was the most successful among their numbers. His was a fairy tale rise to the upper echelons of the international business world, a journey that made him one of Canada's earliest entrepreneurial success stories. By the turn of the twentieth century, McGarvey had made the Austro-Hungarian province of Galicia — now part of Poland and Ukraine — the third-largest oil-producing jurisdiction in the world and expanded his empire to Russia and Romania. He drilled for oil and refined it, manufactured equipment and built pipelines. He was among a handful of individuals responsible for bringing petroleum to the brink of ubiquity; the arrival of the Great War in 1914 would solidify its omnipresent hold on mankind.

As well as establishing his successful business, McGarvey was a giant in petroleum science and technology. He was crowned the Petroleum King of Austria, dubbed Europe's Rockefeller and called upon to advise the British government in the great debate over converting its naval fleet to oil fuel in preparation for the coming war.

The company McGarvey established and led never rose to the heights of John D. Rockefeller's Standard Oil, or the empires established by the Nobels and the Rothschilds. While always a smaller player by that measure, this son of an Irish immigrant was the keystone in a four-generation family saga that centred upon oil. His father started a business that catered to the early wildcatters who put down the roots of the industry in pre-Confederation Canada. His brothers and his son were his support system as he built his domain.

The women in his family were far more than passive beneficiaries of his success. Several of them were strong, proficient and accomplished individuals in their own right. William's first wife bridged the cultural and language gap he faced when they arrived in Galicia, and as a levelling influence, was crucial to McGarvey being welcomed into Polish Galician society. One of his daughters became the true matriarch of the family and struggled through two world wars to maintain her Austrian estate as the place the family was always welcomed into for refuge and regeneration. His two granddaughters became the link to the various branches of the family and the keepers of its archive.

This, then, is the story of a pioneer Canadian family that defied the odds to become an international success – and what became of them.

A note on spelling: "McGarvey" was the accepted spelling of the family name when William's ancestors arrived in Canada from Ireland. Once in Europe, however, the name was often spelled "MacGarvey", with the "a" in Mac. This is also how William frequently signed his own name. Sometimes it became "MacGawey" or just Garvey, and there were occasional other misspellings and interpretations that evolved in German and Polish. For the purposes of consistency, this book sticks to the original, straight-from-Ireland McGarvey, although in some direct quotations, variations will be found.

CHAPTER 1

THE SEEDS OF HIS SUCCESS

The Unfortunate Cow That Inspired An Empire

Billy McGarvey's father had handed him a big responsibility. Take the two cows to the market and get a good price for them. The boy, barely into his teen years, smiled to himself with pride. As he led the animals along the road from his family's home toward the Covent Garden Market in London, Ontario, Billy speculated what he might get for them. He imagined how it would feel when he stuffed the money carefully into his pockets and returned home to a hero's welcome. He would be a man.

The boy approached the tracks of the Great Western and his mind went to the stories he had heard people speaking of not long ago about the terrible rail disaster at Hamilton. A passenger train had gone off the track, plunging into a canal there. Of the one hundred passengers on board, nearly sixty had died in the icy waters. Despite the warmth of this day, Billy shivered at the thought.

Approaching the crossing, Billy heard an engine huffing in the distance and decided he had better be cautious. He would hold the animals back until the train passed. He held on tightly to their leads and his mind again turned to the cash he would be going home with. Billy imagined the big grin on his father's face when his eldest son handed it over.

Just as the train approached, one of the cows lunged backwards, spooked by the strange sound. It brushed against its companion, then further alarmed, it bolted forward, tugging the rope out of Billy's grip.

Billy moved quickly to snatch the rope back up but the cow, now fully panicked by the approaching engine, was too strong. It began to gallop and headed right for the tracks. Billy held on to the lead attached to the other animal and watched, horror-stricken, as the first unfortunate creature ran out in front of the train. The boy cringed at the terrible sickening sound as the cow was struck and, of course, immediately killed.

A lesser individual of such a tender age might well have panicked, perhaps sat down on the ground and cried. But not Billy. He was a sensible lad and within moments he had willed himself into composure. His father had given him a tremendous responsibility and he would do his best to deliver. He determined the best course of action was to continue on to the market and see what he could get for the remaining cow. To his relief, he made a good profit on the surviving animal – so good that his father said little about the loss of the other.

Years later, when Billy McGarvey was grown and better known as Mac, when he had established an immense fortune for himself, he sat in the parlour of a family in Lviv, in eastern Galicia. It was the elegant home of a man he had long partnered with in the oil business and Mac spoke of the incident as marking the beginning of a period in his life in which all that he touched turned to happiness and success. McGarvey was, by his own estimate, a very lucky man.

Lucky, that is, until near the end of his life when the massive machines of destruction representing two nations at war brought everything he had worked so hard to build crashing down around him. Even that misfortune turned around, although McGarvey never lived to enjoy it. He died believing that his corporate empire had expired in a conflagration brought about by the competing firepower of the Russian and Austrian armies. Luck, he believed, had ultimately failed him.

Huntingdon, Canada East

McGarvey was born in the small town of Huntingdon, in what is today the Province of Quebec, twenty-five kilometres from the United States border. It is modest in size, its population of about 2,400 having, if anything, dwindled in recent years.

Before Quebec existed as a Canadian province, for the most part the region around Huntingdon was inhabited by the aboriginal or indigenous people. These were the Abenaki, a loosely connected group of people who spoke the Algonquin language. They continued to hunt and fish and live there for many years after the St. Lawrence River Valley to the north was settled and subdivided into farms under the French seigneurial system. That began to change after 1792 when the British province of Lower Canada, the precursor to Quebec, was divided into twenty-one counties. One of those counties was named Huntingdon.

The counties were further subdivided into townships, and the area that would become Huntingdon village was dubbed Hinchingbrook Township. Due to the pronunciation preference of the locals, the letter "g" was frequently dropped from its spelling and Hinchinbrook came into popular usage.

While a scattering of settlers from New England arrived by way of the Chateauguay River prior to the War of 1812-14, the district remained only lightly populated until 1821, when British surveyors were engaged to blaze a trail south into the territory from the St. Lawrence River. Right afterwards, the first settlers used that trail to penetrate the heavily forested region that lay on the northwest flank of the Appalachian mountain range. This was after the war and the immediate threat of American invasion had receded. Men who had recently retired from the British military were enticed to the area by the offer of land, the reasoning being that they would counter the French-speaking population and act as a buffer against the newly independent American nation, and so help to protect British interests in North America. These new settlers cut down the forests and began new lives as farmers. Others came down the road to establish businesses, including lumber mills and gristmills along the Chateauguay River. Among their numbers were the Protestant Irish families of Edward McGarvey and Sarah Gamble. Sarah's father, William Gamble, was a British military officer who had served with the 17th Light Dragoons in India. Edward's father, also named Edward, was a shopkeeper.

The McGarveys had come from Belfast while the Gambles were from County Armagh, both set in a region of the northern part of Ireland that in the early part of the nineteenth century was beset by economic and religious troubles. The McGarveys and the Gambles fled those troubles and searched for a more peaceful existence in the New World. Both were from what was commonly known as Scotch-Irish stock – families that had emigrated not long beforehand from Scotland and sought new opportunities in Ireland before many of them moved on to the Americas. Edward and Sarah were children when their families arrived and met in Lower Canada. The young couple fell in love and in January 1842 they married, the ceremony taking place at the Episcopal Church – the American incarnation of the Anglican or Church of England – in the village of Huntingdon. That October 24, their first child, a daughter they christened Mary, was born and the following year, on November 24, 1843, William Henry was born. William was followed by James, on July 31, 1846, Ellen on October 25, 1848, Albert on January 20, 1851, Edward Wesley on June 25, 1854, and Thomas Augustus who came along on February 6, 1856.

Huntingdon grew into a thriving farming town. A stagecoach line linked the village to Montreal, seventy-five kilometres to the northeast. Edward earned a good living by operating McGarvey's Sawmill on the Chateauguay River, two miles from the hamlet of St. Michaels in Huntingdon village, in the midst of a region where sugar and red maple, bitternut hickory and ironwood grew sturdy and tall. The children were educated at Huntingdon Academy after it opened in 1851, originally in the basement of a church. The next year a freestanding academy building made of stone was erected.

Soon after Thomas was born, Edward decided to up stakes in Quebec and move to London, a growing community in Canada West, which was a British province that one day would be named Ontario. There he settled in 1857 and opened a shop.

Oil Fever

Edward noticed the London newspapers carried frequent reports about the discovery of oil, a phenomenon that was sweeping the region just west of the city, in Lambton County. One of the earliest stories chronicling the tale of petroleum was this one first printed in the *Sarnia Observer* of August 26, 1858 and reprinted in numerous other journals. It is quite possible this is the very article Edward read while living in London that piqued his interest in supplying those pioneer wildcatters:

> Two weeks ago we noticed the discovery, in the township of Enniskillen, of an abundant supply of mineral oil, which the owner of the land was taking steps for making available for the purpose of light, etc., by erecting works thereon for purifying said oil, and making it fit for use. Since we made this announcement, a friend has brought us a small quantity of the oil as a sample, and which any person desirous of examining can see by calling at our office. The substance is of a dark colour and has a strong pungent smell, but a piece of rag or paper dipped into it and afterwards ignited burns with a strong light emitting as a matter of course, on account of the impurities in the article, a dense black smoke. If clarified, however, we see no reason why it should not make a splendid lamp oil.
>
> The ingredient seems to abound over a considerable tract of the land where it was discovered; in fact, the earth is thoroughly saturated by it, so that a hole dug will collect from two hundred to two hundred and fifty gallons a day, the supply seeming inexhaustible. As yet no works for manufacturing the oil into a merchantable commodity have been erected on the premises, what has been obtained having been barrelled up and sent to Hamilton to be prepared there. But we believe it is the intention of the proprietor, if the article proves what it is expected, to put up suitable works for the purpose, with as little delay as possible.

Devil's tar, flowing gold, black gold: oil was becoming known by a host of colloquialisms. But regardless of what it was called, the smelly substance was starting to excite imaginations.

The "proprietor" mentioned in that article was a Hamilton businessman named James Miller Williams. Williams built wagons and one of his latest efforts was investigating the prospects of supplying train cars to the railways. Then one day in 1857 a man named John Tripp entered his shop and began talking about the "gum beds" he and his brother, Henry, owned in Lambton County, about two hundred and twenty-five kilometres southwest of Hamilton. The Tripp brothers had launched the International Mining and Manufacturing Company to turn the gooey substance into profitable products. One of those products was asphalt, a sample of which they had displayed at the 1855 Paris World Exposition. It had been a sensation, earning the brothers an honourable mention from fair officials. But now the Tripps were in dire financial circumstances and were ready to sell their gum beds.

Williams was suitably impressed and in short order recruited a small contingent of business partners to check out this Lambton County discovery. It took little digging down by hand-held shovel before the Hamilton contingent came upon a supply of free-flowing petroleum and a deal was hatched to purchase the property. Williams and his partners imagined distilling the oil into kerosene and selling it to light homes, factories, taverns and other places of entertainment. The demand was there; all that was needed was a dependable supply.

"Oil Fever" engulfed the region. Overnight, the location where the gum beds had been discovered – Black Creek – mushroomed with the arrival of fortune-seekers from the Canadian colonies and the American republic. It grew from a place of two or three crude shacks to a town of 3,000.

But in the manner that Nature's riches so frequently manage to plant themselves in places inconvenient to humans, Lambton's oil discovery was situated about twenty kilometres south of the nearest railway station in the village of Wyoming. That station had been opened in the latter weeks of 1856 when the Sarnia branch of the Great Western Railway began operation.

Roads into the oil lands were rudimentary and ran through thick and swampy forests. The only way to move the oil out of where it was found was to place it in barrels, then put them onto sledges or stone boats, two barrels at a time, and drag them by oxen up that rustic twenty-kilometre-long road to Wyoming's rail yard.

This, in the mind of Edward McGarvey, spelled opportunity. He was intrigued, not so much by the prospects of striking oil, but by the opportunity that lay in selling the supplies all of those prospectors of this "devil's tar" would need to live and conduct their business. If Wyoming was the place people came to before entering the oil lands, and if it was where the oil was put on rail cars and taken to Williams' Hamilton distillery for conversion into lamp oil and grease, then Wyoming is where Edward needed to locate. He packed up his family and in 1860 moved them to Wyoming where he set up a general store under the banner of Messers E. McGarvey & Co.

Initially the store was a modest undertaking, but with the nearby oil industry feeding its progress, it grew quickly and became a leading institution in retailing. Later, Edward expanded his business interests. Over the summer of 1866, he constructed several more buildings in Wyoming's core and, according to the *Sarnia British Canadian* newspaper of October 24, 1866, they were "bringing him handsome returns in the way of rental."

Messers E. McGarvey & Co. took little time to become a going concern. In 1867, an advertisement hailed it as the largest general store in Canada West. The shelves were stocked with items of hardware of all descriptions as well as crockery, glassware, clothing, boots and shoes, stationary and small wares. In the back sheds, Edward kept a further stockpile of items he had learned were of use to the men who toiled in the oil fields. An advertisement for the store that year boasted: "Having enlarged their store to more than twice its former size, with a very extensive addition to their stock, they have no hesitation in saying that they have the largest and finest general store in the province."

Wyoming, Canada West

The name Wyoming is derived from a Munsee First Nation word that means "big river flat." While the land on which the village was situated was purchased during survey work for the railway, it was only with the discovery of oil to the south that it began to develop. Several hundred people lived there in the early 1860s, nearly all of whom were involved in petroleum in one way or another. Businesses produced timber and made staves for the barrels that were required for the oil industry. Farmers raised grain, plus fruits and vegetables, primarily to supply the local population. By the mid-1860s, there were two churches – one Episcopal and the other Methodist – there was a common school, an agent of the American Express Company, and even a branch of the Montreal Telegraph Company which extended to the community on Black Creek that was starting to also be called Oil Springs.

Wyoming had two general stores – one of which was the McGarveys' – plus four hotels, a post office, a drug store, three shoe shops, three blacksmiths, five cooperages, two butchers, two livery stables, a foundry and machine shop, a gristmill, a carding-and-fulling mill where families could bring their wool to be prepared mechanically, a cabinetmaker, three carpentry and joiner shops, two tailors, two wagon shops, a billiard saloon, two physicians and six small oil refineries.

"Refineries" in those early days of oil were nothing like the giant installations that exist today. They were essentially glorified stills. Initially the oily muck had been dug out of the ground and sent to Hamilton to be boiled down into distillates. Later, stills were erected closer to the source, often on the east side of London. These refining stills consisted of horizontally placed cylinders in which the oil was heated to raise the temperature. Distillates like gasoline came first and because there was no known use for them, they were disposed of, usually by letting them flow away into nearby creeks. It was the next distillation – kerosene – that was so highly prized.

As they matured, the McGarvey boys were brought into the family business, first William the eldest, and later James and Albert. Edward and Thomas were still young children. In short order, the senior Edward McGarvey's cunning choice of location for his new store on Wyoming's Broadway Street began to prove itself. With trains passing regularly through town on their way between Sarnia and London, and with Wyoming the jumping-off point to the oil fields on Black Creek, business boomed.

While the family lived in London, the young Billy McGarvey had already become a great help to his father's business. The incident with the cow was indicative of his strong common sense, a common sense he applied in other business matters. Now with the family relocated to Wyoming, Billy was coming into his seventeenth birthday when his father opened the doors to the new family-run enterprise. It was a busy concern, and he would be heavily relied upon to make things run smoothly. Billy was a smart boy with plenty of native charm who had learned the art of selling at his father's side. In the Wyoming store, he shrewdly picked up on the common business practice of barter, learning how much butter, cheese, eggs and vegetables to ask from the farm folks who called, in exchange for finished goods such as tea, salt, brown sugar and cloth. His father had come to trust his judgment and his younger brothers looked up to him for guidance and training.

By 1864 and at the age of just twenty, Billy – who with growing maturity was coming to be better known as Mac – had taken on considerable responsibility at the Wyoming store and was thinking grand thoughts of a future of his own. Oil prospectors who came to buy supplies filled his head with their stories, stories of how much money they said there was to be made from the thick, gunky liquid they called "ile" that lay beneath the surface just a few kilometres south. Naturally the young man dreamed big. During his infrequent time away from the store, Mac often hopped the daily stage that took the newly finished plank road connecting Wyoming to Black Creek and ventured the twenty kilometres south to see for himself the wells that were scattered thickly across the flats that stretched the length of the waterway.

By his own reckoning, McGarvey began to dabble in the oil business by 1862, before his nineteenth birthday. On his excursions to Black Creek, he observed how and where the older men dug wells, which of them were successful and which were wasting their time. He queried the successful ones and learned from their methods. He was shrewdly gathering information that one day he would be able to use himself. He wasn't ready to jump quite yet, however, and the retail trade would remain his primary focus for a few more years.

Young Mac wasn't the only inquisitive observer who was drawn to this place where oil had been discovered. The town that grew up on Black Creek was a curiosity to those who lived in the cities and the more conventional small towns of the era, too. There were plenty of accounts from the day in newspapers and periodicals that described in vivid detail the boomtown atmosphere that permeated Black Creek. Here is one of the most compelling, found in the December 20, 1862 edition of a British periodical called *The Leisure Hour*:

Leaving London by the 2.40 p.m. train, your correspondent went direct to Wyoming ... The peculiar odor of the oil, which is here stored in large quantities for carriage to the eastern markets, is perceived, especially if the wind happens to be favourable, at the distance of a mile or two. I noticed that the large platform was covered with the blackest and oiliest of barrels,

saying nothing of the hundreds of empty ones which were returned from
the east, and which, in promiscuous heaps, oftentimes twenty feet high,
covered the ground for rods. The rapid importance this place has assumed
is astonishing. A few months ago, and it was no place: now it is *the* place ...
it has stores and shops of every kind. Post office, carpenters, shoemakers,
tailors, blacksmiths ... and two doctors hang out their shingles. A fine
foundry has just been got into operation. There are livery stables and
teams here without number and last, but never least, hotels of a very good
kind. From the crowd of drivers, hotel runners and lounging stragglers,
one would almost suppose himself at the station of a city.

... I took one of the half-dozen stages that run to the oil regions. I am
sure not less than thirty-five or forty passengers went out on the same day
to (the Black) Creek. The road for the first six miles was tolerably good
though, the country being a dead level, with a soil of heavy clay, drainage
is difficult. ... (S)oon, we hope, the labourers of the energetic contractor,
who is building a plank road from Wyoming to Black Creek, will render
the route less wearisome than at present. At a distance of four miles we
come to a store and tavern; this is Petrolia.

There was really little more to Petrolia than that store and tavern so
fleetingly mentioned in this published account, plus a handful of makeshift
shacks. An oil refinery had been built there in 1861 and its name, the
Petrolia Oil Refining Company, was lent casually to the sparsely populated
district. The area was known primarily for farming, while oil continued to
be the purview of the village farther south on Black Creek – Oil Springs.
As the decade progressed and the wells of Oil Springs started to fail, more
exploration moved up the road to Petrolia on Bear Creek.

Mac had spent five years with his father's lucrative enterprise in
Wyoming and felt it was time he started to make it on his own. He had
learned his father's lessons of Wyoming well: there is good money to be
made from supplying the oil men rather than simply becoming one of
them. Not far into his twenties and with his merchant father's blessing,
William opened Petrolia's Mammoth Store in early 1865.

His timing proved perfect. One might even say it was lucky. From
the handful of rudimentary shacks of three or four years earlier, when
William arrived it was still just a little unincorporated community of three

hundred. An influx of Americans, however, was about to swell those numbers. Their own nation was in chaos. In April 1865, Lee surrendered to Grant and Lincoln was shot and killed. These were the incentives to leave the troubled United States; stories of Lambton's oil riches offered an enticing destination.

Newspaper stories and word-of-mouth led to scores of wildcatters flowing in to test for oil along the banks of Bear Creek and led to astonishing growth in the early months of 1866 as fortune-seekers arrived to mine for oil. By 1866, the community grew to 2,300 residents and there were nine hotels. One of them, the American Hotel, was refurbished and stocked with wines, liquors and cigars to entice the big spenders. The *Stratford Beacon* reported in April, in a story picked up by the *Sarnia Observer* on April 27, that "(D)wellings, stores, hotels, workshops, engine-houses and derricks have gone up as if by magic," just six months after a casual visitor would have been hard-pressed to find a meal or accommodation.

Petrolia had joined Wyoming and Oil Springs as a boom town, with a main street that was typical of small Ontario agriculture-based towns of the era: at the retail and commercial heart of the community it boasted banks, general stores, blacksmiths, bakers, shoe and harness shops, churches and pharmacies. It grew with no thought of plan.

But something different lurked behind the main street façades of Oil Springs and Petrolia: three-pole derricks and smelly little refineries. When combined, the two – derricks and refineries – scented the air with the familiar sulphur and pungency of oil. That aroma helped to define them as working mining towns and places of quick wealth.

Despite a mid-decade downturn in oil production, Oil Springs still prospered on Black Creek throughout the 1860s. As new wells came into operation, older ones petered out and were abandoned. Men still had little knowledge of the geological processes that created oil, or the manner in which it spread between rock strata. Drilling was often guesswork and sometimes even directed by "dowsers" or "diviners," who used a divining rod, "oil smellers" and "oil wizards" who claimed a special talent for sniffing out petroleum sources. The early erroneous belief that oil was primarily located near water is the main reason they continued to dig close to Black Creek near the gum beds. But essentially, the early wildcatters simply dug anywhere and everywhere, and dotted the landscape with their familiar three-pole derricks.

From the comfort of a later era when his wealth and status had been achieved, McGarvey looked back at those early methods used for finding oil and marvelled how any progress had ever been made. "The early methods were exceedingly primitive," he said, "and at the present time many of us wonder how with such poor material such splendid pioneering results were secured."

Yet success came in abundance to Petrolia and the new town grew. It was showing every sign of overshadowing its older neighbour, Oil Springs. While the community's retail district remained strung out along a single street, that street was getting ever busier. New stores were being added all the time and there were several hotels. There were four churches – Roman Catholic, Presbyterian, Wesleyan and Episcopal Methodist – and a school. Pride and confidence in the community grew right along with it. When a group of local businessmen, led by oil entrepreneur John Henry Fairbank and supported by McGarvey, failed to convince the railways to build a spur line to accommodate the oil business, they decided they would have to build their own line from Wyoming. The spur vastly improved the hauling of crude and refined oil when it opened on December 7, 1866. Within six months, the branch line had paid for its own construction and operating costs. The Great Western Railway then purchased the line from the builder group.

With such growth and rosy prospects for the future, Petrolia's residents decided it was time to incorporate, and in January 1867, six months before Canada was officially declared a nation, they established the Village of Petrolia. On July 1 that year, Petrolians, brimming with confidence in their community's future, joined other communities across the new dominion in a grand celebration of nationhood. Church bells rang out, military drills were held and under the sunny skies that covered much of the country that day and suggested somehow that God approved, Canadians celebrated with picnics and patriotic speeches declaring fealty to Queen Victoria. In the evening, fireworks displays lit the heavens in declaration of the happy event.

Petrolia had not been conceived of in the same way most other communities were. In fact in the annals of Canadian history, Petrolia was an odd town in that it did not grow alongside a lake for ease of access and transportation, or a flowing stream where mills could be constructed. It grew up away from the only waterway in the area – Bear Creek. But then it was never a normal town.

"It was never intended to be a town, but a place of sudden wealth," wrote two chroniclers of the town's history, Charles Whipp and Edward Phelps, in their book, *Petrolia 1866-1966.*

As a result, while the better-off merchants and professionals in the more solid, established towns of Canada West were building their homes of brick and stone, most of Petrolia's buildings were constructed of wood. Some warned that with the obvious hazards related to the omnipresent oil, the town was leaving itself open to disaster. They advised on regulations to build with brick and talk often circulated about the benefits of a formal fire department as well as underground oil containment tanks.

Before there was time to act, however, two huge fires marked the summer of 1867 as a year to remember. Burning oil spilled from wooden vats, derricks and wells were consumed and refineries were levelled in the inferno. When residential areas were largely untouched, the town's citizenry realized how lucky they had been, and how they needed to be better prepared for the mercurial and hazardous industry to which they had chosen to hitch their prosperity.

Bernard King's Discovery

Bernard King was a Great Lakes ship's captain from St. Catharines. When one of his vessels returned to home port one day, its hull smeared thick in oil, a much-perturbed King demanded to know what had happened. "It's all that oil they have out West," he was told. "It's so thick, it flows down the rivers and into the lakes. It just covers everything. It's so bad, sometimes the creeks catch fire!"

King packed his bags and headed out there to discover the source of this damnable substance. When he arrived in Petrolia in the mid-1860s, the conventional wisdom still was that oil was best found along streams.

King decided to find out for himself and dug a well west of Petrolia's Bear Creek, up a hill and quite some distance from water.

None of the other prospectors could imagine crude might be found any distance away from watercourses and it became a great joke to most Petrolians when "that crazy ship's captain" started exploring farther west on the heights above the creek. They were suitably shocked when King's well came in, in November 1866. It wasn't the first "flowing well" Petrolia had seen, but it was the most prolific to that point and proved to all doubters that oil could be found in more places than they had ever considered.

King's experience was a turning point in the education of oil wildcatters. He had drilled a mile outside the "golden circle" that encompassed the Bear Creek flats and was down one hundred and twelve metres below the surface, a good eighty-five metres through bedrock. The well came in on Friday, November 23. The next day, King sent a telegram to business partners in St. Catharines: "Struck a flowing well last night. Can't control it."

At about the same time that the King well came in, two Enniskillen Township landowner brothers, James and Peter Duncan, sold their farm just north of Petrolia to American C.J. Webster who came from Hartford, Connecticut. Webster was more interested in oil than crops and livestock, but realized he could benefit from advice in matters of oil exploration. He approached Mac McGarvey who agreed to act as his agent. By this time the old foot-treadle "kicking down" method of percussion drilling through the bedrock was being replaced by an American invention that consisted of manila rope cable to which the drill bit was attached. The supporting poles were made from ash, which grew abundantly in the area. McGarvey and Webster decided to experiment. Instead of manila cable, they attached the drill bit to a series (or string) of black ash poles that were attached to one another. To drill deeper, they simply added more poles or rods.

"Although primitive in construction," McGarvey said more than four decades later, "the advantage of the system was recognised, and in a very short time improvements were made and brought it well to the front." While modesty prevented McGarvey from saying precisely who it was who recognized these advantages, it was almost certainly William McGarvey himself. At least that is how J.E. Brantly saw things in his 1971 book, *The History of Oil Well Drilling*. Brantly credits McGarvey with developing the system about 1866, and then later taking it to Europe and modifying it to suit conditions there. Regardless of who was responsible for adapting and developing the drilling method, this was, in McGarvey's estimation, the beginning of what would come to be known as the Canadian pole-tool drilling system. Used as late as the 1920s in some places, it was a system that would revolutionize drilling in many parts of the world and help to make William McGarvey a very wealthy man.

The depths at which oil was found in Lambton County in those days are shallow by modern-day oil well standards. John Shaw's well, the region's first free-flowing well or "gusher," came in at 48.5 metres (one hundred and fifty-nine feet). King's well nearly six years later went down one hundred and twelve metres. Wilfred Durham Keith, known by one and all as Willie, prepared an account in 1950 that describes the average well of the era. While Keith spent most of his life developing oil resources with his family for the McGarvey enterprises, and then themselves, in Eastern Europe, he knew the Lambton wells inside-out and wrote this description of Ontario's conditions:

> The surface strata consisted of about eighty to one hundred feet (twenty-four to thirty metres) of blue clay which was bored out by means of an auger and cased with a wooden conducter. Drilling was then continued to the oil-bearing rock. All the oil was produced from the Devonian or Silurian formation. With such shallow depths it did not take long to drill a well. Within a week's time, the drilling rig was put up, the well drilled, the rock torpedoed (a process similar to what is known today as fracking) and the whole equipment moved to another site. The only thing left to show that some driller had been there would be a bowing walking beam and a tripod derrick.

Willie Keith went on to describe how oil wells seemed to sprout like springtime weeds, even amidst the accouterments of every-day living. "It was no unusual thing in those days to see a flourishing vegetable garden in somebody's back yard in the morning and, the next morning, to see a drilling outfit in the same place ready for action. ... I don't think that there was a back yard in the whole East End of Petrolea (this is the archaic spelling of the town's name) that did not have a tripod derrick standing in it, some silent and forsaken, others with the usual bowing walking beam."

Technology's Steady March

McGarvey and his fellow wildcatters were learning a great deal from their early experiences. While oil was formed over millions of years and its existence had been known to humans for thousands, for most of that time, it had been obtained by scooping it up in ladles, or soaking it up in woollen blankets and wrung out into pails. It was then applied to the wounds of humans and livestock to promote healing, or boiled down and used as a caulking to repair leaky boats. Starting in 1858, people in Lambton County had learned how to drill for oil and then convert it into a range of useful products such as grease, kerosene and lubricants. At about the same time, the process was replicated by the Americans in Titusville, Pennsylvania, and by Europeans in Germany, near Hanover.

In the first years of oil production, individual oil wells were pumped by hand through the use of a spring pole system. This proved highly inefficient and when horse- or steam-power was introduced to replace the man-operated spring pole method, the inefficiencies became that much more obvious. It was too expensive to operate a single well from its own dedicated power source.

John Henry Fairbank, who had entered the local oil business about 1861, knew there had to be a better way. "I had a well too hard to work by manpower," Fairbank told the Royal Commission on the Mineral Resources of Ontario in 1890. "I hadn't an engine, but there was engine power within reach." Fairbank attached a horizontal pole or "walking beam" to connect the engine to the well-pumping apparatus. It worked. Later, he applied the same principle to link a number of wells to a single engine. The jerker-line system had been invented. Fairbank credited a man named Reynolds for introducing a "field wheel" to the system so as to power even more wells from a single source. In this way, he explained, up to eighty or ninety wells could be operated from a single boiler and one or two engines. Fairbank never sought a patent on the system because, he said, it never occurred to him.

In the first decade of their activities, these Canadian oil workers had learned that petroleum need not be found only near water, that wooden poles – which became the hallmark of the Canadian method of drilling – could be linked together to increase the depth of their wells, that multiple wells could be operated from one power source and that by boring to greater depths, new oil-bearing rock could be tapped.

Despite the growing oil boom, William McGarvey still was reluctant to tie his horse exclusively to the oil business. In the town Bernard King was in the process of making famous, the owner of the Mammoth Store, Bill McGarvey had swiftly become one of the most respected individuals and successful businessmen, and a man who knew how to make a good living. He had the qualifications to go far. He was highly likable with a dynamic personality, possessing a jolly countenance and round face. His twinkling eyes, bushy moustache and eyebrows that bobbed somewhat comically up and down when he laughed endeared him to nearly everyone. McGarvey was not a particularly tall man, but his presence commanded attention. He was broad-shouldered and his jovial booming voice was a familiar greeting to those who came by his Mammoth Store to pick up supplies and share news of the day. Not surprisingly, then, when several of the leading citizens gathered to organize the new village, they called upon William McGarvey to serve on the first council.

Not only that, McGarvey was prevailed upon to take over the role of leading that council in the position of village reeve and, at the tender age of twenty-three – and despite his own misgivings – he agreed to their plea. The council's first year of existence in 1867 was a busy time for the new corporation and for the men who managed it. The five-member council met on average every eight days to get the village up and running and the distraction from his commerce proved too much for young William. Barely giving himself time to warm his seat at the council table, McGarvey resigned in March 1867, convinced his encounter with politics had been a mistake that was destined to distract him from his true calling.

While the pressures of operating the Mammoth Store might have been the primary reason given for his departure from council, his retail enterprise was not the only matter that played on his mind and distracted his attention, however. McGarvey had been looking longingly at the oil business and considered it an opportunity too good for him to avoid jumping into fulltime himself. After all, it seemed everyone was striking an oil well and setting up business. There were wells all over the village.

There was still another reason for McGarvey to contemplate ditching his municipal role: thoughts of love. Arriving in Petrolia just in time to capture the young man's attention was a young American woman of half-Polish extraction, Helena Idwega Wesolowski.

CHAPTER 2

THE POLISH CONNECTION

W as it coincidence or destiny that led William Henry McGarvey to meet and fall in love with Helena, daughter of a Poland-born father and an American mother? Was it part of a grand plan? Further evidence of the "lucky man" syndrome McGarvey attributed to himself? In later years that liaison with Helena Wesolowski would prove to be a significant factor in improving McGarvey's fortunes. It was a fortuitous liaison, because when circumstances conspired to bring the Canadian oilman to the Polish countryside in his search for petroleum, his wife's background and knowledge of the language served him well. William never was able to conquer the Polish language himself, a fact he would joke about years later at a grand reception held in honour of a colleague. But Helena had quickly proved to be a hit with the locals – peasants and aristocracy alike – when, in the late 1880s, the couple started to set up a new life in Galicia, a largely Polish-speaking province of the Austro-Hungarian Empire in Eastern Europe.

William's first encounter with the Wesolowskis was through Helena's father, Ludwik, who was hired by the newly incorporated village of Petrolia, with William as its first reeve and leading businessman. Wesolowski, a professional engineer, was hired to apply his surveying skills in helping to plot the new community's layout.

Ludwik Wesolowski was born in Warsaw, Poland on March 3, 1810. Educated at Warsaw's University of Military Engineering, he spoke and read six languages fluently – Polish, English, French, German, Latin and Russian. He joined the Polish Insurrection of November 29, 1830 in which his countrymen sought to toss out the Russians who had partitioned their land with Austria and Prussia. The revolutionaries became known as the Novemberists and Ludwik became a second lieutenant during the fighting which continued for ten months.

The revolution proved to be a lost cause and many of those who had fought on the losing side fled to the West. Ludwik was detained by the Austrians and deported from the port of Trieste on November 22, 1833. By the following March 28, he was in New York, where the Austrian consul gave him thirty-three American dollars and told him to "get lost."

In the summer of 1834 and with a group of fellow ex-Novemberists, Ludwik arrived in Michigan where he was hired as a draftsman to plan locks, bridges, aqueducts and other services to accommodate a canal project. He became a deputy county surveyor and then a naturalized American citizen in 1846. Later, he was elected Macomb County surveyor. In a book by Harry Milostan, *Enduring Poles* (Mount Clemens, MI: 1977, Masspac Publishing Co.), the author declares Wesolowski Michigan's first multimillionaire.

Ludwik Wesolowski married Sarah Jane Fletcher, formerly of Vermont, in December 1838 and they had five children. Helena Idwiga was the fourth, born in 1845. When Wesolowski started doing business for the newly created village of Petrolia, he came to know Bill McGarvey. Wesolowski liked the young man and sized him up as someone who was bound to succeed – suitable marriage material for his daughter, Helena. On his next trip from Michigan, Ludwik brought along the twenty-one-year-old Helena and introduced her to William.

Helena was a stunning beauty, standing five-feet, five inches tall, with dramatic hazel eyes. Her lustrous auburn hair, parted in the centre, was smoothed over the ears and turned up in a bun at the back of the neck in the style of the era. An early photo taken in Petrolia shows Helena in a stylish full-skirted dress, tight at the waist, lace at the collar fastened by an oval brooch. The sleeves, upper arms, waist and skirt were set off by contrasting dark bands. She immediately captured the attention of the shopkeeper and soon-to-be oil man.

The feelings proved mutual and the couple began courting. Marriage was discussed and on July 10, 1867, the ceremony took place back in Mount Clemens, Michigan, at the comfortable six-acre estate of Helena's father. Her mother had died a few years earlier. After the honeymoon, the couple moved to Petrolia to establish a life together.

Oil was in its ascendancy at Petrolia and had been given a huge boost the previous November when Bernard King's flowing well had come in. At the time, the well was the largest ever struck in the province of Canada West. It initially flowed at eight hundred barrels a day, yet there had been no storage facilities established beforehand and the crude flowed untapped, covering the ground and filling Bear Creek to overflowing. As King himself had said at the time: "Struck a flowing well last night. Can't control it."

Modern-day environmentalists would be appalled at the cavalier approach taken to the environment in the oil fields of the 1860s. For the most part, no thought was given to the Earth as anything more than a resource to be exploited for human gain. Unfortunately, there were severe consequences. Early oil drillers did not possess the means to quickly stop up the flow when they struck a gusher and little time was spent thinking about its impact on the living creatures and vegetation, to say nothing of humans, who relied on the Earth for their wellbeing. Yet coincidentally, just as Petrolia was evolving as a centre for oil production, the environmental movement was taking its first baby steps. In 1862, John Ruskin published *Unto This Last*, in which he criticized unrestricted industrial expansion and its impact on people and on the natural world. Two years later, George Perkins Marsh published *Man and Nature*. It was the first systematic analysis of the impact human development was having on the natural environment and, in the words of Lewis Mumford: "the fountainhead of the conservation movement."

However, environmentalism would take many more years to reach the oil industry. With the seemingly limitless profits to be made, oil was becoming king.

Thanks to the success of his Mammoth Store, McGarvey was beginning to put together a healthy stash of cash. He had been dabbling in oil wells for a few years when, in May 1866, he purchased a parcel of oil property at auction for $10,400. Such prices were unheard-of for agricultural land but this was the era of black gold. The land he purchased had been one of the plots connected to the hard-luck Tripp brothers. Located northwest of Oil Springs, the Tripp "jinx" prevailed and according to a report in the Toronto *Globe* on May 3, 1866, it never panned out.

But the fact he was able to find that kind of money proved McGarvey was faring well in the business world, especially for a young man not far into his twenties. And the failure of that first enterprise did nothing to dampen his enthusiasm for petroleum.

Fortune-seekers were rushing into town and McGarvey's store was scrambling to keep up with demand. The village was filled with construction, with oil traffic and land speculation. Enthusiasm remained undampened by the two big fires of 1867 that started from oil spilling from wooden storage vats. Oil wells were wiped out, as were refineries and shanties used to supply the industry. Rebuilding began quickly. With money to be made, there was no time to pause.

Despite the brevity of his first stint on council, in December 1867 McGarvey was prevailed upon again to serve for the following year. "Without you, we don't have enough members to fill the slate," they told him. He was reluctant, but finally agreed. "Should my services be required, I shall serve," he said. This time he stayed, and spent three terms on village council, from 1868-70. But he never lost sight of his desire to immerse himself in the booming new industry. Within a year of his marriage to Helena Wesolowski, William had accumulated a portfolio of eighteen wells. As his interest in oil rose, he shifted more and more of the burden of running the store to his brother, James, who had been enticed down from Wyoming to live with William and Helena. Up in Wyoming, the teenaged Albert was given an expanded position of responsibility for Messers E. McGarvey & Co. while his father maintained proprietorship.

By 1870, sixty per cent of Ontario's total oil production was being exported to Europe. Granted, production was tiny by modern standards: it is estimated that annual production from the Lambton County wells averaged just 200,000 barrels (a barrel held forty-two gallons) between 1865 and 1870. Still, the world was just learning what it could do with oil, with most of it being used for lamplight kerosene and lubricants. Lambton

County alone was supplying all of Canada's oil needs and even producing enough to export to the U.S. It seemed as though the business could know no bounds and new partnerships were formed to take advantage of the thriving industry. McGarvey joined the London-based Martin Woodward and Oliver Simmons in a partnership to start a new refinery in Petrolia on November 1, 1872.

Simmons and Woodward are listed in the articles of partnership documents as oil refiners while McGarvey is called an oil operator. The partnership created Simmons Woodward and Company, described as manufacturers of illuminating, lubricating and other oils, and shippers of crude petroleum. McGarvey does not appear at first to have been an active partner as the other two were. Instead, lending further credence to his growing affluence, McGarvey's contribution was primarily a monetary one: of the $7,000 in capital contributed, half came from McGarvey and one-quarter each from the other two. He was learning the value of diversification.

In later years, McGarvey took on a more active role in the enterprise, which by 1878 was officially known as the Woodward & McGarvey refinery. An invoice submitted by the refinery refers to the company as "producers of crude" and "manufacturers of the products of petroleum." Martin James Woodward would later go on to make a significant name for himself. He was hired by the Shell Transportation Company in 1897 to build a five-million-barrel refinery on the island of Borneo, before working again with McGarvey on a huge oil project.

Besides diversification, McGarvey gained something else of value from his association with the new refinery: connections. Besides Woodward, another of those valuable connections was the American-born Charles Nicklos, who had worked briefly in London, Ontario for the Smallman, Menhenick and Company refinery. When Nicklos came to Petrolia to work at the new refinery, he started off as what was in those days called a "treater" and later came to be known as a chemist. Nicklos and McGarvey became acquainted and in later years, Nicklos would become a key player in the McGarvey empire.

McGarvey might have divided his time between the Mammoth Store and petroleum for the first few years but by the time of the Canadian census in 1871 – the first one post-Confederation – he was officially declaring himself an oil operator. By 1871, James McGarvey was twenty-five, and the census listed him as a merchant, having taken over operation of his brother's Petrolia Mammoth Store. While the town was expanding westward, William and Helena McGarvey were living in a nice home in Petrolia's older east end and, according to the census, had in their employ an 18-year-old servant named Jenny Jackson. Village records show they also owned a dog.

Meanwhile up in Wyoming, William's father, Edward, was still owner of the general store, but Edward's son Albert, aged twenty, was running the place. The 1871 census shows that with Albert in charge of operations in Wyoming, Edward and Sarah had already moved back to London where they lived with daughter Ellen and younger sons Wesley and Thomas. Their eldest daughter, Mary, had married homeopathic doctor Andrew Vanalstyne in 1866 and was also living in London.

There are suggestions, however, that Albert might not have been as skillful and diligent in his business practices as his father had been. For some years, Edward had owned a handful of oil wells and used small on-site stills to refine the crude. This was not an unusual practice among the smaller and part-time oil producers whose wells were liberally spread around the region. The small-time operators welcomed the extra cash the wells brought in and the larger refiners didn't mind the minor competition. In 1872, however, the Canadian Department of Inland Revenue accused Edward of failing to remit the duty he owed on twenty barrels of oil. They swooped in and seized his "refinery" – really little more than a backyard still – and referred the matter to the Justice Department.

As the official owner, Edward was given a steep fine of five hundred dollars, plus costs. The suspicion is that while Edward was living in London and was not in Wyoming to watch over his enterprise, Albert either got sloppy in his bookkeeping, or else attempted to deceive the taxman. His father paid the price.

Albert continued to operate the general store and throughout the 1870s it remained an important part of life to the community. Then a fire at E. McGarvey & Co. in November 1877 marked a change in fortunes.

Perhaps recovering from the fire was too much of a burden for the business to shoulder; perhaps Albert was not as skillful in operating the store as his father and older brother had been. The courts swooped down again. Edward claimed his debt was greatly exaggerated and insolvency was forced on him by greedy creditors and that it had been totally unnecessary, due in large part to a grain shipment. For whatever reason, Edward was forced to declare insolvency in 1879 and even had to sell off some of his oil wells to pay debts.

With Edward and Sarah McGarvey living fulltime in London, the Wyoming business was reconstituted after those proceedings, and the company continued its existence into the 1880s, with regular advertisements appearing in the local and Sarnia newspapers. In 1882, the general store was carrying a full line of clothing, furs, saws and axes, cutlery, tableware, revolvers, shotguns and gunpowder.

Albert McGarvey would soon have new and quite different responsibilities, however, thanks to his big brother, William.

A Family Commenced

William and Helena McGarvey's first child, Nellie Edith, was born on February 22, 1869 and two years later, a son, William Edward, was born on April 25, 1871. William Jr. was about a year old when tragedy struck: he contracted smallpox.

Smallpox is an ancient scourge of the human race, having likely emerged in the human population around 10,000 B.C. Signs of it have been found in Egyptian mummies. By the late 1800s, a vaccine had been invented and the disease was fairly uncommon – except for the Great Epidemic of 1885 in Montreal – and little William catching it was not only a sad, but a very unlucky incident.

Smallpox is an acutely infectious disease that gets its name from the pus-filled blisters, or pocks, that form during the illness. It is accompanied by a severe fever and its early signs begin to appear twelve to fourteen days after infection. The most severe type can kill thirty per cent of its victims. Death usually occurred in seven to seventeen days. William Edward was just over a year old when he died from smallpox on May 14, 1872. He was buried in the Pioneer Cemetery on North Street in east-end Petrolia, not far from the family home.

Ten months later another son, Frederick James, was born on March 18, 1873. It would be Fred who grew into an inquisitive and successful young man, a man of science and of business, and the one who would carry on his father's legacy and maintain the family fortunes for two more generations.

Success

William McGarvey became involved in many successful undertakings in Canada and, eventually, internationally. Of his various Canadian enterprises, probably the most successful well in Lambton he enjoyed a part ownership in was the Deluge, a well struck in 1873 that proved to be perhaps the biggest gusher in Petrolia's history. Once it was under control, the well produced up to six hundred barrels a day.

In an article published years later in the *Imperial Oil Review*, one of the men working on that well described that exciting day when it came in. John Scott, a Lambton County oil man who was later inspector of oil wells for the Province of Ontario, told the writer of the 1930 article he served as the engineer on that well. Scott recalled he was alone, dozing in the middle of the night next to the boiler, when the well blew off.

"The roar was terrific," said the report. "In a moment everything was saturated. Scott's first thought was of a conflagration, and by frantic effort he managed to get the gas lights extinguished and the fire put out. ... The oil covered the countryside – the fields, the ditches, the roads. An American had long-handled ladles made at once, hired men, and scooped up hundreds of barrels from everywhere. It was days before that well was controlled. Finally John Scott went in under the deluge of oil with a log and chains. In a second he was drenched. However, he managed to fasten the log as a lever, and chained down the pump, which had been joyously jumping about in mid-air, and the well behaved itself."

Unlike many of those who went on to become successful oil men, McGarvey spent little time working the fields that he owned. In fact he had become something of a dandy by the time of the Deluge strike, noted for being nattily attired wherever he went. Multiple photos of the man over the years attest to this fact.

John Scott once recounted how one day, the impeccably dressed McGarvey rode his beautiful newly purchased leather-seated carriage into one of his oil fields and stopped to chat with his workers, one of whom was Scott. McGarvey wore a white vest with his new suit. Scott said he and another worker were about to knock the spigot from an oil tank and fill some barrels for shipping. The men were "seized" of the same prank at the same time and asked McGarvey to stop and watch whether they were knocking the spigot out properly. McGarvey obliged and directed the procedure as asked. Suddenly the spigot popped out, a spurt of oil hitting him in the face and soaking him from head to foot.

Allegedly McGarvey was a "good sport" about the whole thing and laughed it off, but was "rueful" about the leather cushions in his carriage, Scott said. We can only imagine!

The story reveals a number of things about McGarvey: He had already achieved success in the Petrolia business of oil and general dry goods sales; he loved fine things and was willing and able to pay for them; he had a good and convivial relationship with his workers; and he was prepared to take a practical joke, even if as the brunt of the joke he ended up having to pay for a new suit.

After all, it was only money. And there was about to be plenty more where that came from.

CHAPTER 3

A STRANGER COMES CALLING

Out of adversity blooms opportunity and triumph. The adversity: dwindling supplies and tough competition from the United States. Together, they spur Mac McGarvey to search for a new challenge. That challenge comes courtesy of a British gentleman, a businessman who is about to make McGarvey a fascinating proposition. Then politics again tugs at his coattails, and Mac is conflicted.

Canadian Oil Stumbles

While the 1860s had been a boom time for the oil industry and the next decade began in a manner that suggested it would continue unabated, the source of the Canadian industry's troubles can be detected as early as 1870, when the American industrialist John D. Rockefeller began to turn the tables on the Canadians. Rockefeller's Standard Oil was ramping up production and with new American discoveries in 1873, Standard's success swamped the tiny Lambton enterprise and relegated the Canadian industry to also-ran status. For a short time, the Lambton oil business came to a near-halt, as reported in the *Sarnia Observer* on November 28, 1873:

> There is an almost complete prostration of business at (Petrolia); labourers are leaving and the work of development is making slow progress. The oil refiners limit their production to the wants of the home market, which means that nearly all of them are shut down, and waiting for a favourable

turn in prices. The effect upon our export trade, though not really serious, will be considerable, as about two million in value of refined petroleum was shipped abroad last year. ... Refined Canadian oil is not worth more than twelve and a half cents to eighteen cents in New York – figures quite below the cost of production.

The result was an oversupply of highly skilled workers eager for new employment opportunities. After a decade of exploration and development, Lambton County and its neighbouring jurisdiction of Kent County had created a seasoned crew of oil experts. They knew how to drill for oil, had come to recognize that it was often necessary to reach to much deeper depths than previously believed, and understood how to solve the myriad of problems that would crop up in the process of drilling for crude. They were not willing to head back to the farm fields or work as labourers after they had been bitten by the oil bug and had come to rely on its superior wages and business profits. And so when the jobs began to dry up due to the loss of markets to American Standard Oil, these oil men searched for new opportunities to practice their skills and maintain the good incomes they had come to expect.

The Foreign Drillers

This is the environment in which Canada's self-taught oil experts found themselves in the latter days of 1873. It is the environment in which the Foreign Drillers evolved and thrived. The Foreign Drillers were the men who took their learned-in-Canada skills to overseas destinations, to take leading roles, time after time, in exploring for, and developing oil resources the world over. It has been estimated that hundreds of Canadian-trained oil workers went to eighty-six separate jurisdictions around the world to apply their talents.

The first out of the gate among these Foreign Drillers was a crew that left Petrolia just after Christmas in 1873 to work in the islands off the coast of Southeast Asia. Mac McGarvey and his wife, Helena, joined their fellow townspeople at the railway station to bid adieu to four men who became the vanguard of a movement when they headed to the islands of the Dutch

East Indies. It was a defining moment in Petrolia's and Lambton County's history. Newspaper accounts reported they "were given a rousing sendoff by the citizens of the town who marched to the train headed by the band."

Those first four men who went were drillers Josh Porter and Len Cook, engineer Malcolm "Mal" Scott and scaffoldman William Covert. The pole-tool outfit they carried with them was furnished by George Sanson and Hector MacKenzie from the Oil Well Supply Company of Petrolia. It is a system that had been refined by William McGarvey and was now widely in use in Lambton County. In the coming decades, Oil Well Supply

would become a significant producer and exporter of oil drilling equipment, with a subsidiary opened in St. Albans, England.

We can imagine Mac and Helena joining the others in the sendoff: the hugs and the goodbyes, then waving farewell as the train headed out, chugging its way toward Toronto. As the strains of the Scottish folk tune, *Will Ye No Come Back Again*, still wafted from the instruments of the town band, they turned and began to walk away. At that moment, did McGarvey have any inkling, any hint that one day he would be heading off to the Foreign Fields himself? Had he given any consideration, fleeting or serious, to the prospects? Perhaps he saw the coming experiences of the Foreign Drillers as something of a trial or test, an opportunity by a shrewd man who had done well in Canadian oil to watch the progress of others in the new direction they took. McGarvey had proved himself a gambler, but he was not impulsive. The risks he took were calculated. Certainly he had not yet given up on the local oilfields and the opportunities that existed there to make a handsome living.

Nor was McGarvey ready to give up on Petrolia civic affairs. He agreed to return to local politics and served as Petrolia's mayor in 1875 and again in 1876. He was reeve during the terms of 1877-79. In January 1879, while serving as reeve and consequently the town's representative to Lambton County council, he was chosen by his fellow county representatives to serve as warden. Under the county system of government, the warden acts as council's chairman and official representative, a somewhat titular position akin to "head of state."

The *Sarnia Observer* reported on the warden's dinner McGarvey hosted, an occasion, it said, "to which not merely the county council, but all who are fortunate enough to receive invitations look forward to with a good deal of pleasant anticipation, as it is very correctly regarded as embodying many of the best features of that outgrowth of modern social life denominated a 'dinner.'"

"The leading minds of the county" were invited to the feast, with warden McGarvey proposing toasts to Queen Victoria, the Prince of Wales and other members of the royal family. A male singer then performed *The Harp That Once Thro' Tara's Halls*. After everyone took up *The Maple Leaf Forever*, toasts were then made to the U.S. president who, one of the speakers claimed, had been fraudulently elected.

(It appears as though he had good reason to make this claim. The 1876 election of Rutherford B. Hayes was as hotly disputed as the election of George W. Bush in 2000 and Donald Trump in 2016, as well as Trump's defeat in 2020. According to the Rutherford B. Hayes Presidential Library and Museum, Hayes' opponent won the popular vote and a majority of electoral votes, a portion of which were obtained by widespread voter fraud. It took a decision of the United States Supreme Court to settle the matter in Hayes's favour.)

Everyone in attendance at the warden's dinner, said the report in the *Observer*, agreed it was better to "live and die under the British flag than under the rule of the United States." (Some characteristics of Canadian's attitudes toward the United States and American politics seem to go back a very long way.)

McGarvey's selection as warden signifies just how widely respected he was among his fellow municipal representatives and upon his return to Petrolia by train after the dinner celebration, he was met by friends at the station and feted with an oyster supper at the home of one of their numbers, C.H. Errington.

Besides his role in the local government, McGarvey maintained a keen interest in politics at the provincial and federal levels, too. He was a strong believer in protectionism under the banner of Sir John A. Macdonald's National Policy and against the Liberals' policy of reciprocity or free trade. He was president of Petrolia's Conservative Association in July 1878 when they penned a letter to Macdonald pledging their support for the policy they believed would help build up Canadian industry. They wrote:

Our warehouses are filled with foreign and often inferior articles. What we want is the right and opportunity to fill our ware-rooms by our own labo(u)r productions, so that they can be seen, known and appreciated; then as the markets become depleted of foreign, the home product can gradually take their place and often at less rates than the foreign demanded. We have witnessed with pride, and hope, your efforts to inaugurate a National Policy ... our hope is that the triumphal call of the country will place you in a position to advance your theories with the brightest prospects of success.

Two months after the letter was written, the nation's voters defeated the federal Liberal government of Alexander Mackenzie, a Sarnia stonemason, and elected Macdonald's Conservatives.

Given his eloquence in supporting Conservatism and its central economic tenet, it was not surprising that when the Conservative party looked around for a candidate to represent Lambton West in the 1879 Ontario provincial election, they came knocking at McGarvey's Petrolia door. What was perhaps more surprising is that he actually won the nomination. James Dibb wrote many years later that when he was a young man he recalled encountering McGarvey and some friends on the train on their way to the party nomination meeting in Sarnia. "Mac had not been seriously considered, but received the nomination," he said. (The fond reference to McGarvey as "Mac" is one that will be used many times, and by many others, over the coming years.)

McGarvey likely believed he would be the party's sacrificial lamb, considering it improbable the Conservatives would unseat the incumbent Liberal. The prospect that he would never have to serve in the Ontario legislature might have played a significant part in his decision to accept the challenge.

The Liberal Oliver Mowatt had first been elected Ontario premier in 1875 and would remain in office for nearly twenty-four years. In Lambton West, McGarvey lost in the June election to the incumbent Liberal member, Timothy Blair Pardee. So firm was the Liberals' grip in Lambton West, a Conservative candidate would not take the riding until 1905.

McGarvey believed in Macdonald's National Policy, a program of protective tariffs designed to help fledgling Canadian businesses and industries develop in a climate of swaggering American growth. Ontario and Prairie farmers tended to support a free trade climate that was prescribed under the Reciprocity banner. (The Liberal party would run under Reciprocity in 1891 and be severely beaten by Macdonald.)

While he lost the election, McGarvey succeeded in making the contest far closer than many had imagined it would be. It was evidence of his tremendous personal popularity that forced many who had previously endorsed the Liberals to select him instead.

McGarvey kept up a correspondence with Macdonald, writing to him again in April 1879, six weeks before the Ontario election in which McGarvey was narrowly defeated, and again two years later. In that second letter, he gave every indication of being ready to try again to defeat the Liberal Pardee. Acknowledging Pardee's superior standing with Roman Catholic voters, McGarvey confided to the prime minister that it would be necessary to pry some of those votes away in order to stand any chance of victory.

McGarvey was a very well-regarded man among the supporters of both political parties. He had served as Petrolia's mayor, remained on council afterwards and was chosen the county warden. As a man of such high standing in his community, and a man who had accomplished much in the oil business, it was not surprising, then, that he would be the one British financier/engineer John Simeon Bergheim would approach when he arrived in Petrolia in 1879 with what must have seemed to McGarvey an incredible proposition.

"Come to Europe with me," Bergheim urged, "and join me in the opportunity of a lifetime."

John Simeon Bergheim

Most Petrolians had never encountered anyone like the sophisticated visitor with the suave English accent and gentleman's manners who stepped off the train that day. Having wired ahead the details of his arrival, Bergheim was met by McGarvey and a small group of the town's leading citizens. The two men shook hands and immediately began to size one another up.

Bergheim was born in 1842, a year before McGarvey, but their backgrounds were strikingly different. While one came from the tiny Canada East village of Huntingdon, was of Scotch-Irish Protestant stock and did not have the benefits of higher education, the other had been born in Jerusalem, which at the time was part of the Turkish Ottoman Empire. Bergheim was the son of a businessman and the eldest of six children, including five boys. In 1856 at the age of fourteen, Bergheim left home and emigrated to Britain. He was determined to get a proper education and after obtaining his diploma, Bergheim entered engineering school. The 1861 British census lists him as an engineering apprentice. He was inducted into the British Institution of Civil Engineers in 1867. In 1871, John became a naturalized British citizen. Two years later, he married the British-born Clara Constance Banting, who called her husband "Johnny." It was a moniker that would be widely applied by friends and associates over the span of his lifetime.

Despite the fact he had been born in Jerusalem, Bergheim listed his place of birth on his naturalization papers as Prussia. (In fact, it was his father, Melville Peter Bergheim, who had been born in Posen, Prussia.) Why did he lie? Might he have chosen to go with a birthplace that was readily believable for someone of his German-sounding surname, and the birthplace of his father, rather than acknowledge his Middle East birthplace and deal with suspicions that he was Jewish? In fact, it is speculated that Bergheim's father, Melville Peter Bergheim, was born Jewish and converted to Christianity in Jerusalem.

It was not in any way advantageous to be Jewish in the Britain of the era. It was only in 1834 that Britain even allowed Jews to become naturalized citizens without taking a Christian oath. While by mid-century things were beginning to look up for Jews wishing to play a role in British society – they were allowed to hold municipal office in 1845 – it was only in 1856 when they were permitted to take a degree at Cambridge University and only in 1871 at Oxford. Bergheim was thoroughly Protestant – he was even a Freemason – but might have preferred to avoid any misunderstanding that could arise from the sound of his name. After all, with the royal family themselves boasting of German heritage, what better way to fit in to British society? However by the time of the census of 1881, Bergheim was acknowledging his true birthplace of Jerusalem.

Misunderstanding seems to have dogged Bergheim all of his life. Over the years, he would be misidentified in reports as a Jew, a Prussian and even an American. A story published in the *New York Times* January 3, 1893, said he was "swindled" out of $100,000 by a "pretend" journalist in Vienna. The report identified Bergheim as "an American mine owner" but offered no details of the swindle.

In the years following his marriage, John Bergheim began to devour everything he could put his hands on about the subject of oil. He read about petroleum discoveries on the continent. He learned about the Nobel brothers' efforts in Russia and watched as Rockefeller extended his reach throughout the United States and well beyond its borders.

So Bergheim – the Jerusalem-born naturalized Briton – was a civil engineer with deep financial connections when he went to Pennsylvania in search of oil experts interested in joining him in Germany to develop oil resources. Why Germany? Two decades earlier, oil had been found in the German village of Wietze, west of Celle and about forty kilometres north of the city of Hanover. Just like the James Miller Williams well in Lambton, it had been hand-dug. The crude oil was transported by horse-drawn wagon to Schwarmstedt and then by train to refineries in Hamburg and Bremen. Later, a small refinery was built in Wietze and a workers' village was constructed. At one time, Wietze fulfilled eighty percent of Germany's domestic demand for oil products.

Bergheim wondered: why should the name "Bergheim" not be played up on the marquis of the world petroleum show, right along with the Nobels and the Rockefellers? Why not begin someplace close to home? In Germany, for example, where oil had already been proven.

Bergheim had the vision; all he needed was to find someone with the expertise to deliver it. He knew that European technology was backward and inefficient. It was North America where progress had been made. And so he travelled to America – first to Pennsylvania – in search of experts to help him exploit the resources he had heard existed near Hanover.

The response Bergheim received there was disappointing. The United States' domestic industry was booming. Under the stern businessman's eye of Rockefeller, Pennsylvania had established itself as the hub of world oil and there were new discoveries in New York, Ohio, Kentucky and Virginia (in the part now called West Virginia). Americans were too preoccupied with their own industry to bother with the rest of the world.

The Pennsylvania oil men's advice was clear: "Go to Canada," they said. "Things aren't doing so well up there." And so he did, arriving in Petrolia where he was introduced to William Henry McGarvey. The men hit it off.

As a Petrolian, McGarvey had an inclination to consider overseas opportunities. It had been the Canadians, with a hobbled industry and brimming with knowledge and expertise, who had begun to travel the globe back in December 1873 in search of places to employ their skills. When those first men returned to Petrolia, they recounted tales of the exotic lands they had visited, of their thrilling adventures and heroic escapades. Certainly the romance of the chase for oil had injected itself into the community's psyche and transformed others into a receptive audience for those who came with the promise of new opportunities. It was these circumstances that instilled a wanderlust in the Canadian wildcatters that made them receptive to Bergheim's invitation. It was this wanderlust that would place its stamp on the town's self-image for generations to come, a self-image that exists to this very day.

In Petrolia, Bergheim encountered a Canadian frontier town that had matured considerably in the past fourteen years, yet it was far removed from his own experience back in the UK. At least his short stopover in the wild oil outpost of Titusville, Pennsylvania would have prepared him. Petrolia was a town of forty-nine stores, ten hotels, many saloons and billiard halls and various shops and liveries. Belden's *Illustrated Atlas of the Dominion of Canada for Lambton County* reported at the time: "The general character of the buildings of Petrolea (note the archaic spelling) is inferior, there being very few which are really good, the majority being of wood material ... The Vaughn block, completed last year, was the first really fine business block ... though there are already quite a number of very good private residences." One of those "very good" private residences belonged to William Henry McGarvey.

There was another feature of the town that set it apart from Bergheim's experience: the oil wells that were drilled on seemingly every space that was available. Everything smelled and tasted of oil, Belden's description continued; everything was covered and smeared in it. "You hear nothing but oil spoken of in the cars, in the hotels, in the public offices."

This was indeed an oil mining town, although at least it was taking on a more permanent appearance by the time Bergheim arrived. With the recent erection of the Vaughan Block, there was finally one "truly permanent business building," according to the book, *Petrolia Canada 1862-1908*, written by oil pioneer and leading citizen J.H. Fairbank.

Bergheim's visit was a big event. He was most definitely a VIP. His host, Bill "Mac" McGarvey, Petrolia's reeve, warden of the county and one of the region's leading oil producer/refiners, ushered him around town and explained the ins and outs of the local industry. Dinners were held in his honour and there was even an official photograph taken in a local studio by the Toronto-based photographers Pringle and Booth. In it, Bergheim stares resolutely into the camera as a man who knows what he wants. McGarvey, in contrast, is gazing far off and out of the picture, as though he is contemplating with great intensity his options for the future.

It is also revealing to see who else is featured in that photo. Bergheim (whose name is misspelled "Burgheim" in a caption published in 1930 with a copy of the photo in *The Imperial Oil Review*) and McGarvey are there, of course. In addition, at least eight of the nine others are known to have ended up in the foreign fields – some within months of the photo. The eight are: Cyrus Perkins, Alvin Townsend, John Martin, A.E. "Angus" Slack, Eugene Yager (also spelled Yeager), Neil Sinclair, George MacIntosh and George Fair. It is not known whether the ninth man, Angus McKay, ever left the country to pursue the business of oil.

The following May after Bergheim came calling, the Italian-born Count Carlo Ribighini, who had first arrived in Petrolia in search of oil riches during the rush of 1865, hired a small group of Petrolians to go with him back to his native Italy and search for oil. Among the men who went were Neil Sinclair and his brothers, Duncan and John, as well as George Fair and Angus Slack. Also included in the crew were R. Jackson, J. and

N. Andison, two Wade brothers and Roddy McDermid. John Sinclair recounted years later, in a 1924 story published in the *Advertiser-Topic,* some of the details of how most of the group returned home within three years. His brother Neil, however, stayed for two decades, leaving Italy for Germany, then Romania, where he worked in petroleum.

Some of those men who toiled in the foreign fields became extremely successful. Cyrus Perkins, featured in the Bergheim photo, was one of two brothers – Jacob being the other – who made a fortune in Europe both operating oil fields and manufacturing drilling equipment. George MacIntosh partnered with Cyrus Perkins in the oil-drilling equipment business. They were later joined by Cyrus's son, Charles, who still later became a senior executive for a British oil company and represented the British government on a post-war commission to reorganize Poland's oil industry. As well, Alvin Townsend was a highly regarded oil manager who made his name in several European fields.

(As a sidebar, one of the Foreign Drillers in the photo, Angus Slack, came within a whisker of sailing back home on the ill-fated *Titanic*. At the last minute he handed his ticket to a friend so the man could get home to visit his sick wife. The man, James McRie, was one of the 1,503 who perished after the ship struck an iceberg off the coast of Newfoundland and sank.)

Bergheim was a highly curious man and a man of science. He had done a great deal of reading on the subject of oil and was familiar with all of the evolving theories about how it was formed, where it was located and how best to mine it. As McGarvey ushered him around Petrolia to inspect the oil fields and poke around the refineries, Bergheim became increasingly convinced that the Canadian methods were just what were needed to tap into Europe's supplies. He asked McGarvey to put together a team and come back with him.

"You're the one," Bergheim told his host. "Come back with me. We can be set up in Germany and commence drilling in no time at all."

McGarvey was intrigued by Bergheim's offer, but remained cautious. He was not yet prepared to make the leap and abandon his Canadian enterprise. If he was going to leave and start a new career in Europe, there were loose ends to clear up first and after all, he had a young family to consider. Disappointed yet hopeful, Bergheim went on his way and returned to London. The two men vowed to remain in touch. Each had made a lasting impression on the other. McGarvey believed that indeed, they could do business together under the right circumstances.

A Sophisticated Town

By the time of Bergheim's visit, Petrolia was a town at the centre of an industry that had grown and changed greatly since its founding less than two decades earlier. Three-pole derricks dotted the landscape in all directions, and oil was being pumped to the surface at a brisk rate despite competition from the Americans.

On the refining side of the business, a newfound maturity had evolved. Five years earlier, an American-born entrepreneur named Jacob "Jake" Englehart had purchased Petrolia's Big Still Refinery, which he operated in conjunction with a refining business he owned in Hamilton. In 1878, Englehart decided to centralize his operation close to the source of oil and started constructing the Silver Star Refinery. Set on ten acres at the northerly approach to Petrolia, between the Great Western and Canada Southern Railways, each end of the shipping shed faced one of the lines. The refinery's underground tank stretched forty feet in diameter and fifty feet deep. The agitator, believed to be the largest on the continent, could treat 1,750 barrels at a time, according to the *Petrolia Advertiser* of April 4, 1879.

"This refinery is at present shipping 3,000 barrels of refined oil to Germany, 2,000 to England and 20,000 cans to Brazil, China, Japan and Italy," the paper reported. Oil was big business here.

The newspaper account described in detail the safety aspects employed in the refinery for the benefit of the workers and the town itself. There were ten hydrants situated around the property connected to water tanks. Workers were organized into the refinery's own fire company and were frequently drilled on their duties in the event of an outbreak of fire. The lessons from the great Petrolia fires of 1867 had apparently been learned.

"In addition to the Silver Star Refinery, Mr. Englehart is a very extensive oil producer, in fact the largest producer we have in the district, sixty-two wells being the property of this gentleman," said the paper. He employed a staff of thirty-three.

However, it was Mac McGarvey who had seized John Bergheim's attention. When he left town, Bergheim was more convinced than ever that McGarvey was his man, and Canadian technology was the key to unlocking Europe's petroleum wealth. He waited eagerly for McGarvey to come around to the same way of thinking.

CHAPTER 4

WEIGHING HIS OPTIONS

M ac McGarvey was a significant force in Petrolia's business life but could not compare in importance to either the refiner, Jake Englehart, or the chief oil producer in town, John Henry Fairbank. McGarvey was a combination of the two, but placed no higher than second spot in either field. On the civic front, he served on town council from 1875 to 1880, first as mayor, then reeve and finally the lower and less onerous position of councillor. Meanwhile, he continued to operate a growing oil business as both a driller and a refiner, while his younger brother, James, handled the general store.

Politics vs. Business

With his charismatic personality, it is quite conceivable Bill McGarvey could have become a highly successful politician. In the 1879 provincial election, he had come closer to unseating the Liberals than anyone could have imagined – including McGarvey himself – and with perseverance he might well have won in another try. But he chose not to try. Politics would not be his true calling. McGarvey continued to do his duty at the municipal level but being a successful oil entrepreneur had become his overriding goal in life. It is interesting to speculate where someone with his charisma and persuasive talents might have ended up if he had chosen a political path instead of the oil business.

By the dawn of the 1880s, Petrolia and area was fulfilling ninety percent of all of Canada's petroleum needs, from pumping it out of the ground to refining it. Yet the previous months had not been particularly good ones for the local industry. With exploration in the United States expanding at breakneck speed and more and more fields coming into production there, the Americans, under the leadership of John D. Rockefeller and Standard Oil, were driving down the price. The Canadians were finding it difficult to compete.

There had been a surplus of 375,000 barrels in May 1879 and the price-per-barrel hit rock-bottom at fifty cents. By November, the price had recovered to $1.40, making it at least economical to take it out of the ground. But in order to try to stabilize the price, Lambton producers cut production in early 1880. An article in the *Sarnia Observer* on January 30 predicted that huge surplus from the previous year would likely disappear by summer. On June 25, the newspaper reported that it was no longer possible for Lambton's wells to keep up with growing Canadian demand for oil products; imports would be required.

On the social front, Mac was active in the Petrolia Literary and Musical Association, both as a board member and a performer. Adding a touch of fun to culture, a masquerade ball was held at Christmastime 1878. In 1879, Mac delivered a stirring oratory from Hamlet's Horatio and the year afterwards, he did another reading at the annual event held at the centre of Petrolia's social and community scene, the Oil Exchange Hall. The Oil Exchange Hall bore witness to all types of entertainment, from comedians and magicians, to dramatic readings and Shakespearean performances. McGarvey also belonged to Petrolia's "Washington" branch of the Odd Fellows. He had been a member of the Masonic Order of Canada since 1866.

The McGarveys enjoyed an esteemed place in Petrolia's upper crust and William was often called upon to take the lead in important projects. As a leading businessman, he joined the mayor in engaging with the Grand Trunk and the Erie and Huron railways about the prospects for improving service to the town.

As a respected businessman and politician, McGarvey was frequently called upon for advice and leadership. His expertise in mining was sought by a representative of the Dominion government in the summer of 1880, in the form of a request that he embark on a trip to the Turtle Mountain and Souris River country of southwestern Manitoba to prove up a suspected coal resource there. This was the era of the surveying, routing and construction of the trans-Canada railroad and all along the route, testing was being done to determine whether there might be valuable natural resources that could be exploited.

The request to McGarvey for exploration help came from Dr. Alfred R.C. Selwyn, who had been appointed director of the Geological Survey of Canada after Sir William Logan's retirement. Throughout a quarter-century career with the agency, Selwyn proved aggressive in his efforts for Canada, spending a great deal of his time exploring remote corners of the country, including the route of the railway, to map the geology and search for mineral resources.

(Just how would one get from Petrolia to southwestern Manitoba in 1880? An advertisement in the *Sarnia Observer* on June 25 of that year indicated steamships left Sarnia every Tuesday and Friday for Duluth at the head of Lake Superior, where they met up with the Northern Pacific, and St. Paul and Duluth Railways. The train could be taken to Dakota and then to Manitoba. The rest of the trip could be done via steam-powered riverboats, horseback and/or wagon.)

McGarvey was joined on the expedition by another Petrolian, John Highman, a British-born contractor who had lived in the town for more than ten years before accepting Mac's invitation to join him on the trip. Highman had also been a next-door neighbour of the McGarveys in the east end. According to Selywn's report, test drilling was done sixteen kilometres east of Roche Percée, about four hundred kilometres west of Emerson, Manitoba. Work started on July 8 and a pit was sunk. Eventually, they drilled to two hundred and ninety-five feet (ninety metres).

"(A) seam of coal six and one half feet thick was struck, which proved to be of rather better quality than that which crops out at the Souris River, where Mr. Sutherland's mine is located ..." said the *Emerson International* newspaper. "Mr. McGarv(ey) is of the opinion that the finding of coal at this depth demonstrates that it will be found much further eastward, and thinks that it will probably be found near the surface at Badger Creek, about one hundred and fifteen miles (one hundred and eighty-five kilometres) west of Emerson."

Second and third tests were planned. McGarvey spoke enthusiastically of the Turtle Mountain and Souris River sections "and says they are adapted for agricultural purposes. Mr. McGarv(ey) … is of the opinion that whatever explorations are made will have to be done by private enterprise."

McGarvey returned to Petrolia without any evidence of further riches and with no plans to return. He had done the exploratory work for which he was contracted. Later, he remarked on the difficulties involved in hauling the necessary equipment in to such remote areas and then getting out any resulting finds of coal or other mineral riches. The Oil Well Supply Company, from which the drilling and exploration equipment had come, was simply too far removed from the wilds of Saskatchewan to make it feasible for further exploration at that time. After McGarvey's exploratory work, it would be three years before the Canadian Pacific Railway linked Saskatchewan to Eastern Canada. While the railway came in time to transport Canadian troops to fight Louis Riel in the mid-decade North-West Rebellion, it would not be of any help to McGarvey.

Did the limited success of that exploratory trip west represent the tipping point in McGarvey's decision to seek his fortune overseas? Back in Petrolia, Jake Englehart had led a group of business partners in the formation of Imperial Oil in the spring of 1880. After initially establishing its headquarters in London, the company moved to Petrolia three years later. McGarvey had not been a part of it. The Lambton industry was doing well but its prospects for expansion seemed limited. And McGarvey's visit to the West perhaps convinced him that for the time being, at least, the opportunities in Canada for resource development were constrained by distance and isolation. It was the ideal time for him to think further about Bergheim's visit and the offer to join him in Europe.

The census of 1881 continued to place McGarvey's home in Petrolia, where he lived with wife Helena and children Nellie, Mary (Mamie) and Frederick, who turned, respectively, twelve, six and eight years old that year. Helena's younger brother, Charles, was living with them and was listed as an engine driver, indicating he too was working in the oil fields. There was also a new servant in the household, Dorinda "Dori" Raven, age nineteen.

That same year, McGarvey made his decision. He contacted Bergheim to let him know. Mac now believed he would never be able to break out and make it really big in Canada. It was time, he said. Time to go to Europe and determine once and for all just how successful he could be in the oil industry. McGarvey left for England to meet his new partner. Together the two men, with sky-high hopes, headed for Germany.

The Canadian Pole-Tool Drilling System

While some oil had been found around Hanover in the vicinity of Celle, it wasn't until the summer of 1881 that Adolf M. Mohr discovered large quantities farther east at Oelheim, with the strength of the gushers drawing others to the region. Two of those who came that summer were McGarvey the oil man and Bergheim the financier-scientist. Once the men arrived in Germany, McGarvey was appointed director, or manager, of the Continental Oil Co. Ltd., tasked with the objective of exploring for, and bringing in oil resources at Oelheim.

With him and with Bergheim's full support, McGarvey brought the tools that he had used for drilling in Canada, a "kit" that was quite foreign to the Europeans and which had started to be called the Canadian system or the pole-tool method. The kit, which came from Petrolia's Oil Well Supply Company, represented the first time the Canadian system was ever used in Europe and it was about to revolutionize the search for oil there.

The Canadian system would be spoken of often, and be highly praised in the coming decades as the best method for tapping in to the resources of Eastern Europe. It was, in the mind of Polish petroleum engineer and historian Stanislaw Szafran, the underlying reason Galicia's industry rose to the top tier of world production by the latter years of the 19th century.

So just what was the Canadian system and how did it work?

The methods created by those early Canadian pioneers of oil for locating, drilling for and pumping out petroleum were in no small part the reason that the Canadian oil men's expertise became so highly valued the world over. It was a system devised in an environment of conjecture and speculation as to precisely where the resource was located and how best to obtain it. There were no geology experts on oil exploration at the time, at least not in the modern sense; the methodology for locating petroleum was something that would take many years to develop. It evolved in no small part from the experiences of William McGarvey and his fellow Canadian Foreign Drillers.

Once a decision was made about where to drill, drilling commenced with the use of an auger tool that would break through the top-laying clay or soil. After this was achieved, the pole-tool equipment was brought in to "punch" or break through the rock.

The pole-tool system consisted of drilling equipment or "tools" that were suspended from attached rods and "paid out" or dropped down as the exploratory well was deepened. This occurred by way of a pounding action that used the weight of the drill string to grind its way deeper into the bedrock. The drill bit was attached to the end of this drill string. From time to time, the debris would be scooped up from the bottom of the well. When the drill bit became "bald-headed" or dull from the constant pounding, it was removed from the string of poles, resharpened by "toolies" and re-attached to the drill string.

The pole-tool rig rods were initially made of black ash, which grew in great abundance in central Lambton County. In later years, the black ash poles were replaced with iron rods. The rods were linked together by use of an iron (later steel) connector.

The whole apparatus was suspended from a wooden derrick that was built overtop the well. These were the three-pole derricks that would come to dot the landscape of Lambton County and later be omnipresent in the oilfields of Europe. While initially the drill was operated by hand and then by oxen or horse power, by the 1880s, the whole apparatus was steam-driven.

The Canadian pole-tool system differed from the American standard system, which relied on rope or cable that attached to the drilling tools. This brief description of the American standard system is taken from a book called *The Story of Oil*, written by Walter Sheldon Tower and published in 1909: "The drilling tools in the American system are suspended by means of a hemp rope or wire cable, which passes through a pulley wheel or block at the top of the derrick."

Conflicted Thoughts

After his first summer drilling season in Germany, McGarvey had not yet made up his mind about whether he would stay and continue the search for oil. From Hanover, Germany, he wrote a letter to his idol and inspiration, Sir John A. Macdonald, on November 26, 1881, in which he hinted that politics was still on his mind. McGarvey congratulated Macdonald on his good health and wished him many more years of life. It was about this time that Macdonald, the notorious drunkard, opted to go sober after a health scare. He lived to govern Canada for another decade.

McGarvey then revealed to the prime minister: "I expect to be home in the county of Lambton before the next general election." That would suggest a return in 1882. He went on to further indicate he might even take another run at the provincial seat of Lambton West, the seat he had narrowly lost in 1879. With his family still in Petrolia, no doubt homesickness was also top of mind.

By early 1882, however, McGarvey had set aside thoughts of politics and decided instead he would be staying in Europe for a prolonged period. Still, Mac was determined to reunite with Helena and the children. He missed his family, but the hard work of establishing Continental Oil and getting it on its feet required him to remain in Germany. Letters were exchanged between William and Helena and serious discussions were made about their family's future. How much longer would work keep Mac in Europe? How successful would his business interests prove there? And if he was in Europe for a prolonged period, what about his family – Helena and the children, who were seriously missing "Papa?"

It was a difficult decision for many of the oil workers – to bring the family along with them or to leave them at home in their more familiar surroundings. Many chose to leave their wives and children while they earned a living in a far-flung corner of the globe. Typical was the experience of Bill Cole, whose daughter, Dorothy Stevenson, grew up in her mother's single-parent home in Petrolia while her father spent much of his working life overseas. While he tried to leave it behind, the lure of the fields was just too much for Cole. Dorothy Stevenson recalled: "When he'd come home, he would say, 'I will not go again.' And mother would then get a house and they would settle in it, and he would take a job. But before long he'd come home and say, 'I've signed another contract.' Then things would go in storage and she'd go back to life with her parents."

In early 1882, the McGarveys decided that Helena would leave Petrolia with the children and go to Germany to spend a few months with Papa. Packing only a few personal possessions – "they produce fine pianos and furniture and such in Europe," William assured his wife – the family made the twelve-day trip from New York to the northern German port of Hamburg by steamship, before continuing on the rest of the way to Hanover by rail.

Then, even before they had had time to properly settle in to their new home in Hanover, tragedy struck. Quite unexpectedly, the McGarveys' first-born child, Nellie, took ill. The blue-eyed, curly-haired little girl had always been smaller and more delicate than the other children her age, always dainty, and some compared her fair complexion to that of a porcelain doll. Yet she was eternally a happy girl, popular among her Petrolia friends and eager to take part in local scholastic and cultural activities such as the literary society that her father so loved. The illness quickly worsened and Nellie died on June 28, 1882 at the age of just thirteen, according to the *Sarnia Observer* of July 7.

Despite the grief he felt for the loss of his little Nellie, duty called out to him. Mac must continue to give his full attention to his and Bergheim's oil interests. Progress had been slow thus far and if they were going to succeed, McGarvey must soldier on despite the heavy heart Nellie's unexpected death had left him with.

Helena did not settle in easily and quickly to life in Germany and she had been severely shaken by Nellie's death. When she learned she was again pregnant soon after Nellie died, Helena reasoned with William that she should return to Petrolia to have the baby. There, she would be surrounded by friends and family. She feared the consequences of giving birth in a strange land, surrounded by people and conditions she did not know. William reluctantly concurred and in late 1882 as winter began to set in, Helena took the long trip back to Petrolia along with young Fred and Mamie, as well as a servant girl to keep watch over the family.

Nine months after Nellie's untimely death, on March 31, 1883, Sarah Katie McGarvey was born – in the friendly confines of the McGarveys' Petrolia home.

Kate's birth became a harbinger of good things to come and her father's timing in leaving Canada now seems perfect. A further flood of American discoveries in 1883 would cut into the Canadian market even more and contributed to the Canadians' growing interest in overseas opportunities.

In comparison to Canada's economy generally, which was suffering through a prolonged recession, Petrolia and Lambton County's dependence on oil allowed them to fare far better than most Canadians. In fact in 1884, according to the Canada Geological Survey Annual Report of 1903, Canada was even able to export some refined petroleum to the United States despite Standard Oil's predominant position (Ottawa: 1905, Part S, p. 101). Even in its somewhat depleted form, the business of oil was serving the citizens of Lambton County very well.

For the McGarveys, however, the success that lay just over the horizon in Europe would dwarf their experiences in Canada's Lambton oil fields.

CHAPTER 5

GALICIA

Disheartening early drill results fail to curb William McGarvey's efforts in Hanover. With John Bergheim's continued enthusiastic encouragement, the Canadian crew drills on, confident that their methods will eventually pay off. Then an unexpected visit from a Polish man, educated in Western Europe, opens up a whole new world of opportunities.

Another Invitation, Another Country

The birth of Sarah Katie in March 1883 was a great joy to Bill and Helena McGarvey, still devastated by the sudden loss of their first-born daughter, Nellie, the year before. But Helena had insisted she return to Canada with the other children for the birth and now, as Mac and his partner, Johnnie Bergheim, began their third drilling season in Germany with sky-high hopes, Mac missed his family who were so many miles away in Canada.

As the season progressed, the partners put on a concerted push to develop the petroleum resources around Hanover. Despite those efforts and the expenditure of large sums of money, however, their findings fell far short of their grandiose expectations. A small gusher at Oelheim that for a while had created pandemonium failed to lead to further discoveries and the partners grew disheartened.

While McGarvey was disappointed, he remained convinced that their failure to secure a reliable and steady supply of crude was not because of deficiencies in their Canadian methods or equipment. Bergheim backed him up in this opinion. Both men continued to have unwavering faith in the Canadian system they had introduced to Europe. As stated years later in an obituary for McGarvey published in a European magazine: "J.S. Bergheim and MacGarvey did not have any great success with their wells in Germany, but this was less because of the quality of their machines, their equipment and their methods, than of the local conditions." In other words, there simply wasn't enough oil to be found near Hanover.

One of the essential contributions McGarvey made to the petroleum world was to introduce a level of professionalism those who sought petroleum in Europe had never before witnessed. These Canadians had put the business of oil on a new footing, one based on the body of knowledge they had gathered over the course of nearly a quarter-century in the North American fields. Back in North America, Canadian and American oil drillers had, in very short order, learned a great deal about how best to obtain crude: how to locate it, how to drill for it and how to get it to the surface where it could be refined. With practice and learning to read the signs, "the percentage of lost holes has been reduced to such a minimum as hardly to enter into the calculations of producers," McGarvey said in 1910. Not only was this done with certainty, but with safety too, he said.

Oil exploration was evolving into a science, and yet there remained more than a modicum of intuition in its practise. The expert oil driller, it was said, developed a "sixth sense" that allowed him to read the sound of the steam engine, the behaviour of the walking beam and the cable. The job was not one that could be performed by any inexperienced labourer, but only by a man of intelligence, energy and physical strength, Andrew M. Rowley wrote in an article for *The Oil and Gas Journal* of Tulsa, Oklahoma in 1923. "He must be able not only to sense and avoid dangers, exercise patience and constant vigilance, but also solve numerous puzzling problems."

These Canadian Foreign Drillers were quite capable of doing just that. Canadian oil men were experts of the "bush fix" — figuring out what was wrong and what they needed to do to repair it and get back to work. They possessed a level of character and skill that made them a valued resource on any crew. The late and longtime Petrolia oil man Arnold Thompson, who spent most of his career in Lambton County but took a one-year contract in Cuba, explained it this way: "They just weren't drillers. They were blacksmiths and … if something went wrong with their tools, they didn't have to send them away to be fixed. They fixed them right there on the job. Drilling was a profession alright, but you couldn't carry out your profession if you didn't know how to keep the drill working. This is the success of the Petrolia drillers. They were ingenious men. There was nothing that came up they wouldn't tackle and be successful."

As John Henry Fairbank put it to the Ontario Royal Commission in 1890: "…they can tell what is going on down below one thousand feet as well as if they were there."

Stanislaw Szczepanowski's Plan

When he commenced operations in Germany, McGarvey and his workforce of Canadians became known as the go-to experts on drilling methods. One day in 1883, during his third season drilling near Hanover, as he contemplated the continued drain of his resources into the German countryside with little discernible reward, a man came to his office at Continental Oil with an offer. "Mr. McGarvey," the man said. "Have you ever considered coming to Galicia? We need you there."

The man was a Polish engineer by the name of Stanislaw Szczepanowski. Szczepanowski told McGarvey he was certain that with the correct equipment and know-how, Eastern Europe had the potential to become a significant producer of oil. He had heard about the Canadian pole-tool drilling system and despite the limited success McGarvey had had with it in Germany thus far, Szczepanowski shared McGarvey's and Bergheim's enthusiasm. He fervently believed the Canadian system was the key to unlocking all of the potential he was confident remained buried in the Eastern European rock formations.

Szczepanowski described to McGarvey the primitive manner in which oil was being collected in Galicia. It had been known to exist there for a very long time, he said, pooling onto the surface where it made its way, of its own volition, from the depths of the Earth. Up until that point, however, Szczepanowski said, the production of oil in Galicia had consisted of skimming crude from those surface ponds, and hand-digging shallow wells. He described how itinerant peasants and farmers used horsehair brushes to collect the oil by hand. The horsehair held the sticky material until it could be wrung out and drained into buckets. A bucket would be hung from each end of a pole that was slung across their shoulders. In this way, the buckets were carted off to market and the material was sold to farmers to lubricate their wagon axles and treat wounds and skin conditions on their livestock. This passive system of obtaining oil sounded familiar to McGarvey. It was strikingly similar to the early methods used in his own country, he told Szczepanowski. Methods, however, that had long since been replaced by those far more efficient.

While these primitive methods might have been acceptable practice in an earlier era, the demand for kerosene oil for lighting was growing, and the region of the Carpathian Mountains abounded in signs that oil was present, Szczepanowski explained. To begin with, he believed, the places where oil seeped to the surface indicated far greater resources lurked at far greater depths. It was only a matter of digging deep enough. The American drilling system had been applied sparingly, and with little success, with Galicia's difficult subsurface conditions proving too much for the handful of Pennsylvania drillers who had tried.

McGarvey conferred with Bergheim and the partners agreed it was worth a visit. Leaving the bulk of their workers to continue their efforts at Hanover, they travelled to Galicia with Szczepanowski and a small crew of Canadians.

At the time of their arrival, Galicia was a backward and little-noticed province of the Austro-Hungarian Empire. This was the old Habsburg empire that had been reorganized into the Dual Monarchy (Austria and Hungary) in 1867. The reorganization recognized two separate and equal states – Austria and Hungary – bound together by a common monarch who sat as the kaiser or emperor of Austria and the king of Hungary. The two entities shared an army and had common ministries of war, foreign affairs and finance. Otherwise, each functioned separately with its own parliament. This system remained little changed from 1867 until the Dual Monarchy's breakup at the end of the First World War in 1918.

While it was united politically, Austria-Hungary was not a single-minded entity. While Hungary remained stoically conservative, German liberals moved in to dominate Austrian thought during the 1870s. They introduced free compulsory education, enacted statutes of free speech, press and assembly, and emancipated Jews.

Physically, Galicia sat as far northeast as the empire extended, nosing its way into the region that is today partly in Poland and partly in Ukraine. Historically, Galicia for four centuries was subject to the Polish crown; that ended in 1772 when the Austrian empress, Maria-Theresa, with the aid of the Russian czar, incorporated it into her holdings.

When McGarvey and Bergheim first arrived to poke around in Galicia, the province's 2.6 million inhabitants included nearly 19,000 families of Polish nobility, comprising 95,000 individuals. Seven out of ten residents were serfs, the overwhelming majority of whom held only small or no land holdings at all. About forty-five percent were ethnic Poles, nearly as many were Ukrainian and one out of ten were Jewish. There was a smattering of Austrian and German nationals, the Austrians holding down the administrative positions.

When it took over Galicia, Austria fully understood that in order to control the land, the authorities required the support and co-operation of the Polish nobility. In exchange for achieving this goal, Austria agreed to grant the noble families a strong say in Galicia's affairs. After this occurred, the nobles' support then became crucial to the continuance of the national government in Vienna. The nobles knew they were a crucial element to the system and in exchange for their support, they demanded Galicia be operated under a system of laws that were unique in Austria-Hungary. While the decision to grant that special status seemed convenient at the time, it would later come back to haunt the Austrian national authorities.

Just as in many places across the globe, oil had been discovered bubbling to the surface throughout Galicia. Szczepanowski's description had been bluntly accurate: From the beginning of time and on into the 1880s, peasant workers laboriously dug out the muck, tossed it into caldrons overtop open wood fires and boiled down the material to form a black, tarry substance they called "ropa." The system was a replica of the one that had commenced in Canada's Lambton County, and in other corners of the globe, years before.

As in other places, this substance was at first placed on the cuts and bruises of animals and humans alike to promote healing, and dabbed in cracks of boats to make them water-tight. In a different form it was used as lubricating grease for wagon wheels and, when made thinner still, to treat leather. It might have had a pretty raunchy smell, but it seemed to work.

With the coming of the industrial revolution, human knowledge and endeavor began to make great leaps and bounds. Incredible discoveries were being made on a regular basis and in the 1840s the Canadian physician and geologist Abraham Gesner developed a process for refining fuel obtained from coal, bitumen and oil shale. Gesner created the Kerosene Gaslight Company in 1850, installing street lighting in Halifax, Nova Scotia, and later expanding his operations into the United States. It was this discovery that had fuelled the massive hunt for, and development of petroleum resources in Canada and the United States.

Galicia's Jewish Link

Much the same discoveries were occurring on the other side of the Atlantic Ocean in Austria-Hungary. Ignacy Lukasiewicz (1822-1882) was a Polish-born chemist who studied at the Jagiellonian University in Krakow, Galicia. In similar fashion to his Canadian counterpart, Gesner, Lukasiewicz invented a substance from the distillation of petroleum that, when burned in a lamp, gave off a soft white light. The substance was known by some as kerosene, by others as paraffin or coal oil. Lukasiewicz installed his first kerosene-burning lights in a hospital in Lviv, in the far east of Galicia and which today sits in Ukraine.

The light source that Gesner and Lukasiewicz had created proved far more reliable and less dangerous than candles and open flames. The issue, then, was to find sources of this substance that could be mined to obtain this fascinating new product. Lukasiewicz's lamp was well received at the Exhibition of Products for German Industry, held in Munich in 1854, about the same time that the Tripp brothers were showing off their Canadian asphalt at the Paris Exposition. Unbeknown to each, they had kicked off a sort of race between East and West to see who could take a leadership role in petroleum.

When he heard about Lukasiewicz's discovery, Austria's Emperor Franz Josef was smitten by the idea of the new burning oil and when he saw it demonstrated, he ordered the replacement of tallow (made from animal fat) lamps with kerosene lamps, fitting out Vienna's Nordbahnhof train station with the new apparatus by the end of 1858. Other train stations and buildings followed and Austria clambered for new oil sources to feed the growing demand for oil. While the uses it could be put to were minimal when compared to the twentieth century, oil was at least beginning to command new respect.

Still, while oil mining was taking on a modern feel in North America, it remained very much a cottage industry in Galicia, dependent on the labour of peasants and the capital of small-time operators. In Galicia, men dug down by hand and when a vein of oil was found, others scurried to scoop it up in ladles, pans and barrels. It was a chaotic business, and proved to be a totally unsatisfactory method in an era of increasing industrialization and the kind of advancements that were being enjoyed in Canada and the United States.

Why did Galicia not at first follow those advancements that were revolutionizing the North American petroleum industry? It was primarily due to that special status Austria had granted the province to maintain the support of its noble class. While some large players wished to take control of the oil industry and establish a system of oil leases that would allow them to modernize, Galicia's nobles were free to defy all government efforts to intervene. Small-time operators had the upper hand and this is where the special status the landowners enjoyed became a hindrance to economic development.

Special status helped to perpetuate that impractical system. The mineral rights governing petroleum in the ground belonged to the landowners in Galicia who were usually the Polish nobility. Leases and drilling rights were granted to private companies for a specific period of time, such as twenty-five to thirty years. Those who held the drilling rights were required to start the first hole within a set timeframe. This period of time could be renewed and the compensation thus calculated at a rate of perhaps fifteen to twenty percent.

One result of this chaotic system is that by 1874 there were eight hundred and seventy-four separate and mostly minuscule companies in Galicia's oil industry, operating 4,000 shafts and employing 10,500 workers. It was a business begging for rationalization. But it was also a business that worked to the poor Jewish peasants' advantage.

In earlier years, Galicia's Jews had been barred from working in the petroleum industry but with the coming of Austria's new more liberal laws in the 1870s, that ban was lifted. At a time when demand for petroleum was increasing, Jewish peasants began flocking to the oil business as a welcome new way to make an attractive living. They weren't afraid of the backbreaking work that came with hand-digging and hauling the oil to market since they knew the rewards would make their labour worthwhile.

All of this worked against the rationalization of the industry. Small-time collectors of oil – many of whom were Jews – maintained the upper hand.

This anachronistic system was allowed to continue as long as little attention was paid to Galicia. It remained a poor, backward corner of the empire, of little national consequence. But then the Austrian emperor, Franz Josef, paid a visit in 1880 and everything began to change. Franz Josef returned home to Vienna, told his council there were riches to be exploited in Galicia, and they had better get to work to ensure it happened. By 1884, a new law was in place giving Vienna the right to inspect lease terms and working conditions. It was the beginning of a system that would bring order to the chaotic business of oil and paved the way for the arrival and success of William Henry McGarvey.

McGarvey and Bergheim arrived in Galicia at just the right moment. While there are some references made in the industrial records to the partners bringing Canadian pole-tool drillers to Kryg and nearby Lipinki as early as 1882, the stronger evidence is that it was 1883 when they first arrived with Szczepanowski and started hunting for oil. With some early discoveries and Vienna's introduction of new regulations, the partners felt the time was right for them to concentrate on these fields farther east. After all, Hanover was getting them nowhere fast. McGarvey and Bergheim wound up operations at The Continental and transported the drilling plant, as well as most of their Canadian workers, to Galicia.

Stanislaw Szczepanowski had high hopes for modernizing Galician industry in general and, according to Polish academic and petroleum historian Stanislaw Szafran, can clearly be termed the reformer and the founder of the modern Polish oil industry. Szczepanowski was educated and trained in London and Western Europe in science and economics and looked upon the resource-rich and cash-poor Galicia as a place where he could experiment with his ideas. Having heard of the Canadian drilling system that was in operation not far away in Hanover, Szczepanowski decided McGarvey and Bergheim were the vehicle for putting those ideas into motion.

Would McGarvey and Bergheim have made the trip and applied their methods in Galicia at the time they did, had it not been for Szczepanowski's invitation? No one will ever know for sure but as far as Szafran is concerned, Szczepanowski deserves the gratitude of his countrymen for recognizing oil-based industrialization could benefit Galicia, that it was in serious need of a new approach, and that McGarvey and Bergheim were the men who could deliver results.

British oil expert Thomas Boverton Redwood, looking back at the Galician industry mere months after McGarvey's death many years later, wrote that there was "no considerable development … until … the Canadian drilling system was first introduced into Galicia at Kryg by Messrs. Bergheim and M(a)cGarvey, and this field became for some years a very important centre of the industry."

In 1915, Dr. Leon Rymar wrote in *Galicyjski Przemysl Nafty (The Galician Petroleum Industry)*: "The Canadian system became the main reason for the fast drilling of oil in Galicia." Galicia influenced the world because of the technology of drilling introduced by McGarvey, he said.

After his initial drilling efforts at Kryg, near the town of Gorlice, McGarvey and his partner were sufficiently optimistic about the drilling opportunities there that they established Bergheim & McGarvey as a private drilling company. In short order, the men agreed McGarvey, the oil expert, would be the company's feet on the ground while Bergheim, the London-based financier, would develop contacts back in Vienna and his home country of Britain, and contemplate ways to expand the business.

The Canadian Contingent

To ensure their search for petroleum proved successful in this new country, McGarvey travelled to Galicia with his own crew of Canadian roughnecks

– drilling crews that covered every position, from engineers and drillers, down to toolies (driller assistants) and roustabouts (labourers). Among the crewmen who went was Malcolm "Mal" Scott of Petrolia, who had been part of that first crew of Foreign Drillers who went to Southeast Asia in 1873. Mal Scott and his son, Elgin Fredrick Scott, eventually built a large home at Ropienka which became a popular boarding house and place of entertainment and camaraderie for the Canadians as they came to, and left the Galician oil fields.

Mal Scott first came to the McGarvey works in Ustrzyki, north of the Carpathian Mountains and just southeast of Gorlice, and wrote a letter home on April 30, 1884. The letter was printed in the *Petrolia Advertiser* on May 23. Scott reported that his party had left America on the *SS Italy* and spent seventeen days on a cattle ship, sharing quarters with two hundred and fifty Texas steers. From London, they passed through Holland, Germany and Austria, stopping in Berlin and Breslau (today known as Wroclaw, Poland).

Once he arrived in Galicia, Scott wrote: "Where we are located here in Austria (Galicia) is a very pleasant place. You breathe the pure mountain air which is most invigorating." McGarvey led Scott on an inspection tour of the oil district and invited him home to dine. "He showed us the flowing well he struck a few weeks ago. Forty barrels a day. Mac is in excellent spirits and on a fair road to making a fortune."

It was just McGarvey's second year in Galicia but already all the indicators were positive. A further letter from Scott to a friend was reprinted in the *Advertiser* that August in which he offered some observations on the establishment of the quickly growing petroleum industry, saying developments in Galicia "are in their infancy." He declared the equipment they used to be poor and surmised the entrepreneurs would probably be producing more if they had a decent pump. McGarvey would soon supply such a pump – and far more.

This time Scott located himself in the town of Uherce, just outside of Ustrzyki and Polana, where he said McGarvey had put down five wells, the best of which were producing forty barrels a day. About the same distance to the northwest, he said, were two wells that had been pumping for five years while he was told that farther east, some were pumping up to two hundred barrels a day.

"We are all in the best of health and fat as pigs," Mal Scott told his friend back in Petrolia.

All of this activity meant that McGarvey required more workers. On November 13, 1885, he ran an ad in the *Petrolia Advertiser* calling for drillers and rig builders who were willing to relocate to work for him in Galicia. The ad read: "Applications from Drillers and Rig builders wishing to engage with Bergheim & McGarvey, of Austria, in Europe, will be received by the undersigned until Nov. 20, 1885." The undersigned was William's younger brother, Albert, who, the ad noted, was staying at the Tecumseh House hotel in Petrolia. Albert would do the hiring and then accompany the men to Galicia.

Having disposed of his father Edward's Wyoming business interests, Albert had now entered the family firm alongside big brother Mac. Their other brother, James, appears to have remained in Canada for a while longer, likely until about 1890. *The Farmers and Business Directory for the Counties of Elgin, Essex, Kent and Lambton* records James, along with William, as landowner in Lambton's Enniskillen Township as late as 1889. Thereafter, their names both disappear from Lambton's property records. James in the meantime had relocated to St. Thomas, Ontario, where he was still engaged in oil production and refining.

Excitement in Petrolia was rampant at the news McGarvey was hiring foreign drillers and rig builders. One of the oil men who came, Wilfred Durham "Willie" Keith, recalled: "a cry went up for Canadians and Canadian drilling equipment for the exploration of the Galician oilfields which from 1860 had been worked by very primitive means such as hand-dug wells and collecting from seepages on the hillsides." Willie Keith's father, Admiral Nelson Keith, and his uncle, Lafe Keith, were approached by Elgin Scott to join him in his Galician adventure with McGarvey.

"Canadian specialists were then greatly in demand," explained Willie Keith.

Keith's diary entries seemed to suggest that it was only after his father, Admiral Nelson Keith, his brother, Charlie, and Mal Scott, along with Mal's son, Elgin, went to work for McGarvey that they struck a successful well. He recounted one story about McGarvey's famed good luck and about how the group ended up striking it rich.

The men were in a McGarvey field in Wietrzno, about fifteen kilometres south of Krosno, which was about to become a thriving oil town. "After drilling maybe four wells without striking any pay oil, things began to look rather gloomy. McGarvey, taking off his bowler, or rather his Churchill hat, threw it into the air and said, 'boys, since you are willing to help me drill a well on the spot where my hat lands, good luck to you.'

"This well was drilled by my father (Admiral Nelson Keith) and (his elder son) Charlie and it proved a real gusher. The production was so great that there were not adequate means to handle it. The oil was transported to Krosno in barrels – five barrels to a cartload. The production of the well was about 1,000 barrels per day and all the small farmers in the vicinity were engaged with their little horses and carts to transport the oil."

William McGarvey's good luck had apparently served him well again.

Willie Keith's brother and father then moved on to nearby Libusza, sixteen kilometres east of Gorlice, which was becoming the centre of most of the drilling activity under McGarvey and Bergheim's supervision.

Gorlice is situated in the Ropa and Sekowka River valleys, a place tucked among several subranges of the Carpathian Mountains. To the east of the town sat the tiny but impressively named village of Glinik Mariampolski. As it was set squarely in the centre of the oil producing region, McGarvey and Bergheim decided this would be the spot they would build their company's first physical installation. They received permission to erect an administrative building and small refinery to accommodate the crude oil they were pumping from wells in the area, including Kryg.

The partners purchased an old brick distillery building in Glinik Mariampolski – frequently known simply as "Mariampol" – converting and expanding it into their first refinery, which they christened "Glimar," a contraction of the town's name. It was small by later standards, and by the standards of Pennsylvania and Ontario, but it was evidence that the rudimentary methods of old Galicia were being replaced by those of the modern era. When the Glimar refinery was opened for business, it initially employed sixty men, while the process of refining was fuelled by natural gas and oil waste.

The partners were happy to confirm the Canadian drilling system, with some adjustments, was well suited to the geological conditions of Galicia.

Initially, their business was to drill for other landowners. It took little time, however, before income derived from the drilling of those early wells and refining the oil allowed them to start acquiring their own land and drilling rights by 1885.

Drilling equipment and central refining were not the only modern touches McGarvey brought to Europe. The Canadian jerker-line system, by which a number of oil wells could be pumped from a single power source, was also introduced. As in Lambton County, jerker-lines can be seen operating in Poland's historic oil fields to this day.

Oil drilling and refining were going to be just a part of the new operation. Demonstrating their genius and farsightedness, McGarvey and Bergheim laid down the early framework for creating a multi-armed, vertically integrated corporation. They believed that true success and wealth lay in not only owning the mineral rights that allowed them to take the crude petroleum out of the ground and refine it, but in manufacturing the necessary drilling equipment. There would be no further need to import their equipment from the Oil Well Supply Company of Petrolia, Ontario. They could manufacture and use the equipment themselves, as well as market it to other drilling firms. This was a crucial step in their long-term path to success in Europe. And just to make sure of that success, they would also produce the barrels and storage equipment, build pipelines and sell storage space to competitors.

The Bergheim & McGarvey partnership would do it all.

CHAPTER 6

A NEW HOME

William McGarvey had not experienced immediate success in Europe and even though he had faith in his methods, he was relieved when it became clear the gamble he had taken leaving Canada for Europe showed every sign of success. When his drilling began to deliver good results in Galicia, William's letters to Helena spoke glowingly of future prospects. It was time, he told her, for the family to make the move. First, however, he would pay one final visit to Canada to close out his affairs. This time when he returned to Europe, the whole family would be with him. There would be no more splitting them up between two continents.

McGarvey smiled. He was a very lucky man.

Farewell To Canada

In the summer of 1884, William sailed to Canada. It would be the final time he would ever see his homeland. Since the family would be returning permanently with him to Europe, preparations were made to sell their home and the July 4, 1884 edition of the *Sarnia Observer* contained this report from their Petrolia correspondent: "The residence of W.H. McGarvey, Esq., at the East End (Petrolia), is offered for sale, that gentleman having determined to settle in Germany. Mr. McGarvey will be in town shortly, and will take his family to Germany when he returns."

(Apparently, McGarvey did not end up selling the home. Instead, he rented it out and put it up for sale again in 1888. However no sale ever occurred during his lifetime, and in a typical example of his generosity, McGarvey finally offered the home to the widow of a former employee, rent-free.)

Even though the focus of his efforts was to be Galicia, the newspaper declared that McGarvey was on his way back to Germany. At first, that might hint that he was not yet fully committed to building a business in Galicia, but that was not the case. The family's home would be in Hanover, a sophisticated European city in north-central Germany, where they could live a genteel existence in a more central and less isolated location. McGarvey was not prepared to subject his wife and children to the harsh conditions he had himself experienced on his trips into Galicia, even though he would be spending much of his time there.

Kate was just over a year old, Fred was eleven and Mamie just eight when the family accompanied Papa from Petrolia to Hanover. A trip to Europe was definitely a "journey" in those days, but far more pleasant than it had been in the days before coal-powered steamships. The McGarveys likely chose the common route of Canada's Foreign Drillers: take the train from Petrolia to New York, then depart from Ellis Island for Europe by steamship. Steamship travel was far speedier than old-style wind power, with a passenger vessel normally taking a dozen days to go from New York to the Port of Hamburg.

(We can only speculate now, but it is fair to wonder how much time McGarvey spent during his ocean crossing contemplating how the fuel he was helping to produce might be applied to powering these huge vessels. While in the U.S., Civil War-era experiments indicated oil-fired ships were faster than those powered by coal, conversion was rejected by the secretary of the navy, not to be implemented until the Spanish-American War of 1898.)

Once they docked at Hamburg, there was another train ride to their destination of Hanover, one hundred and fifty kilometres south of the port city. With German unification in 1871 under Wilhelm I of Prussia, transportation links had been rapidly improved and that portion of the trip was largely seamless and fairly comfortable.

For the McGarveys, this was a journey of reverse migration. William's ancestors had left Ireland for a new life in the Americas six decades earlier. Now, William and Helena were counting on the Old World for a new start.

The family settled down to life in Hanover and bid Papa frequent goodbyes as he often made the arduous journey into the Galician wilds. Just east of Gorlice, William had chosen a site at the village of Glinik Mariampolski for his new industrial complex.

From a member of the Polish nobility, he purchased a piece of property on a rise overlooking that complex. A simple Polish-style "country house" was already there and McGarvey approved it as a place that was suitable for him to lay his head during the infrequent moments he was off-duty while he strove to build his business.

But McGarvey knew he would be settling there permanently and yearned for his family to be nearby. Once he had shown sufficient success with his Galician operations, Mac and Helena decided it was best to settle the family there. In fact in the words of their son, Fred, it was "mother deciding" Mariampol would be their home. So William, honouring his wife's wishes, set about to have constructed a more regal home in the neo-classical style. Upon completion, Mariampol would welcome the whole family into far more luxurious surroundings. When the new one was finished, the original was used to accommodate the company managers.

By 1888, with the company of Bergheim & McGarvey firmly established and production going well, their new home was ready. While she had never been there, Helena knew of "old Poland" thanks to the childhood stories told to her by her father, Ludwik Wesolowski. She had heard about his growing up in Warsaw and knew Galicia would be primitive compared to the life she had become accustomed to in Hanover.

She might not have anticipated the trip to get there, however. The journey from Hanover to Gorlice is nine hundred and seventy kilometres and today it can be driven in nine and a half hours. Not so in the mid-1880s. East of Germany and beyond Vienna, railways were few and primitive. The first rail link as far as Drohobycz and Boryslaw had not come until 1873 and it was only in 1885 that the state-owned Galician Transversal Railway finally linked Gorlice with Jaslo, Krosno, Sanok and Stryj, in a route along the north side of the Carpathian Mountains. The latter was a project that had been encouraged and championed by McGarvey. The primary purpose of the Transversal, however, was to move crude oil and the military, and passenger service was spotty at best.

Once travellers arrived at Krakow, the nearest significant centre, they were still one hundred and thirty kilometres from Gorlice and Mariampole, a trip that would have been taken via coach and horses. Beyond the railways, there were few paved roadways, with the bulk of them being dirt, which turned to mud for large parts of the year. The winter freeze came as a blessing. In many places, logs were put down to create a type of corduroy road into which wagons would not sink, although the resulting ride was jolting at best.

Then there was the matter of what awaited them. When Petrolians Jake and Jennie Perkins arrived in Galicia with their family in 1887 to work with McGarvey, they discovered a country where peasant villages consisted "of straw-thatched huts – two rooms in the largest – where a miscellaneous assortment of pigs, chickens, people and cows all lived under one roof," their son Wilfred, wrote years later. Cooking was done not by way of the cast iron wood-burning stoves that were by then common back in Canada, but over open fires. Most cottages had mud floors and thatched roofs.

William made sure there would be no such rusticity in store for Helena and the three children. The new McGarvey home was Helena's sanctuary in her new land. She found the view south from her new residence an exercise in stark contrasts. Immediately below the house on the flats of the Ropa River lay the industrial complex that had grown quickly in the past four years. Yet beyond the complex and south of the river rose the beautiful Carpathian Mountains, cloaked in verdant shades of green. It was an enchanting sight.

The McGarveys and the other Canadian Foreign Driller families found the mountains a beguilingly beautiful place. When spring came and melted away winter's heavy snows, the ground beneath the still-bare branches of the beech trees came alive with wildflowers: corn poppies, globe flowers and Siberian iris grew in profusion. The locals appreciated the beauty of the wildflowers and the Canadians learned it was a common courtesy for visitors to pluck a bouquet of the blooms to present to hosts when they paid a visit.

Apart from the occasional smattering of oil wells and rudimentary refineries, much of Galicia was still in its bucolic glory when the McGarveys arrived. Heavily forested, the foothills and, beyond, the

Carpathians themselves, leant the landscape a primeval, pre-industrial feel that belied what was about to happen to the region. It was a district far from the increasingly sophisticated cities of Europe, a community where just one in four could even read and write.

Coming from Petrolia, Ontario, where well-off families such as the McGarveys enjoyed the advancements of late-Victorian society, William and Helena were drawn to the handful of noble families that lived in the area as those closest to having the standard of living they had enjoyed back in Canada. And yet they selected the edge of William's industrial complex as the location where they would build their first home. To offset the rough industrial basin that sat behind and below the home and establish William's image as a successful man of affairs, he adopted the Polish nobility's practice of creating a "plantation" or landscaped park that led up to the front door. This plantation of trees consisted of some species that were not naturally known in Eastern Europe. The trees, carefully selected and positioned as they would be in a public park, included maples – the iconic Canadian tree – and tulip trees from the Carolinian forests of mid-southern North America. The milieu complemented the locals' sense of being at one with Nature, while establishing a unique feel that bordered on the exotic – a message that eloquently communicated this Canadian family's arrival in their midst.

The McGarvey homes — both the initial single-storey cottage-style residence that housed William during his early years there, and the later estate manor — were still standing in 2007 when this author visited. A plaque on the original home states: "Here lived William Henry McGarvey in the years 1895-1914." While the period of residence is not correct – McGarvey lived there from 1888 and was primarily resident of Vienna by 1897, leaving the home to son Fred – the sentiment is what is important. It is because of the research and hard work of Maria Mockal, who was for many years a chemist at the Glimar oil refinery, that the house was identified as that of McGarvey and so recognized. Mockal gave this author a tour of what remains of the house and grounds, and regaled him with stories of the region during his visit to Glinik Mariampolski in 2007. She also shared her extensive research on McGarvey's early industrial installations.

The later home was a much grander and more fashionable structure than the original. Interior photos from 1900 depict a home that would not be out of place on a Victorian-era English country estate. A tennis court was built to one side of the home.

On Helena's wise advice to her husband, the McGarveys tread a fine line between wealth and ostentation. Helena understood from growing up in her Polish-born father's home that if her husband were going to build a successful petroleum empire, he would need the help and support of the local citizenry who were primarily simple Polish peasants. Helena understood that there was no better way to lose the support of the locals than to "show off." McGarvey needed to demonstrate he was a man of the people and not an outsider who had come to join the Polish nobility who, while respected and obeyed, were not widely liked. As an outsider, McGarvey needed to be liked.

There would be plenty of time and other ways to enjoy their wealth, the McGarveys ultimately decided. They would send their children to Europe's finest schools and take in the great entertainment and social functions that awaited them in cities such as Vienna, Paris and London. McGarvey occasionally spoke of enjoying examples of that high-end lifestyle, such as when he told a Polish family he was visiting in Lviv of being carried decadently through the streets of Paris in an elegant cart pulled by ostriches. But once they were at home in Glinik Mariampolski, they must revert to being just plain folks – albeit rich ones.

Still, Helena was determined to turn the property into something special. As well as the impressive plantation William created that led from the road up to the McGarveys' Mariampol home, she oversaw the creation of an English-style country garden around it. With the typical larkspur, St. John's Wort, roses, rosemary and lavender, the home was enveloped in a cocoon that protected it from the harsh and bleak industrial complex that grew up on the back side to the south.

Despite the industry that rose on the spot, there were also stunning natural surroundings at Glinik Mariampolski and the children came to love the outdoor delights that surrounded them. They charted the comings and goings of the wood grouse that favoured the pinewoods near the Carpathian lakes and watched with delight as the trout leaped for mosquitoes, with the great dark forest forming a dramatic backdrop. In winter, they put on their skates and glided across those lakes, just as they would have back in Canada. They grew up to be avid equestrians. Fred especially adored donning his tweeds and deerstalker hat and riding into the nearby countryside. It was a pastime he took with him when, as an adult and family man, he left the Galician countryside and moved to Vienna.

Helena and William came to love their new home. They often hosted lavish parties there and welcomed members of the Polish nobility who lived in grand estates in the vicinity. One such gathering occurred in 1892, this one as a surprise to the couple who were celebrating their twenty-fifth wedding anniversary. The event demonstrated how highly thought-of the couple was in their new community and provides interesting details of their life in Mariampol.

News of the occasion was published in their hometown newspaper, then called *The Petrolia Advertiser and Canadian Oil Journal*, which reported on the event in its August 19, 1892 edition. The McGarveys had been married on July 10, 1867 and by the time of their silver anniversary they had been living in their new Galicia home, together with their three children, for four years.

An entire committee had been established in May 1892 to plan the festivities. Committee members decided one of the gifts would be an album consisting of various paintings that depicted their home, the countryside and McGarvey's oil wells and refineries. While the children appeared to be in on the planning, apparently the committee did its work in such a high degree of secrecy that William and Helena were taken by total surprise when the occasion was thrust upon them. Adding further to the surprise was the fact the party was held a day before their anniversary.

That morning, the couple were awakened "by the sounds of music, and in a few moments appeared in sight, winding through the beautiful park surrounding the residence of Mr. McGarvey a splendid military band composed of forty-five musicians in the Austrian uniform and followed by over eighty Canadians, many dressed in the new uniforms of the two Austro-Canadian (baseball) clubs."

As mentioned earlier, the "park" that surrounded the McGarvey home was the property or grounds that went with the estate, and the manner in which it was landscaped as a "plantation." It was created as a small nod to the McGarveys' immense wealth, something that suggested a level of nobility. The trees shaded the house and provided a striking entranceway along the winding driveway up to its front door. In the brilliant mid-summer sunshine, light filtered down through the heavy canopy of leaves and dappled the throng of well-wishers as they approached the manor.

The country manor where William and Helena lived up until 1897 and which then became the home of their son, Fred, contrasted starkly to the urban surroundings of the Vienna residence to which the McGarveys later moved. Today, while the Glinik Mariampolski houses remain, unfortunately most of the "park" is now gone, the property has fallen into disrepair and much of it is overgrown.

We can imagine William and Helena rushing to the entranceway of their grand home to investigate the cacophony that had so early on that Saturday morning awakened them and there, at the front door, they were greeted by their old friend, Jake Perkins. Perkins, who had accompanied McGarvey on his move to Europe and managed some of the drilling functions for his company, took the lead in wishing the couple a happy anniversary. He then invited the couple, as well as their children – Fred, Mamie and Kate – to join the procession to the nearby estate of a friend. Once there, they were greeted by the wives and children of the Canadian workers.

"The park where the festivities were held is justly celebrated for its beauty, and willing hands had made it a scene of splendour and gaiety by the erection of a tent fifty feet wide and two hundred feet long," the newspaper account continued. There was a second tent for the band. Wreaths, flowers and flags – Austrian, Polish and the Union Jack – were added to the scene. Reportedly there wasn't a cloud in sight as "a refreshing breeze from the Carpathian Mountains tempered the summer heat."

A baseball game was held and a lavish dinner was prepared. Floral arrangements bedecked the tables when it came time for the one hundred and fifty in attendance to sit down to enjoy the feast. Toasts were made, including one given by McGarvey to Canada, which "was received by the Canadians present with three hearty cheers."

Perkins, the transplanted Petrolian, presented the official toast to the happy couple. The newspaper report said:

He alluded to the efforts of Mr. McGarvey in introducing the Canadian system of drilling in Europe, his unwavering kindness toward the Canadians, and his solicitude for their welfare, as was evidenced on every occasion by both words and deeds. He concluded by uncovering and presenting the album of views, which as a work of art, both as to the paintings and the cover, reflects the greatest credit on the Krakauer School of Art as to the paintings, and to the firm of Weidmann and Co. of Vienna, who are the manufacturers of the cover.

The paintings, fourteen in number, sixteen by eighteen (inches), are true to nature, painted in watercolours from sketches taken on the grounds by three first-class artists, finished and tastefully mounted. The album was of plush silk and tied with an ornamental silver band. In the centre of the cover was a silver plate, the years 1867-1892 engraved upon it. The inscription stated: 'On his Silver Wedding day by his fellow workers in Galicia, wishing him and her long life, prosperity and every happiness.'

(Unfortunately, all evidence of the album has been lost.)

McGarvey's reply to Perkins's toast referenced the success the Canadian crew had achieved and generously attributed it to "the honest, faithful service of those happy smiling faces" before him. Another Canadian, George MacIntosh, then offered a toast to the ladies.

As evening approached, the band led a procession back to the McGarvey residence for more socializing and music. At nine o'clock, a second band arrived as part of a torch-lit procession of about one hundred and fifty others, representatives of the oil workers and refiners. A foreman delivered congratulations on behalf of McGarvey's entire staff. Later, there was a fireworks display.

There was yet another procession, this of Gorlice firemen, who offered their own congratulations to the Canadian couple.

The newspaper report concluded: "Mr. McGarvey's services to the country as the founder of a great and growing industry are so well known and appreciated that no less than sixty-four congratulatory telegrams were received during the day, among which many from Members of (Austria's) Parliament and high officers of the government."

Further gifts were presented from friends and colleagues across Europe.

CHAPTER 7

EDWARD MCGARVEY'S FAR-FLUNG FAMILY

In Canada, Edward McGarvey, family patriarch, continues his entrepreneurial ways with a series of strategies to earn a living. The early 1890s bring tragedy, before a visit from grandson Fred, born with a scientist's mind, lifts the elderly man's spirits.

In Europe, his granddaughter marries into German nobility.

New City, New Plan

After he left Wyoming in 1871, and now happily ensconced in London, Ontario, Edward McGarvey showed he was never lost for an idea. Leaving the general store in son Albert's hands, Edward created a new career for himself. In London, the 1881 census listed his occupation as iron merchant. In 1883, the London city directory listed him as a hide dealer. Real estate, too, would play a part in Edward's plan. For the rest of their lives, he and Sarah lived in one of a group of terrace homes Edward owned at 115 York Street, between Talbot and Richmond. The area came to be identified on city maps as McGarvey's Terrace.

Sarah Gamble McGarvey was five years her husband's senior. She suffered a stroke in 1888, which left her with general paralysis. She died February 20, 1892 in London, and was buried at Mount Pleasant Cemetery. As if her loss was not enough of a shock for the family patriarch, the next year, a horrible accident left Edward McGarvey reeling.

Thomas was the youngest of the McGarvey brothers and chose to remain back in Canada rather than follow his elder brothers to Europe. Born in 1856 in Huntingdon, a year prior to the family's move to London, Thomas was still a teenager when his parents left Wyoming for London.

Thomas married Louisa Taylor and made his new home in Massachusetts, although he did a lot of travelling and was frequently found in London, Ontario. He was on his way from Chicago back to Boston when the train he was travelling on collided with a westbound express train at Battle Creek, Michigan on October 20, 1893. Newspaper accounts told of the tremendous impact of the crash that telescoped coaches together and ignited a fierce fire that added to the destruction. The reports contained gruesome details of the crash and resulting inferno.

Twenty-five people died in the crash and many more were badly injured. Thomas was described as "mangled and burned to death." The reports said either the conductor or the engineer on the eastbound train disobeyed orders and the result was "the two engines were driven into each other and were a total wreck."

After the loss of his wife and a son, Edward McGarvey was more than pleased when a letter came in 1895, telling him that his granddaughter was about to marry a German count.

A Noble Wedding

A Countess! One of Canada's fairest daughters to grace the Austrian court.

Count von Zeppelin, an officer of the Emperor's Guard, woos and wins the daughter of William H. MacGarvey.

Brilliant event consummated in the presence of a royal assembly.

It was a breathless newspaper account of William McGarvey's daughter's Viennese wedding that greeted readers back in Petrolia days after the big event. On December 19, 1895, the front page of *The Petrolia Advertiser and Canadian Oil Journal* was emblazoned with photos of the countess, the count and McGarvey.

"By the courtesy of an esteemed contemporary in Vienna we had placed at our disposal a special society reporter who has sent us a full report of the marriage of Miss McGarvey to Count Eberhard von Zeppelin, lieutenant to the Uhlan regiment of Kaiser Wilhelm II (of Germany). It will be remembered that we announced the nuptials (on November 14) and that we promised our readers a full report of the event. The letter of our special correspondent has just arrived, and we are therefore in a position to give the following account of the marriage."

The report went on to say that this "Canadian lady's" marriage into the family of "a European count of royal lineage is an honour to Canada, but that the bride should be the daughter of a Petrolian is a matter of special pride to us and to every citizen of this town."

McGarvey, it said, would be remembered "as an old and highly respected resident who was for several years mayor of the town and as many more warden of the county." McGarvey and his family left Canada "to seek his fortune in a foreign land. A few of our readers know how fortune has favoured him. His conscientious business principles, his active brain and ready wit, his exceptional tact, and the prompt manner in which he always grasps the opportunity when it presents itself has won for him an enviable position and ample fortune. There is no greater illustration of Shakespeare's immortal words uttered by Brutus: 'There is a tide in the affairs of men, which, taken at the flood, leads us on to fortune.'"

The McGarveys hosted a reception the night before the wedding "at the princely apartments of the Grand Hotel in Vienna, after which a sumptuous supper was served in the palatial dining room, which by the way, is one of the finest halls in Europe." This was followed by dancing to the "enchanting sounds" of a famous orchestra. Festivities continued "until the small hours of the morning."

The main event began at noon the next day, Tuesday, November 12, when "the lavished guests were assembled in the German Protestant Church of Vienna to witness the ceremony. The church was beautifully decorated."

"No handsomer couple ever pronounced the inevitable 'I will.' The bride was gowned in an elegant dress of moire silk, trimmed with lace and orange blossoms. The bridesmaids were Miss Maggie Lake, the charming daughter of Colonel Lake, ex-president of the Incorporated Law Society of London, England, and Miss Kate McGarvey, sister of the bride, who wore blue and white silk dresses. The groom was supported by (members of his military regiment in full uniform)" of the Guards Cuirassiers.

Later, there was a "princely breakfast" back at the Grand Hotel. "Money was lavishly expended by a generous hand." Speeches and toasts took up the afternoon, until the couple left at five for their honeymoon in Budapest.

"The festivities still went on, and the flow of wit, mirth and music continued until seven o'clock in the evening. As a minor illustration of the esteem to which the young couple is held, no less than seventy-two telegrams and cablegrams of congratulations were received from all parts of the world while the party were at breakfast."

Among those in attendance were the other McGarvey children, Fred and Kate; the captain of the czar's imperial guard; the groom's mother, the countess Sophie Zeppelin; and several of McGarvey's colleagues in the oil industry, including Robert de Biedermann and August Gorayski. Several guests also came from Southwestern Ontario and there was an old family friend from Detroit.

Mary "Mamie" McGarvey was aged twenty when she married Eberhard Friederick Alexander Joseph Edward von Zeppelin, twenty-six. Mamie, the Petrolia-born daughter of the wealthy Canadian industrialist, made an exquisite bride for the handsome nephew of the German founder of the Zeppelin airship company. Eberhard, who came to be know by the family as Ebert, was the eldest son of the brother of the founder, Ferdinand. It marked the marriage of new colonial wealth and old European nobility. Whether the Petrolia newspaper's reference to the Zeppelins as "royalty" was warranted, is arguable, but certainly by any measure Mamie had married into German nobility.

Schloss Graschnitz: A Tradition Is Born

As a wedding gift to the couple, McGarvey purchased Schloss Graschnitz, a castle that sat within a twenty-acre estate north of Graz in the Austrian region of Styria, for a reported $70,000. The equivalent in modern-day terms would be more than two million. The house would prove to be an excellent investment, one enjoyed not only by the Zeppelins, but by the whole family. Not only did Mamie live in it for the rest of her life, but it became the go-to place for other family members as well, a sort of McGarvey family compound. Mamie's sister, Kate, moved there after her husband died and brother Fred and his wife spent a great deal of time there – including summer vacations – over the years, as did their daughters, Molly and Leila.

Mamie's marriage to Ebert lasted less than a decade. But thanks to William's intervention, Schloss (which means "castle" in German) Graschnitz remained in the countess's hands until she died in 1962.

Graschnitz Castle dates back to the twelfth century but it was only in the fifteenth century that it was rebuilt and raised to its regal status. It has undergone many changes in ownership and it was only in the latter half of the nineteenth century that it began to resemble the estate McGarvey purchased for his daughter and son-in-law.

The main focus of the castle consists of an elongated building with two perpendicular connecting structures. The estate is dominated by a tower that was built in the nineteenth century and rebuilt in 1917 to reflect its current appearance. This is when the dome of the turret lost its original rounded form and was turned instead into a more angular structure. The remains of the original castle walls that surrounded the courtyard can still be found as part of the foundations.

Inside the main house, beautiful Renaissance-era wood panelling in the former dining room and breakfast room were preserved. Behind the castle was a well-kept park, guarded by two resting stone lions that were added in the late nineteenth century to lend a decidedly British touch to the property's character. Extensive agricultural buildings were constructed in the twentieth century. "Mamie went on farming enthusiastically" for many years, according to Patricia Lindsay, a cousin of her sister-in-law.

A Proud Mother

Helena McGarvey kept up her correspondence with friends and family back in Petrolia and Lambton County while she lived in Hanover, Mariampol and Vienna. The year 1895 was a busy one for her and she felt compelled to apologize to an old friend, Ann Reese of Edys Mills in Lambton County, when Christmas was missed and her apparently normal gift package was late arriving.

On December 27, Helena wrote to her old friend, acknowledging a letter she had received from the woman and sending her regrets she had taken so long to respond. The family had spent Christmas at their Glinik Mariampolski residence, where the Canadians celebrated the festive season with a variety of English-Canadian, Polish and German traditions. On Christmas Eve, there was the traditional German tree and the Canadian custom of the opening of the children's stockings hung on the hearth. The small contingent of Canadians had gathered for the singing of carols. Roast beef and plum pudding leant a decidedly English flavour.

In her letter, Helena quickly got to the point of her tardiness and confessed herself a proud mother of the bride. Under the letterhead of William's Galizische Karpathen-Petroleum-Actiengesellschaft, (Galician Carpathian Petroleum Joint Stock Company) Helena wrote: "We have lost our little Mamie. Not really lost, but gone from our house. Married, but as she is so happy I must also be contented. She has a lovely husband. We love him. Also I shall send you a photo of them."

Helena McGarvey proceeded to provide the weather summary and commentary. "We are having some snow and it looks a little like Xmas today. But we had very mild weather this fall and so far."

Helena sent news of her sister-in-law, William's older sister, Mary Vanalstyne of Winnipeg. She remarked that her own "little Kate is a very large girl, taller than I am, and a very good industrious child." By 1895 Kate was twelve, still a decade away from her own marriage.

Helena continued with a reference to her annual Christmas package and apologized for it coming late. "I am sending you a little slice of my dear Mamie's wedding cake and a little photo. A photo on the bill of fare at wedding." Helena ended with: "Enclosed please find the $1 Xmas box and photo."

The letter demonstrated that contrary to some claims, Helena's English was very good. It has been said by some over the years that she spoke in heavily accented English. That would not make sense since while her father was Polish-born, she was born, and grew up in Michigan. Helena did, however, grow up knowing the Polish language and was instrumental in paving the way for William's quick acceptance into Galician society.

Edward McGarvey Jr.

Little is known about the second-youngest of Edward and Sarah's children, Edward Wesley. Born in 1854 while the family was still in Huntingdon, he was six years old when his parents moved to Wyoming and there are no indications that he ever worked in the store there. He moved with his parents back to London in 1871 and in the late 1880s is found in city directories living in a separate home on McGarvey's Terrace, three doors down from his parents. His profession is listed as a wood and ashes vendor. The younger Edward married Annie McLeod but he died on February 11, 1896 at his father's London home, leaving Annie a widow for the last dozen years of her life, and a frequent companion to her father-in-law.

The 1890s were active ones for the McGarvey clan and after the deaths of his wife and two youngest sons, Edward, the patriarch, lived to enjoy the sight of the rest of his children growing up, marrying, raising families and creating successful careers for themselves. A letter he wrote to his nephew, James, in Alliston, Ontario, dated March 6, 1897 – three-and-a-half years after Thomas' tragic death and a few months after the death of Edward Wesley – demonstrates just how proud of his family he was.

Edward references a visit he had paid to his nephew in the recent past. "I am happy and thankful to inform you that I have enjoyed good health since I was at your place," wrote the then-75-year-old Londoner. He noted that he remained active and attended church twice each Sunday with Annie, Edward Wesley's widow.

Mentioning the frequent letters he received from William, Edward indicated he was looking forward to an upcoming visit from his grandson, Fred. Fred had been born in Petrolia in 1873 and was three years older than Mamie and ten years Kate's senior. All three of William's surviving children – Nellie had died suddenly in Hanover, Germany at the age of thirteen in 1882 and William Edward died at just over a year old in 1872 in Petrolia – were educated at private schools in Germany and England, and all grew up learning the German language as fluently as they did their native English. There are also suggestions that all three children had a far better command of the Galician Polish language than their father.

Once the family was living in Mariampol, Fred was sent to obtain a proper English education at Cranbrook Academy in Kent, England. Census records show he was in the residence in 1891 and Fred later recalled he finished his Cranbrook education in 1892. Founded in 1518, at the time of Fred's attendance it was known as one of the finest grammar schools in the country. After graduation from Cranbrook, Fred attended the Karlsruhe Institute of Technology – a leader in engineering and natural sciences – and obtained his diploma. Then it was on to Heidelberg University, perhaps the finest school of higher education in Germany, where he said his main objective was the study of chemistry. He also studied geology and physics and obtained his PhD.

William McGarvey had never had the opportunity of a good formal education but believed firmly in its value and encouraged his son to continue his studies. The business of oil was changing and Mac felt Fred would benefit from professional studies as he was being groomed to take over the company. The proud father looked on as Fred was awarded his doctorate. Fred would be as well prepared for running a petroleum company as education could ensure.

Fred was proud of his Heidelberg education and tried years later to convince a young North American cousin, Dan Chew, to take advantage of his fluency in German and attend Fred's alma mater.

After graduating from Heidelberg, Dr. Frederick McGarvey was invited to join "Professor Engler," head of the chemistry school at Karlsruhe, on a scientific expedition to Egypt's Sinai, Palestine and Syria. Fred recalled the trip involved scientific work on the shores of the Red Sea and a trip up the Nile. The plan, outlined by his grandfather in the letter he wrote to his nephew in Alliston, was that when Fred returned from the Middle East in April 1897, he would pay a visit to England and then would be off to explore North America and see his Canadian family. When Fred again returned home to Galicia, he would "settle(s) down to business." Already by 1895 and while still attending university, Fred had been appointed a manager at the Glinik Mariampolski works in what must have been at first a largely titular position, designed to prepare him for the more active role he would assume after graduation.

("Egyptomania" reached epic proportions in 1890s Britain. In 1894, Oscar Wilde published a work on the subject. In 1897, the year Fred went, T. Cook & Sons of London published *Cook's Tourist Handbook for Egypt, the Nile, and the Desert*. For Victorians who had their own sometimes morbid take on death, something in the Egyptian ceremonies and rituals around death seems to have struck a chord. Well-off and curious Britons were flocking to Egypt.)

Fred recalled years later that on his return from Egypt, he travelled through Constantinople and Romania, then back home for a couple of weeks. Then he left for England before sailing for Canada and the United States. During that trip, he crossed Canada from Quebec to British Columbia, then down the coast to California and east through Salt Lake City, Chicago and on to Petrolia for a visit. After stopping to see his grandfather Edward in London, Fred returned to England aboard the *Umbria,* out of Quebec City, which returned him to Liverpool, before he continued the trip back to the Continent.

Edward said his plan was to accompany his grandson on his return to Europe. He expected to be back home in London, Ontario in time to greet his nephew at the time of the local fall fair.

Fred did make it to his grandfather's home during his cross-continent odyssey that year and from a family photo taken at Mariampol afterwards, it is clear that Edward was able to join his grandson on the return trip and take that planned European holiday. In the photo taken on the rear steps of the McGarvey manor home, Edward, William and Helena are joined by Mamie and Ebert, Fred and Kate, as well as an unidentified young man who might have been a friend of Fred's.

Other photographs taken of family occasions at Mariampolski reveal much about the events and visits that took place there. The house conveys an elegant Victorian atmosphere, its drawing room filled with Persian rugs and furnishings, its walls and tabletops overflowing with family photographs. Outside scenes show Fred and his future wife mounted atop riding horses, picnics in the garden and people walking through the manicured vegetation with tennis racquets. This was a clearly wealthy family enjoying their gains.

CRUDE GENIUS

The elderly Edward McGarvey was back in London on June 23, 1900 — when he died at the age of 81 from "chronic heart and kidney trouble." The obituary in the *London Free Press* mentions that he still lived at the "terrace" off York Street that bore his name and that he was engaged in the wood ashes and pressed hay trade that he had joined in partnership with his late son, Edward Wesley.

From sawmill operator, to shopkeeper, to iron merchant, to a trade in wood ashes and pressed hay – Edward had lived a life of varied careers and life experiences. The son of an Irish immigrant from Belfast, he had shown grit and determination in establishing his own businesses. He was a true entrepreneur and a model to his children. In the words of his grandson, Fred, "he was a typical colonial pioneer and a great optimist. His business activities varied greatly. At times he was prosperous but many of his schemes resulted in losses."

As for Fred, once back in Europe, it was now time to settle down and take a more active position with his father's company, the Galician Carpathian. Over the years, Fred became a valuable asset to the company. But his father's dream of Fred managing the company through another generation would not come true.

CHAPTER 8

VIENNA

6 6 The city was a dream, and the emperor a dream within the dream."
So wrote author Hermann Broch about *fin de siècle* Vienna, which had evolved into one of Europe's truly great centres of civilization. It was a place of grand avenues lined with buildings adorned with elaborate Baroque ornamentation, superb opera houses and coffee houses where intellectuals debated the political and social issues of the day. A plurality of races, religions and beliefs poured into the "Imperial City" from across the empire, creating a cosmopolitanism the likes of which Europe had not experienced before. With them they brought copious talents in all fields of endeavor, and it became the fourth most populous city in Europe.

Kaiser Franz Josef's Creation

Vienna was dominated, and the modern city shaped by Emperor Franz Josef. Throughout his long reign (1848-1916), Franz Josef demonstrated an openness to diverse beliefs and opinions. A Roman Catholic himself, he expressed an acceptance of German liberal thought. Jews were welcomed to worship as they pleased and to take a full part in society, with the emperor once saying: "The civil rights and the country's policy is not contingent on the people's religion."

When he took the throne, Franz Josef was considered a man of modern ideas. He ordered the demolition of the city walls and battlements, replacing them with the Ringstrasse, dubbed by some the most beautiful avenue in the world. The boulevard was lined with five kilometres of neo-Gothic and neo-Baroque buildings, including the Museum of Fine Arts, the Renaissance Revival Vienna Opera House and the Burgtheatre.

Helena McGarvey adored Vienna and paid many visits during the years she lived in Glinik Mariampolski. She would usually stay at the Grand Hotel, strolled the Ringstrasse, adored the spate of beautiful department stores that opened during the roaring 1890s, and loved attending the art museums and the opera house. She and William danced under chandeliers of fine crystal to Strauss waltzes played on exquisite violins. Helena saw to it that her children were exposed to Vienna's social milieu. Fred and Madge would eventually move there and lived in the city for many years, as would his sister, Kate and her husband, Erik Jurié. One of Fred's daughters would one day perform at the concert hall.

Feeling somewhat stifled by provincial Galicia, Helena wanted a permanent Viennese address and was instrumental in convincing William to move their household to the city. Plans were already afoot to move the company headquarters there. Certainly the Karpath had outgrown its humble Galician beginnings; if it was going to prove its competency to be considered one of the world's great petroleum and manufacturing corporations, it would be much easier to do so if headquartered in what was widely recognized as one of the world's finest cities. With Helena's influence and William's business acumen, the move to Vienna now seems preordained.

McGarvey chose as his company headquarters a utilitarian, two-storey office building in downtown Vienna at 29 Graben. A market street off Graben to the west of the office building led directly to the emperor's palace. Wolfgang Amadeus Mozart had lived at the same address in 1784 when it was still used as a residential building. When fire destroyed the building in 1910, it was quickly replaced by a five-storey, equally non-Baroque-looking structure, one more in the style of the groundbreaking Viennese architect, the stark minimalist Adolph Loos.

For their Viennese home, the McGarveys selected something quite different in style. William and Helena took one of the six apartments in a beautiful newly built neo-Baroque edifice at 2 Gusshause. The elegant three-storey structure was completed just before the McGarveys moved into their new home in 1897. The city apartment was a gargantuan departure from the estate home they had built at Glinik Mariampolski and no doubt satisfied Helena's desire to truly enjoy the refined Viennese lifestyle. Once they lived in the city, there was no further need to prove themselves simple country folk. Helena loved to throw lavish parties and take part in the privileged lifestyle that the emperor's capital city had to offer.

Emperor Franz Josef epitomized Vienna's nineteenth-century liberalism and as a Canadian-born Protestant with simple country roots, McGarvey was of a like mind. In Galicia he found himself surrounded by Catholics and Jews and maintained a generous openness to their beliefs that was in keeping with the kaiser's philosophy. McGarvey seemed as comfortable meeting and conversing with the most humble and unsophisticated of his employees (although his knowledge of Polish was rudimentary) as he did to the German-speaking Polish noble landowners who inhabited the grand estates that dotted the countryside in Galicia, and to the great families of Europe – including the Zeppelins – with whom he was often becoming involved.

While he loved the sophistication of Vienna, McGarvey never tired of visiting his industrial installations. There is a photo of a smiling McGarvey visiting the Glinik factory and posing with the plant officials and workers, dressed in his signature vested suit and Churchillian bowler hat. A more demure Fred is seated to his left, arms crossed in the style that was his signature in his early years as superintendent.

McGarvey arrived in Austria in the midst of the revolution of thought that swept Europe between the 1880s and the 1920s. It was a revolution that was no more intense than in Vienna and in turn it sparked a more extreme reaction, said *The Economist* in a 2016 article. It was a time when mutton-chop whiskers were giving way to clean-shaven faces as well as atonal music and Freud's psychoanalysis. The juxtaposition was no more obvious than at the spot where the neo-Baroque Hofburg Palace, home of the ruling Habsburgs, sat across from the Loohaus with its straight lines and smooth, non-ornamented façade. While built just two decades apart, these structures represented the intense pressures that were growing inside the empire, pressures it would ultimately prove incapable of harnessing.

McGarvey's openness and "liberality of thought" began to be challenged with the coming to power in 1897 of the anti-Semitic

Viennese mayor, Karl Lueger. Franz Josef loathed Lueger and used his prerogative to delay his swearing in for as long as he could. Eventually, the emperor could stop him no longer and once in office, Lueger was a progressive politician in everything but race relations: he introduced municipal gas and electricity works, created a public transit system including streetcars, implemented a social welfare system, and built parks, hospitals and schools.

Vienna became a hotbed of new ideas, some good and some bad. Only in Vienna could a joke possibly begin: " Freud, Klimt, Trotsky, Lenin and Hitler walked into a coffee house." Because, in fact, they all did.

It is here in Vienna that Freud developed his theories of psychoanalysis and first described the Oedipus Complex. Here, Gustav Klimt created his symbolist style demonstrated in *The Kiss* and *Portrait of Adele Bloch-Bauer I*. Trotsky and Lenin honed their political theories and a young Austrian painter named Adolph Hitler decided he had no future in the arts. Theodor Herzl, the father of Zionism, studied at the University of Vienna and edited an influential newspaper. Composers Gustav Mahler and Arnold Schoenberg, authors Stefan Zweig and Arthur Schnitzler and philosopher Martin Buber all lived in the city during the era. It was a wonderful city that captured the imagination of three generations of McGarveys and left an indelible impression upon them.

Helena Wesolowski McGarvey

Helena Idwiga Wesolowski McGarvey lived to see the marriage of her eldest daughter, Mamie, to Count von Zeppelin, but had precious little time to enjoy her incredible wealth and the beautiful Vienna apartment she and William had moved to in 1897. She had been in poor health throughout 1898. William suggested she get out of the city and travel to Schloss Graschnitz for the clean air and to visit daughter Mamie and son-in-law Ebert. Mac was worried about Helena. In her younger years, she had been so vibrant and fun-loving but she had been ailing for quite some time. Illness meant she had not had much opportunity lately to take part in the Viennese lifestyle she so adored. William hoped that a visit to the beautiful Austrian countryside and some pampering by Mamie would do her good. He hoped that breathing in the fresh mountain air around Graz would be just the tonic.

While visiting at Schloss Graschnitz, on Tuesday, December 13, 1898, Helena took a turn for the worse and died. Her body was brought back to Vienna for burial in the Protestant section of the main city cemetery. Helena's presence and her sparkling personality had been an incredible comfort and benefit to William in his efforts to become acclimatized to, and accepted by his adopted country. Helena was fluent in Polish, the language of her father, and eased her husband's way into the society where he needed to be accepted by not only the Polish nobility, but the serf and peasant class as well, who comprised the majority of his workers.

Back in Petrolia, the *Advertiser and Canadian Oil Journal* reported Helena's death in its December 21 edition. While no cause of death was indicated in the newspaper article, it did mention her "poor health for a long time." It is worth noting that, in referencing William McGarvey's fame overseas, that story is the first known place where he is referred to as the "petroleum king of the great Austrian fields."

After she died and even though the McGarveys were Protestant rather than of the Galician province's predominant Roman Catholic or Orthodox faiths, McGarvey donated stained glass windows to a Catholic church near Gorlice in his wife's memory. It was one of many acts of kindness and generosity for which the Canadian petroleum industrialist was known and beloved.

Fred McGarvey Marries

Margaret Fanny Salome Bergheim was known as Madge to most of her friends and family and was the niece of William McGarvey's partner, John Simeon Bergheim. Born in Jerusalem where her father, Peter, had been a noted photographer, she and three siblings were orphaned after Peter was murdered in 1885 and mother Martha died two years later. Madge and brother Peter Jr. were sent to live with their Uncle Johnny and Aunt Clara Bergheim, while the other two siblings went with relatives on their mother's side.

Even though they lived far apart, Fred and Madge grew up frequently socializing with one another, but it seems to have taken them many years, and apparently several other less serious relationships, before they decided they were in love.

By the time Fred and Madge married, he was twenty-eight years old and she was twenty-three. Like the McGarveys, the Bergheims were incredibly wealthy by this time and lived in a beautiful home in Belsize Park, London. On July 10, 1901, Fred and Madge were married in the Anglican Church of St. Peter in Belsize Park, London. Fred's sister, Mamie Zeppelin, served as one of the witnesses while his younger sister, Kate, was one of the bridesmaids. Madge's uncle, Reverend Nigel Bergheim, was the officiating clergyman.

As wedding gifts, Fred presented his bride with a roofed carriage known as a brougham, and dressing bag (a small cushion or pad over which the hair was "dressed") with silver settings. Madge gave Fred a set of pearl studs. Other wedding gifts included a diamond necklace, comb and brooch from Papa William, plus a sizeable cheque, a diamond and ruby ring, and turquoise and diamond bracelet. (It should be recalled Papa had already given Fred his Mariampol estate after his parents moved to Vienna).

The event was described in a report in the *Petrolia Advertiser* of July 31, 1901. "After the ceremony, a reception was held at Belsize Court, the residence of the bride's uncle (John Bergheim), and later in the day the bride and bridegroom left for Scotland, where the honeymoon will be spent," said the report.

The newspaper explained its extensive coverage of the wedding was "because of the important and honorable connection which the families of MacGarvey and Bergheim have with the petroleum industry of Galicia." It continued that the couple "are both popular and highly esteemed by the workpeople on the well-known Galician properties, so successfully founded and built up by Messers MacGarvey and Bergheim."

Fred and Madge lived in the family home at Mariampol where he had lived alone since 1897, when William and Helena moved permanently to Vienna to be closer to the bright lights of the city as well as his company headquarters. While Mac directed operations from the head office, Fred stayed behind to manage and keep a close watch on the centre of production as superintendent of the oil fields, the main company refinery and the equipment factory. William's only living son had taken on a huge responsibility in the company Bergheim and McGarvey had built. The founders were paving the way for a smooth succession.

Fred was known for his Victorian charm and deadpan sense of humour. While he and Madge lived in Mariampol, Madge's younger brother, Peter, would often pay a visit. On one such visit, Fred, a passionate horse-lover, took his brother-in-law for a ride in the countryside. Peter spotted some unfamiliar droppings along the way and asked Fred what sort of animal might have left them. Fred replied with a twinkle in his eye: "Those are from a peasant, living on potatoes."

Fred was articulate, unpretentious and down-to-earth, recalled American cousin Dan Chew. He wore cozy sweaters around home and in the outdoors was forever seen in an old fedora, the brim of which he wore straight, even in a later era when men more fashionably turned theirs down.

Fred's early shyness is reflected in photos showing him posed with crossed arms, clearly as second-fiddle to his confident and beaming father. In later years, Fred adopts the pose of a more confident and worldly man, one who has grown comfortable in his own skin and feeling capable of the huge managerial responsibilities bestowed upon him.

He was also known for a dictatorial streak when it came to managing his children. In later years, Fred's younger daughter, Molly, would fall victim to her father's dictates, as will be discussed later in the book.

According to a note in Fred and Madge's guestbook, the couple lived at Mariampol until February 1910. That is when, said the note, they left "the dear old house" that had been the McGarvey family home since 1888 and they, too, moved to Vienna, living in a luxurious apartment that overlooked a city square along the Arenberg Ringstrasse 16. It was a fashionable address, one befitting the wealthy scion of the petroleum king of Austria. Fred was now William's assistant in all company matters.

Kate McGarvey

Sarah Kate, youngest of William and Helena's children, remained a somewhat mysterious figure, quieter and far less flamboyant than sister Mamie, yet not averse to having a bit of fun on occasion. Peter Bergheim,

Madge's younger brother who is one of the family members who changed his name to Lindsay, remembered the many times he and Kate, in their younger years, used to go out and "paint the town red." She was remembered by other cousins, nieces and nephews as a fun-loving character who enjoyed showing off the sights of Vienna.

Kate became engaged to Erik Jurié von Lavandal in the spring of 1904 and they were married on October 4 back in Glinik Mariampolski. (In German the term "von" is used to denote a level of nobility.) Erik Jurié was from a less wealthy and lesser-known Austrian family than Mamie's husband, Count Ebert von Zeppelin. When he married Kate, Erik was a hussar (light cavalry) officer in the Austria-Hungary army, assigned to Bosnia and Herzegovina. His father, Gustav, was a doctor and university lecturer who boasted of his membership in the Sovereign Military Order of Malta.

Kate adored the simplicity of the Galician country lifestyle and chose to hold her wedding back there rather than in the glitzy big city. It was a typical show of independence that set her apart from her sister, Mamie. A photograph in an album that was kept by Fred McGarvey's daughter, Molly, shows Kate and Erik in traditional Galician wedding costume, Kate in a peasant dress and Erik in a long military coat and woollen hat. The detail with which the weddings of Kate's older sister, Mamie, and brother Fred were reported is missing for the youngest McGarvey.

While their wedding was held in Galicia, once they were married, Kate and Erik made their home in Vienna, at 8 Karntner Ring. Erik was brought in to the Galician Carpathian corporation as a member of the board of directors in 1913.

The couple is recorded together as visitors to Fred and Madge's home in Glinik Mariampolski, and then Vienna, up to November 1917. After that time, Kate paid her visits alone. However, up until June 7, 1921, Kate still lists her home as Vienna. On her next visit, which was on January 22, 1922, she presented her home as Schloss Graschnitz, Mamie's palatial residence. We can only speculate what became of Erik sometime between November 1917 and 1921 or 1922. Did he die? Was he killed in battle?

While Kate adopted the peasant costume of Galicia for her marriage ceremony, that is not to say she did not enjoy more formal attire too.

A photo taken at a Viennese studio about 1920 shows Kate in a beautiful ivory gown, layered in lace at the bodice, and conveys the gently beguiling smile for which the family came to know her.

After Erik's death, Kate never remarried and lived at Schloss Graschnitz with her sister for the rest of her life. She died January 28, 1934, at the age of fifty.

Eleanor Hamilton

William lived alone for a number of years after Helena's death. He spent much of his time on company business but in his off-hours the loneliness was difficult for him. The Bergheims would often invite him to their London home and were well-known for their gatherings to which they would invite talented young performers to help entertain their guests. Clara Bergheim was not beyond a little matchmaking and would occasionally invite unattached friends and acquaintances in the hope of helping William find a new mate.

The oil tycoon would politely tolerate Clara's efforts and gently admonish her, but did not seem to be in any hurry to find someone with whom to share the rest of his life.

That changed the day McGarvey was out with friends at an event in Vienna and a stylish young Englishwoman of means and refinement named Eleanor Emily Hamilton was in attendance. More than 30 years his junior, Eleanor Hamilton was a vivacious woman who lived in London's fashionable Cadogan Square, known still today as one of the city's most desirable residential addresses, a neighbourhood of red brick homes collected around a central garden. Cadogan Square is named for Earl Cadogan whose family ownership there goes back centuries.

With the wide gap in their ages, it never occurred to friends that the two would hit it off, but William was smitten. The Bergheims, while undoubtedly taken aback by the age difference, were pleased for their old friend. On October 10, 1905, William McGarvey and Eleanor Hamilton were married in St. Columba's Church of Scotland in Chelsea, Reverend Archibald Fleming presiding. John Bergheim signed his name as one of the official witnesses.

The petroleum trade journal *Nafta* reported: "William M(a)cGarvey, a well-known and highly respected oil industry executive and vice-president of the Galician Carpathian Petroleum Company, married Miss Eleanor Hamilton in London on October 10. In sharing this news with our readers, we send Mr. M(a)cGarvey our warmest wishes."

By all accounts, Eleanor made William very happy. He began to enjoy social outings again and would frequently travel with Eleanor back to his old home in Glinik Mariampolski, where son Fred was living with his wife, Madge, and their two daughters, Leila and Molly. *Nafta* reported the bride and groom dropped in to the Galician office for a visit soon after their wedding. "At noon on November 20, 1905, Mr. William M(a)cGarvey arrived in Glinik Mariampolski after his recent marriage, with his bride, Miss Eleanor Hamilton. The factory gateway was decorated in triumphal fashion with white and red flags and factory managers and workers gave the new couple a warm welcome. Amidst wonderful weather and to the sounds of the Wieliczka Salt Mine Band, the newlyweds were greeted with the traditional (Polish) bread and salt."

McGarvey was clearly touched by the appreciative welcome and spoke about his fondness for his adopted country and second homeland, a place filled with good friends. There was a lantern-lit procession of workers to the old McGarvey home and factory management held a party for workers in one of the company buildings. McGarvey toasted the prosperity and development of Poland and expressed his deep appreciation for all that the people there had done for him. Eleanor looked on with pride.

The couple would be living in Vienna and Eleanor knew no German, so she hired a tutor and began to pick up the language. They chose not to live in the Vienna home William had briefly shared with Helena at 2 Gusshaus, and instead selected one half a kilometer away at 8 Lothringerstrasse, about a six-minute walk from where his daughter, Kate, and her husband, Erik Jurié, lived. However, William kept his original apartment as well. Closer to the age of William's children than her husband, Eleanor continued to call upon Fred and Madge in Vienna long after William's death and was a frequent guest at Mamie's Schloss Graschnitz estate.

The Vienna newspapers' society pages were filled with references to William and Eleanor McGarvey. There were frequent charitable events and mentions of Eleanor attending garden parties where she took tea with some of the city's other leading and noble wives. William was never known for taking vacations but he was apparently inspired to buck that trend in the late winter of 1912. A Prague newspaper, *Prager Tagblatt*, reported on April 3 that Mr. and Mrs. McGarvey had just arrived home from a visit to Portoroz, a resort community on the Slovenian coast of the Adriatic Sea. The couple had stayed at the Portoroz Palace Hotel. It had been established in the late nineteenth century as a health and spa resort.

A Life Of Mission And Service

While Mac's capitalist intentions were never in doubt during the years he built the Galician Carpathian Petroleum Company, he maintained a generosity toward his friends and his employees that guaranteed a genuine warmth toward him. While less scrupulous operators suffered frequent labour unrest, McGarvey's companies were relatively free of such strife.

While he was never overtly religious, as a man of notionally Methodist upbringing, McGarvey believed in and practised the concept of "social holiness." He believed Man's life on Earth was as important as any life after death. Faith in the Wesleyan tradition equips and mobilizes us for mission and service in the world, he believed.

McGarvey's generosity became legendary. Beata Obertynska was a poet and writer in the Polish language who was born in 1898 near Lviv, which is now in Ukraine but at the time was part of Galicia, right in the midst of McGarvey's oil empire. Her father, Waclaw Wolski, was a wealthy business associate of McGarvey's whose portrait hung in the company's Mariampol office. Wolski frequently welcomed the Canadian into his home. It was a home of great privilege, a place filled with books and art, and a place often visited by men and women of the arts.

As a young girl, Beata Wolska Obertynska remembered McGarvey's frequent visits to her home. He was kind-hearted, a man of great generosity, she said, a man who came laden down with gifts. But those gifts often came with unexpected and sometimes humorous consequences.

Beata Obertynska's father was a great believer in physical fitness. He would keep the windows open year-round and instruct his children on the benefits of walking barefoot in the cold, dewy grass. "Once we even had our own gymnastics teacher," Obertynska said. "My father was a great athlete. He swam, rode a bike, played tennis, fenced. He was an avid hunter. An oil man himself, Father had business dealings with the millionaire oil man, McGarvey."

McGarvey, knowing Wolski's penchant for physical fitness, once sent the children a set of Canadian hockey sticks, boxing gloves and a punching bag. The children had never seen a punching bag, which was designed to be strung by rubber bands between two poles. "Each time we'd strike it, it snapped back furiously, coming at us in unforeseen, unpredictable directions."

McGarvey's gifts often left the Wolskis wondering what to make of them. "An unusual parcel came to us on one Christmas day. McGarvey sent our father literally an entire rail car filled with domestic and wild birds. Ducks, partridges, pheasants and species that were totally unknown to us. The shipment came from Baku in the Caucasus Mountains. It looked as though someone had shot an entire paradise of birds that were then frozen and sent to us. It was a real disaster, not a gift, although we children had a lot of fun with these birds. The whole kitchen up to the ceiling was filled with them. That year, our angels' Christmas toys had wings made from real feathers rather than paper ones."

Then there was the cheese. "An entire huge round of cheese, so big the postman could not roll it into the house. The aroma was so strong we had to find an unused portion of the house to store it. Luckily, because we lived in a remote area and not all of the windows came equipped with security bars, the strong smell of the cheese at least had the beneficial effect of deterring thieves."

One day McGarvey sent a couple of five-kilo tins of caviar. "It was a dizzying amount of caviar. How to eat such a quantity? The family took bets on who could consume the most." The maid prepared the boys' sandwiches for school with a large dollop of caviar in the centre, but it was so big the rolls could not be closed. "When the school's headmaster saw the caviar, he sent a polite but firm letter to Father with the request that they not show such luxury in front of the other children."

"The kind-hearted McGarvey was forever sending us gifts. Then there were the plants: datura, tuberose, nicotiana, caprifolium, cinnamon, lilies. Whatever you wanted. The calla lilies were so big, their blooms were bigger than gramophone horns. At dusk they sprayed their scent throughout the house. The exotic scent carried on the breezes for miles.

"The datura came to us as a flower but it was so big, I swear we were quite comfortable seating ourselves in its crook – they were like miniature boughs of trees. I cannot recall what happened to it; I suppose eventually it withered and died."

Obertynska remembered McGarvey perfectly. "Not a tall man, grey-haired, with small, cheerful eyes, thick eyebrows, and a grey moustache that made him look like a walrus. He was always filled with amusing stories."

Every time he paid a visit to Lviv, McGarvey always reserved a table at a fine restaurant and hosted lunch with the entire Wolski family. He seemed to truly enjoy his visits. During one of his stays, he recounted the story of his early years in Canada, including mention of the cows his father told him to take to market. He told the Wolskis how one was struck and killed as they crossed a railroad track. But the second sold for such a price his father said nothing about the loss of the first animal.

McGarvey was somewhat wistful on that occasion. He said he felt himself a truly lucky man, a man whose good fortune seemed to increase with every turn of his life. He recounted the time he found himself riding through the streets of Paris in an ostrich-drawn carriage, the height, in McGarvey's mind, of privilege and luxury. The older he was, the more money he made.

"I am quite sure," said Obertynska, "that in place of that unfortunate cow, McGarvey will be leaving his family the golden calf."

Papa's Grandchildren

Fred and Madge presented William with two grandchildren in the early years of the twentieth century. Leila Helena Margaret was born on August 15, 1902 and on April 9, 1906, just a few months after William and Eleanor were married, a second child, Molly, was born. While Fred and Madge lived in Mariampol, it was decided the births would take place in larger centres. Leila was born at the Bergheims' London home and Molly's birth took place in Vienna.

There were less happy events occurring in the family, too. Within months of his own second marriage, William's daughter, Mamie, finally had had enough of the philandering Count Eberhard von Zeppelin and advised her lawyers to prepare the appropriate divorce proceedings. While Austria is primarily a Roman Catholic country and divorce was not permitted for Catholics under any circumstances, Mamie and Ebert had been married in a service at the Protestant Church of Germany. That made everything different: under the Austrian divorce law of the era, a non-Catholic divorce was permitted either by mutual consent, or when one party had committed adultery. Nevertheless, the whole matter ended up costing William a great deal of money to pay off the count and persuade him to forego any legal claim to the matrimonial property.

After the divorce, Mamie maintained her title as the Countess von Zeppelin, and signed her name that way for the rest of her life. She never remarried.

Zeppelin did marry again, in 1916, to a cousin named Gabriele Ludmilla von Wolff. He died in 1926 after contracting dysentery that required an operation. While the operation was a success, during recovery Zeppelin developed an inflammation of the lungs, which killed him.

A Meeting of Kings

Vienna's British population was a substantial one during the pre-war period, with estimates ranging upwards of 1,000 or more. There was both an Anglo-American Club (which consisted largely of Americans) and an Anglo-American Society, to which the McGarveys and many other Canadians and Britons belonged. William occasionally served on the society's board and was president for several years. In 1903, Buckingham Palace announced that King Edward VII, son of the late Queen Victoria, who succeeded her when she died two years earlier, would pay a visit to the Austrian capital. It was a grand occasion, designed to cement the friendly relationship between the British Empire and the Austro-Hungarian Empire, a relationship based on the connections between the two royal families. At a state dinner, the kaiser and the king toasted one another's good health. The *Illustrirtes Wiener Extrablatt* newspaper featured a line drawing of the monarchs' meeting on its front page on September 2.

King Edward dropped in to the British embassy to pay homage to the British colony in Vienna and when newspapers reported on the event, McGarvey's name headed the list of attendees. Perhaps McGarvey had the opportunity to remind the king that in 1861 when he was the Prince of Wales, he had visited the petroleum lands of Lambton County.

Gifts presented to the king by Vienna's expat community included several silver-framed watercolour paintings, including views of the K.K. Hofburgtheater and the Austrian parliament.

But there was an ominous backdrop to the whole event: turmoil in the Balkans on Austria-Hungary's southeastern frontier. It seemed minor at the time, a mere inconvenience to the great Habsburg empire. It would be slightly more than a decade before those troubles threatened the friendship that the two monarchs had come together to celebrate.

CHAPTER 9

A MODERN COMPANY

From oil drilling, to refining, and manufacturing their own equipment, to pipelines, storage tanks and supplying businesses around the world, William Henry McGarvey's business is transformed into an international concern.

Building a Reputation

"Mac" McGarvey and "Johnny" Bergheim fully believed the best way to ensure their company's success was to create a self-sufficient and integrated business that could do everything itself, without ever being beholden to other suppliers. They were equally determined to conduct themselves in the most honorable fashion. McGarvey led the building and development of his enterprise in a manner that adhered to "the most scrupulous business practices," a fact that earned him an "exemplary reputation," according to a translation of Volume 1 of the *History of the Polish Oil Industry*.

Wrote the Lviv-based journal *Nafta* on the occasion of McGarvey's sixtieth birthday: "His industry and skill and the resulting successes have brought McGarvey position and respect; his charm and friendly nature have touched the hearts of all; and thanks to his preeminent qualities, he has been able to find in this, his second home (Galician Austria), an excellent and agreeable life. McGarvey has always observed the interests and characteristics of the country in which he was to find his life's work, and his attitude in our midst brought him a measure of respect which is only accorded to one of true worth and nobility of character."

Part of that reputation was based on his penchant for operating under "gentlemen's agreements" whereupon he would seal a deal with nothing more than a handshake. When the Polish-language *New Reform* newspaper of Krakow reported on McGarvey's death, it quoted longtime friend and petroleum colleague Robert Biedermann as saying he had conducted business with the Canadian for many years based only on oral agreements and nothing formally written. (*Nowa Reforma*, 1 December 1914).

Oil production had been the genesis of the Bergheim & McGarvey partnership and continued to take a leading role in its success. The company opened properties in Wietrzno and Rowne in 1886-87 and in 1888, Weglowka was added. Then came oil fields at Krosno in 1890. Chemical engineer and renowned British petroleum expert Thomas Boverton Redwood visited Krosno in 1894 and later wrote: "I was impressed with the character of the results achieved. Somewhat deep drilling was necessary here, but oil and gas were met with under great pressure, and spouting wells (gushers) of a remarkably productive character were not uncommon. One well was drilled to a depth of 2,140 feet (six hundred and fifty-two metres) and was at the time the deepest producing well in Europe." Redwood said that field peaked at 68,000 tons (about 486,000 barrels) in 1901.

Throughout the 1890s and first decade of the new century, the company continually made new oil discoveries. McGarvey was a pioneer in the opening of the huge Boryslaw oilfield in 1892, which came to be recognized as one of the best producing in Galicia's history, according to the American *Oil Weekly* magazine of January 20, 1923. In a short time the area was covered in oil wells, the stench of petroleum filled the air and Boryslaw became known as "the Galician hell." It was a hell, however, paved with gold for the oil producers and those who catered to their needs. From a village of five hundred before McGarvey's discoveries, Boryslaw grew to 12,000 inhabitants by 1898. McGarvey had created an oil boomtown, one bigger than Oil Springs and Petrolia back in Canada would ever become.

McGarvey's 'Other Son'

It was during the development of Boryslaw when Mac met the acquaintance of, and developed a fond friendship for a young man named Wladyslaw Dlugosz. Their relationship became symbiotic, of great benefit not only to McGarvey, but to his company and to Dlugosz.

Galicia's oil lands became known as the "Galician Klondike," not a place of gold fever, but of oil fever. The region attracted thousands of people on the hunt for a share of the great riches that were literally pouring out of the land. Wladyslaw Dlugosz was one of the young men who came in search of success. Dlugosz was born in Krakow, the son of a Polish judge and a Swiss mother. He took his technical studies education in Prague before beginning his adult life as a gymnastics teacher in Gorlice.

But he had a hankering for a future in petroleum. Dlugosz took on jobs as a blacksmith's assistant and then a driller. He graduated to mine manager and came to the attention of McGarvey when he was looking for skilled workers at Boryslaw. McGarvey appreciated the young man's keen intellect and expertise. The two men struck up a friendship. Less than a decade older than McGarvey's own son, Fred, Dlugosz came to be looked upon by the elder McGarvey as not only a valued employee, but as another son.

Dlugosz progressed quickly through the ranks of the Galician Carpathian Petroleum Company. He was appointed a director and oversaw a significant time of growth in the company as it expanded its reach beyond Galicia and, when oil production began to wane in its home province, the diversification into other products. He was a trusted right-hand man of McGarvey's, valued for his boundless energy, decisiveness and diligence. Together with Fred McGarvey, Dlugosz represented what the company founder believed would be its next generation of leadership.

Dlugosz recorded his own recollections of McGarvey which were incorporated in a book published in 2000 called *Boryslaw In Okruchach Wspomnień (Fragments of Memories From Boryslaw)*. He wrote that he came recommended to McGarvey as "a special man" by the landowner from whom the Canadian entrepreneur had obtained oil leases. When he began working for McGarvey at Boryslaw in 1893, Dlugosz said, conditions were still as primitive as they had been in the rest of Galicia a decade earlier, before McGarvey's arrival. Peasant workers were paid in vodka and lived in shelters concocted from potato boxes. There were so many of the old hand-dug wells that the land was caving in. The entire place had fallen into a state of decay. "It was a squalid picture indeed," he said.

Dlugosz soon sized McGarvey up as an "uncommonly noble man" who could be key to his own future success. "I learned a lot of lessons and learned to follow his principles of frugalness, total devotion to his work and adherence to duty." McGarvey's character was such that, despite being a foreigner, he was able to work together with his Polish staff and earn their respect.

Dlugosz recalled his first encounter with McGarvey in March 1893. The pair was headed to the recently opened oilfields of Boryslaw. "We spent the night sitting on the chairs in a hotel in Drohobych because it was impossible for us to put up with the dirty bedsheets." The next day as they entered Boryslaw, "our first impressions were terrible," Dlugosz said, recalling the rows upon rows of half-collapsed cottages. "When we set up a mine, we had to build a long walkway from the blacksmith shop to the shaft so the workers knew where to walk to avoid the collapsing ground."

Crime was rampant and Dlugosz feared for his own safety. He went to bed at night, in a church basement, with an iron pipe in his hands and a St. Bernard dog at his side that was ready to rip anyone's throat out. Yet Dlugosz was encouraged by his prospects for success.

McGarvey's plan was to send back to Canada for more drilling experts, something he had done many times before to great success. This time, Dlugosz had other ideas. With the assistance of a friend who had just returned from drilling in Argentina and a local driller named Jan Raczkowski, they built their own test rig. McGarvey was so impressed, said Dlugosz, that he laughed and said Dlugosz would have to show the Canadians "how it was done."

Dlugosz stayed at Boryslaw until 1896 when the company sent him to Bitkow for new drilling. Then in 1902, he led the drilling team in Tustanowice. He watched the first shaft go down 1,160 metres with no success and word came from McGarvey at the company's head office to cease drilling. But Dlugosz had a hunch and continued drilling. The results far exceeded expectations. Afterwards, McGarvey praised his young protégé's efforts often and joked about how he had refused to follow the boss's orders. McGarvey's reaction speaks to his respect for rebels who were not afraid to break the rules or, in this instance, the chain of command, provided they could prove they knew what they were doing.

Dlugosz's interests also lay beyond the Galician Carpathian company, and these interests would eventually add to his value to the corporation. In 1908, he was elected to the Austrian national parliament and became known as a social reformer who acted to improve the conditions of the people. In this, he was in sync with his boss. In 1911, Dlugosz was appointed the government minister responsible for the Galician province. In the latter days of the Great War, Dlugosz was made president of the National Oil Company and after the war, the newly created Republic of Poland appointed him president of the State Oil Council. He eventually was elected a national senator.

Beyond Boryslaw

Drill rigs and oil derricks rose across the Carpathian countryside, and the pungent aroma of crude oil permeated the landscape. One account of the scene at Boryslaw described the mines that sat in a broad valley, closed at one end by forested hills. An account from the *Geographic Dictionary of the Polish Kingdom and Other Slavic Countries,* published in 1892, reported: "This whole valley is excavated in its length and breadth, has thousands of holes, and is filled with piles of stones and mud among which rise small wooden sheds which cover the wells and the numerous distilleries which line the road to the neighbouring Drohobycz. The atmosphere is filled with coal gases."

Significant additional holdings were picked up in 1893 when McGarvey and Bergheim bought out the Polish oil industrialist Klobassa Zrecki. Zrecki had accumulated considerable holdings himself, before several fires hobbled his plans. McGarvey made a lucrative offer which included hiring several of Zrecki's family members. From the time of their arrival in Galicia until 1894, Bergheim & McGarvey drilled three hundred and seventy wells in forty-three locations.

After Boryslaw came discoveries at Schodnica and Humniska in 1898 and Bitkowa in 1899, finds that kept the company well-oiled while it awaited the arrival of the biggest find yet, at Tustanowice, near Boryslaw, in 1902. McGarvey was initially lured to Tustanowice by several eruptions of natural gas. Over time, production shifted from West Galicia to the Boryslaw and Tustanowice fields of East Galicia, so that by the time war broke out in 1914, the bulk of the province's oil – more than ninety percent – was coming from the east. Here, McGarvey held the bulk of the resources.

By the early 1900s, McGarvey was drilling wells as deep as eight hundred and nine hundred metres and achieving excellent flows. By 1909, Galicia's best production year, the wells produced more than ten million barrels – some reports estimated as high as fourteen million. That year, the Boryslaw/Tustanowice region produced an estimated five per cent of the entire world's petroleum. Most of it was under McGarvey's name.

While Galicia remained the company hub, the McGarvey empire had begun to spread out beyond the province soon after its inception. In the summer of 1886, William's brother, Albert, was charged with opening up a Romanian branch of the company. Back home in Petrolia the *Advertiser* reported on July 16, 1886: "Mr. (Albert) McGarvey leaves on Tuesday next (July 20) for the Ro(u)manian oil fields. He takes with him Messers Robert McKaig, William Hopkins, David Slack and James F. Ward. They are getting a regular army of Canadian drillers in that country and if a secession wave was to strike that province, we fancy the Canadian element would nearly predominate."

Training and Worker Safety

The "Canadian element" did, indeed predominate. A host of skilled positions needed to be filled to bring in the oilfields, among which drillers and stokers were the most important. But plenty of other positions needed to be filled and sufficient numbers of Europeans had not yet been trained adequately to fill the posts. Canadians were brought in as tool dressers, blacksmiths, boilermakers, iron lathe operators, boiler attendants, welders, fitters and other metal workers, as well as machinists, barrel coopers and carpenters.

The hiring of Canadians was all done with the utmost in professionalism. Canadian workers hired on by Bergheim & McGarvey were required to sign a contract in which they committed to serve overseas for three years. Once engaged, the workers acknowledged they could be transferred to any of the "allied companies," which could entail being reassigned to Russia or Romania, for example.

The contract stipulated that travel expenses were covered, second-class, by steamer and train, at an estimated cost to the company of seven hundred Guilders. Initial salary was five hundred Guilders a month, with payment commencing the moment the employee reached Galicia or Vienna. A half-salary was paid for travel time, both to the destination and, provided the three-year-term was completed, back home again. The company covered the cost of lodging and medical care.

The contract warned that an employee could be terminated for misdemeanor or incapacity. Should the employee become incapacitated as a result of their employment, they would be paid three months' salary and transport expenses home. Such a system of workers' compensation was nearly unheard-of at the time.

Wages and employment conditions were generous by the terms of the era, but it was becoming increasingly hard to find enough Canadian workers. Despite Albert McGarvey's recruiting efforts, there were insufficient numbers of Canadians back in Lambton County to fill all of the positions the growing company required. It was clear to management that more workers needed to be found among the local population. After several years of relying on Canadians for the key non-labourer positions, it was decided a system needed to be established to ensure local workers were properly trained to take on some of the important jobs.

The National Petroleum Society (Krajowe Towarzystwo Naftowe) of Galicia had been created in 1877 as a "society for the care and development of the oil and mining industry," with Ignacy Lukasiewicz serving as the first president. In 1885, McGarvey approached this society of professionals and encouraged officials to throw their support behind the establishment of a school to train workers locally. McGarvey would finance it.

The Practical School of Canadian Drilling was opened in Ropianka in 1885. Three years later, it was moved to Wietrzno and renamed the

Drilling School of Wietrzno. Further professionalization came in 1892, when the Austrian government endorsed McGarvey's call for the introduction of lectures on oil drilling and petroleum technology at the Polytechnic of Lviv. Then in 1896, the drilling school was moved from Wietrzno to Boryslaw where the National Mining School already existed. The combined institution was renamed the National Mining and Drilling School of Boryslaw.

McGarvey was the principal force behind introducing training, knowledge and professional methodology to the oil industry in Eastern Europe. The training facility was commonly known simply as the McGarvey school. Dr. Stefan Bartoszewicz of Warsaw wrote in 1934 that "there was not a senior manager in the business who had not graduated from McGarvey's petroleum training school." In the estimation of the Lviv-based *Nafta* journal, McGarvey's training of oil executives became the "model" for others (December 15, 1903).

The school's aim was to prepare the hundreds and thousands of workers who would be needed to maintain the drilling operations, machine factories and other related skills that were required to maintain the growing industry. But the knowledge that it was going to be impossible to import sufficient numbers of Canadians to fill all of the positions was only part of the schools' genesis: Training local workers to conduct business in a safe manner was also a key goal.

Drilling for oil had been a risky venture from the beginning. Hugh Nixon Shaw, no relation to John Shaw who drilled Canada's first gusher at Oil Springs back in 1862, had himself fallen victim to those dangers. Shaw died after being overcome by fumes when he had himself lowered into his well to perform a repair.

Safety was no less a problem in the European fields. "The digging and the deepening of the wells is not without danger," reported the *Geographic Dictionary of the Polish Kingdom* back in 1892. "From the ground soaked with oil rise toxic deadly gases. This has led to the introduction of ventilators or air-mills. (As well,) miners work in pairs, with the digger fastening himself to a strong line which is tied to a post driven into the ground next to the well. The other watches him from above in order to pull the digger to safety should he lose consciousness." The lesson learned from Shaw's demise had been learned well and the solution was practised in McGarvey's Galician fields.

There were other sorts of mishaps as well. A steam engine explosion in 1890 at Wolanka near Boryslaw killed eighty people, while an uncontrolled burst of oil at Schodnica near Boryslaw five years later polluted the Stryj River, according to an article titled "The Chaotic Saga of Oil."

It is not known whether these occurred at McGarvey installations, but we do know many smaller and less-scrupulous companies sprang up as a result of his success and many paid far less attention to worker safety. At many of them, worker housing was built right next to oil storage facilities and fire could have a devastating impact. A fire that started in Boryslaw in November 1902 could not be extinguished until January. Then in July 1908, lightning struck what was at the time Galicia's most productive well – which was one of McGarvey's – and burned for four months. Throngs of sightseers poured in and had to be kept at bay.

Danger lurked beyond the fields, and safety in the refineries was another concern. Most refineries were poorly ventilated and the air was contaminated by the vapors from the distillation process. McGarvey recognized standards needed to be improved and adhered to if the industry was going to move forward. Through professional organizations, he pushed for more stringent rules and sought government support to enforce them.

Safety regulations were of little assistance when lightning struck, however. On the night of June 27, 1911, a fierce electrical storm hit the Gorlice region. A bolt of lightning ignited a fire at McGarvey's refinery.

"A terrible fire raged all night," reported *Neues Wiener Tagblatt* the next day. "The vast quantities of smoke made any approach quite impossible. The walls of the reservoirs were melted by the intense heat and the burning oil poured out in a great firestorm in all directions, flooding roads and railroad tracks and setting everything on fire." As of later that day, the area remained cut off from the outside. Rail traffic was halted when two bridges burned down. Telegraph and phone service was cut off. Residents were evacuated, but humans were largely powerless to intervene in the midst of the fearsome inferno. Only when the fire began to burn itself out about 24 hours later was it able to be brought under control.

Formation Of The Joint Stock Company

In 1895, McGarvey and Bergheim decided to turn the privately held enterprise that they had created more than a decade earlier into a publicly traded, joint stock company and on July 4, the Galizische Karpathen Petroleum Actiengesellschaft (a publicly traded joint stock company) was created with a capital of ten million Austrian kroner. The founding meeting was held on August 12 at the headquarters in Mariampol and a secondary office was established in Vienna. According to plan, shareholders chose August Gorayski as president and McGarvey as vice-president. Among the board of directors were John Bergheim and Robert Biedermann.

The new corporation's holdings included the oilfields at Weglowka, Bobrka, Wietrzno, Taraszswka, Lezyny, Golcowa, Kryg, Woleylanka, Straclwcina, Boryslaw and Potok, as well as the Glimar refinery and the Glinik factory at Glinik Mariampolski, and other unspecified holdings. Its first annual general meeting was held in Mariampol on June 15, 1896.

The industrialist-financier Gorayski was selected for the company presidency to satisfy the Austrian legal requirement for publicly traded companies to prominently feature local officials. But make no mistake: the name behind the company, the trusted presence that assured investors and those it did business with, was William Henry "Mac" McGarvey. Whenever the firm was referred to under its new name, it was also called "vormals Bergheim & McGarvey," the German equivalent of "formerly Bergheim and McGarvey." William's sterling name would continue to be featured front and centre in the newly minted enterprise, including on all of its letterhead and correspondence – even the company's stock certificates. Every newspaper and periodical article and every advertisement featured both names.

Over the years, the Vienna office took on a more prominent role in the joint stock company that became known far and wide as the Karpath, although Glinik Mariampolski remained the official headquarters for several more years. William served as refinery and factory director from 1885 until 1895 when Fred McGarvey, who was still attending school, was named to the post and held the position until after the war.

When William moved to Vienna in 1897 and took over as general manager and vice-president of the newly incorporated joint stock company, Fred McGarvey was appointed manager at Glinik Mariampolski. Fred took a significant step up the corporate ladder when the *Neue Freie Press* of Vienna reported on December 5, 1903 that he was elected to the Karpath's board of directors. He was thirty years old.

As time passed, more of the company-wide business was conducted from Vienna and after William moved there in 1897, the headquarters resided in the Austrian capital in all but name. Finally in 1910, the headquarters was officially moved there. That same year, Fred left Mariampol and moved to Vienna as his father's assistant, taking on responsibility as superintendent of the company's Galician oilfields, refinery and machine shop.

For its first few years of existence, the joint stock company remained a tightly held entity with virtually no trading in its shares and little improvement in its share price, although it paid handsome annual dividends. Then in 1899, with a regular flow of good news reports, trading on the Vienna exchange opened up and the share price doubled in short order, adding handsomely to the partners' and shareholders' on-paper wealth.

While the Galician Carpathian Petroleum Joint Stock Company had been established by two foreigners, it was always treated as an Austrian, Polish or Galician firm, says Polish oil engineering historian Stanislaw Szafran of Krakow. There were advantages to that and the firm prospered in no small part because of it. Much of that was due to McGarvey's convivial personality and willingness to get along with the locals. He had been helped considerably by the guidance of wife Helena whose father was Polish-born, although William himself was never able to grasp the local language and conducted business in English and the German language he picked up much more effectively. In time, he became as capable in conducting business in German as he was in English. When Gorayski retired as company president, McGarvey delivered the tribute totally in German.

Despite his language difficulties in Polish, McGarvey bonded with his Galician home. "He was emotionally attached to the territory," said Szafran. "This was in stark contrast to the Rockefellers and other foreign interests that tried to get established in Eastern Europe. He was emotionally connected to the people. He had a sense of responsibility to them."

McGarvey's generosity to his workers and to his community was well known. Despite his immense wealth, he never took a superior attitude and was aware of the importance of maintaining a close personal connection to his employees. He opened a day care facility at Glinik Mariampolski where his employees could obtain shelter for their children when necessary and funded construction of a school in the village. He also provided the land for the school. The teachers were given lodging and a garden on-site, according to materials provided by the Malopolski Instytut Kultury (Malopolski Cultural Institute) of Krakow.

A Methodist himself, McGarvey knew full well the majority of his workers were Catholic and to recognize his respect for them, he built a chapel for them at the Glinik Mariampolski refinery and factory site. He established a child protection fund under the Sisters of the Stewards of Stara Wies, which used the money to build an orphanage. Then he built a brick residence for members of the order. The sisters were given the responsibility of providing care for the younger children and educating the older ones.

To honour his first wife, Helena, McGarvey donated stained glass windows to a Polish Catholic church near Boryslaw, dedicating them to St. Barbara, patron saint of the oil workers, and over the years he built and renovated numerous roadside shrines frequented by his workers.

McGarvey also maintained an openness and respect for his Jewish employees and in this he was reflecting the social attitudes demanded by the Austrian kaiser himself. While religious differences would eventually harden, and in the early twentieth century workers and peasants were known to clash over their religious beliefs, McGarvey always demanded tolerance and acceptance.

On the civic front, McGarvey also contributed to the construction of a light rail line through the Gorlice region, which vastly improved public transportation.

Were these strictly altruistic acts? Were they the acts of a Methodist who was simply practising what his religion called on him to do? McGarvey wanted to take actions that would lessen the burden on the family lives of his workers because he knew that those burdens were adversely affecting their production. It also benefited his public image to be so overtly generous. In his early years in Galicia, McGarvey found it difficult to maintain a workforce of locals since many of the peasants would simply work until they obtained the income they sought and then head back to their homes. The addition of schools and welfare programs, plus seemingly generous donations, was a new concept to native Galicians and helped to further improve his image with them by creating a sense of community.

But while he became a much-loved philanthropist of the highest order, McGarvey was never shy about his intent. He was once quoted as saying: "I didn't come here (to Galicia) to introduce capital, but to make millions in this country." (Translation from *Przemysl Naftowy* periodical, Lviv, 25 February 1933.)

At this he was succeeding to an unimaginable degree. By the turn of the twentieth century, the Galician Carpathian Petroleum Company pumped crude from its own wells, refined the petroleum along with gasoline, various lubricating oils and paraffin, and manufactured a range of equipment, from steam-powered drilling engines and drilling rigs, to boilers, pumps, core drillers, winding machines, portable cranes and the eccentric drilling bits McGarvey had developed and patented himself. His company employed six hundred to seven hundred men, who were supervised by about thirty mostly Canadian principal managers.

With the joint stock company paying its shareholders fifteen percent dividends, the future looked incredibly bright for the Petroleum King. Europe's Rockefeller was progressing well.

Expansion

Going public in 1895 provided much-needed expansion cash and opened up lucrative new opportunities for McGarvey and Bergheim by extending their reach, and extend, they did.

In oil's early days, "refineries" were small operations, set up right in the fields next to where the crude was collected. Over time, methods became more sophisticated and refineries became larger, established to process the oil from many wells at a central location. McGarvey and Bergheim introduced the concept of much larger, centralized operations where economies of scale could be applied. This they did at their Glinik Mariampolski location.

By applying the most modern methods, the Glimar refinery was, at the time of completion, the largest in Europe. The adjacent Glinik factory produced the best quality machinery and drilling tools and soon had branches in Boryslaw, Tustanowice and Vienna. Pipeline was constructed in the Boryslaw and Tustanowice plants. All of these facilities were required, with big oil discoveries coming on a regular basis and other companies the world over clambering for their machinery and other manufactured goods.

New associated companies were established, with the Austrian Petroleum Company (Oestereichische Petroleum Industrie Aktien-Gesellschaft or OPIAG) opened up in Vienna in 1905 and, entering the Russian fields in a big way, the Anglo-Terek Petroleum Company and the North Caucasus Oil Company (Severnokavkazkoe Neftepromyslonnye Obscestvo).

Despite the success of the training schools, Canadians continued to hold down many of the important managerial positions. Besides William's brother, James, for example, Charles Wallen of Oil Springs entered the Russian fields, taking over as field manager for North Caucasus in 1911. Wallen was a globe-trotter. Having originally gone to Germany in 1894, in the interim he had also tried his luck in Java in Southeast Asia before accepting the significant position with McGarvey's North Caucasus.

In 1910, McGarvey and Bergheim created Vaterlandische Mineralolaktiengesellschaft in Budapest. The company was a key participant in two large refinery operations in Hungary and another in Vienna. In 1913, William was chosen president of Vaterlandische and Fred was elected to the board of directors. This is the time when Erik Jurié von Lavandal, husband of William's youngest daughter, Kate, was chosen as a Karpath company director.

It is also interesting to note that while McGarvey left Canada in 1881, later, he was indirectly involved in two other groundbreaking oil projects in North America that did not fare as well during his lifetime as his European enterprises did. One, Canada's Athabaska oil sands, will be discussed in more detail later as it pertains to the campaign to supply Britain with oil sourced from within the British Empire, in preparation for the First World War. The other was the California Oil Refineries project on San Luis Bay, about three hundred kilometres northwest of Los Angeles. Under chief director Simon Symons, McGarvey served on the board of directors. His world-renowned reputation meant he was being sought as an adviser thousands of kilometres from his home.

The California project is described as an "ill-fated oil port and refinery" that once during its short existence employed more than five hundred. Commenced in 1905, it was shuttered two years later, just two weeks after its completion, when a giant tidal wave destroyed the half-mile pier and wrecked the refinery.

Many innovations can be credited to William McGarvey's genius and he personally piled up dozens of patents for the equipment his companies manufactured. Having made his reputation on the Canadian pole-tool method of drilling, which he continually refined over the years, in 1905 McGarvey decided to experiment with the Pennsylvania or American Standard drilling rig, based on machinery they imported from the United States. The American Standard method used cable – initially made from manila rope and later from steel. After directing some adjustments be made to accommodate the unique Galician conditions, he began to manufacture his own American Standard equipment.

But attempts to patent the "eccentric" (or off-centre) drilling machine he had created for this purpose proved to be one of Mac's few setbacks. In 1913, McGarvey led the first attempt in Galicia to use the rotary system that had been invented in the United States. Within a short time his factory was building the new drilling equipment, with both a permanent or stationary model and a portable one designed for ease of transport. After he registered the patent in Europe, however, an American manufacturer launched a patent challenge and, since it was found to be a design by that time widely utilized in the United States, the European patent was tossed out.

The setback was a small one for the petroleum empire-builder. By 1914, factory production at Glinik Mariampolski amounted to three million Austrian krona. An estimated two-thirds of that was exported to other countries, with Galician Carpathian-produced machinery and equipment showing up in the United States, Mexico, Romania, Russia and even India.

Doing Battle With Standard Oil

William McGarvey was clearly a self-made man. He had built a sizeable fortune in Canada's Lambton County, first as a general store owner and then as an oil producer and refiner. In tough economic times, he had agreed to join forces with other producers and refiners in a series of largely unsuccessful attempts to control prices. His experience in Galicia had followed the same path: He started out as an independent entrepreneur and then in 1895, agreed to join a loose "syndicate" of corporations that was created to jointly promote their shared interests. McGarvey and colleague August Gorayski were appointed to the syndicate's board of directors.

McGarvey and Bergheim had shrewdly understood that the path to success lay in vertical integration. They knew that they must not only own and drill for the oil, but that they must refine it in all of its forms, sell it, transport it and even build the equipment that was required to make it all happen. The international giant Standard Oil had built its success in a different manner: by swarming and overwhelming its competition in production, refining and transportation. It often used questionable methods to achieve this. The Karpath was miniscule compared to the mighty empire that had been built by John D. Rockefeller in the vicious bear-pit of American capitalism.

As a large but still primarily regional entity, the Galician Carpathian corporation was becoming a victim of its own success as the first decade of the 20th century progressed. New efficiencies in production and new discoveries were flooding the market with crude oil and prices were falling. Arriving at the "grow-or-die" moment, the Karpath knew that the only way to grow was through exports. And as the company established a blueprint for capturing more of the European market, it garnered the attention of a wary Standard Oil.

Founded by Rockefeller and Henry Flagler in 1870, Standard had spread its influence the world over, but had not been able to achieve a foothold in Eastern Europe where McGarvey, supported by the Austrian government, encouraged the other independents to stand their ground – at least those independents that he did not buy out himself.

By the time he retired as chairman of Standard in 1897, Rockefeller was the world's richest man. His company had taken over most of the Canadian industry when it purchased Imperial Oil in 1899 and moved the resulting Canadian subsidiary's headquarters from Petrolia to Sarnia. In much of Europe it had been equally successful. With its economies of scale, Standard was able to undercut Galician oil prices in Germany and had consumed much of the petroleum industry in that country.

As he tried to expand his company's reach, a frustrated McGarvey fumed that Rockefeller's Standard Oil "will not allow us in any country in Europe."

McGarvey also knew it was only a matter of time before Standard moved on Galicia and attacked his own home market. They were already expanding resolutely into Romania, limiting opportunities for the Karpath there. At a meeting of crude oil producers in Lviv in January 1902, Galicia's largest corporations agreed to step up their efforts to create a co-operative effort that could better fight off their growing competition from Standard.

This next small step proved ineffective as well and in 1903, the Karpath's annual general meeting discussed potential remedies: lobbying government for higher tariffs on imports, converting locomotives to oil burners, increasing storage capacity and seeking Germany's support to sell more product in that country. It was even suggested the company offer to build a new refinery in Germany in exchange for greater access to its market.

But the problem required immediate action and later that year, McGarvey reluctantly agreed to take part in an Austrian cartel of independents called the Petrolea Oil Society. The organization was created to trade in crude oil and other mineral oil products both domestically and abroad. It was also charged with installing and owning pipelines and storage facilities, as well as acquiring more property and drilling rights, drilling wells and establishing refineries, plus the manufacture of equipment. In essence, it covered all aspects of the business that McGarvey headed at the Karpath. The new entity announced relatively modest initial capital holdings of one million kronen.

Despite his disinclination to engage in a cartel, McGarvey was still the most important figure in Austrian petroleum and as such was asked to head the organization. He reluctantly agreed, while his old friends, colleagues, fellow Petrolians and oil field owners Cyrus Perkins of Stryj and Elgin Scott of Ropienka, were elected to join Mac on the board of directors.

Standard had clearly been the target of the cartel. This was about the time that the U.S.-based *McClure's* magazine published an exposé by Ida Tarbell revealing Standard's predatory business practices in the United States. The series, which was later published in book form, was a key factor in the U.S. government's order in 1911 that the Standard trust must be broken up into 34 units.

"Standard" was definitely a dirty word in Galicia. There had been a bloody oil workers' strike in the Galician oilfields in 1904 – one that hobbled McGarvey's company profits that year – and rumors spread that Standard had been behind it, although there seems little proof of this.

It had been back in 1899 that Standard made its first move into Austria when it registered a "Trojan horse" company by the name of the Vacuum Oil Company. Five years later, pushed into action by high Austrian tariffs, Vacuum Oil built a refinery in Austrian Silesia (an area that today is divided among Poland, the Czech Republic and Germany.

At the urging of its McGarvey-controlled petroleum industry, in 1904 the Austrian parliament held an inquiry and heard proposals for legislative reform. McGarvey told the inquiry his company could only survive and continue to prosper if it had access to the German and French markets, which Standard was seeking to control. In fact, he said, Standard's goal was to consume the Galician industry as well. The only way the domestic industry could survive was to merge oil producers and refiners, he said. "It is our duty to not waste the infinite treasures of crude oil deposits that exist in our own Austria, and to not allow the lands of Galicia to fall into the possession of the foreign petroleum industry." It was an eloquent defence of protectionism that was consistent with the position he had taken years earlier back in Canada when he endorsed Sir John A. Macdonald's National Policy. It is also a clear indication that McGarvey expected to be viewed as an Austrian entrepreneur, and not as a foreign carpetbagger who had come to Galicia to plunder its resources.

As part of his campaign to create a united defence against Standard, McGarvey led the creation of OLEX (Aktiengesellschaft fur Osterreichische-Ungarische Mineralolprodukte), a joint stock company aimed at organizing export activities. OLEX was headquartered in Vienna and was initially focused on the sale of kerosene to the railways of Austria-Hungary and Germany. Later its reach was expanded to include gasoline and other petroleum fractions. In time, OLEX established seven German subsidiaries and included oil holdings in Romania.

McGarvey's hand can be seen clearly in the establishment of OLEX as a joint stock company in the same manner he and Bergheim had created the Karpath. It had been a highly successful maneuver when they did it in 1895 and McGarvey must have thought it could be equally successful again. Within the OLEX organization, however, the independents continued to function under their own organization and ownership, making it in effect more of a co-operative than a "company" in the traditional sense of the word.

The Galician petroleum industry succeeded in convincing the Vienna government authorities to impose on Vacuum a complex series of laws and practices that awarded certain important preferences to the domestic operators. The United States protested through diplomatic channels, sending their ambassador in Vienna to ask the Austrian government to suspend "the proposed oppressive measures."

While Austria cared little about relations with the Americans and would have been prepared to ignore the protest, they did care about relations with France and it so happened that a French company had been caught up in the same OLEX-Austrian legal chicanery. When France pulled its underwriting of a loan that Austria's imperial partner Hungary had been counting on, Vienna caved and a compromise was reached with the French.

McGarvey and his colleagues were able to convince Austria to delay withdrawal of the sanctions on the Americans, however, and despite pledges to remove them, Vacuum remained singled out for discriminatory treatment. As Austrian foot-dragging extended well into 1912 to McGarvey's delight, Vacuum began to feel the pressure and finally agreed to limit its incursion into the Austrian kerosene and gasoline markets.

After long negotiations in Hamburg and Vienna, Vacuum agreed it would purchase the surplus of Galician oil that was suppressing prices. In addition, Austria agreed to McGarvey's demands to give him favoured access: use Galician oil for its railway fleet and finance new storage facilities and a refinery, the Polmin, at Drohobycz. "The situation was saved," declared the Karpath's Wladyslaw Dlugosz.

It was just a partial victory, however. McGarvey and his colleagues had retained their favoured access to the relatively small Austrian market but they had not been able to stem the flow of Standard Oil's products into the greater European market. It was an experience that demonstrated clearly the importance of government intervention on behalf of domestic industry – both for the Austrians and the Americans. And it was a clear victory for the big multinational oil companies over the smaller independents such as Galician Carpathian. It was also a clear signal to McGarvey and the Karpath that they would be destined forever to remain a smallish independent, albeit with a series of subsidiaries and partnerships in other oil-producing countries.

Despite his appeal for government support, McGarvey relished the image of the feisty independent and bragged that he was able to stave off takeover by Standard, Royal Dutch Shell and the London-based giant, the Premier Oil and Pipeline Company – the managing director of which was the Canadian, Charles Perkins, nephew of McGarvey manager Jake Perkins and son of Jake's brother, Cyrus. In order to achieve that, McGarvey had agreed to join in the establishment of the Petrolea cartel and the OLEX joint stock company, proving that when faced with a predatory international corporation and weak prices due to over-production, he was willing to join forces with other small producers.

It was not a comfortable position for him, though, and he resisted other attempts to be brought into other syndicates and co-operatives. He favoured independence whenever possible. When he was erroneously linked to a bid to create a syndicate of pipeline owners, McGarvey bristled. He felt compelled to write to *The Times* of London to correct the public record. Speaking as managing director of the Karpath, McGarvey wrote: "my company, quite contrary to the statement made in the article mentioned, is not in any manner interested in the combination of the Pipe Lines. ... As I do not wish my company to be connected with the combination proposed, I trust you will give the same publicity to this letter as you have to the article to which I have referred." (April 4, 1911).

Bergheim, the engineer-turned-capitalist financier, left such business details to his partner and never expressed an opinion. According to an obituary written for Bergheim, "He remained neutral in negotiations over cartel matters as well as national petroleum organizations like *Ropa* and *Petrolea*, preferring to leave such matters to McGarvey due to his greater experience."

Labour Relations

While he played up his Austrian credentials when it suited his purposes, McGarvey truly considered himself a capitalist, not specifically a Canadian, British or Austrian capitalist. When nationality became a rallying cry in the fight against the U.S.-based Standard Oil, a Polish producer pointed out that McGarvey himself was a foreigner – a Canadian. McGarvey's response was: "I came with foreign knowledge, but not with foreign capital."

McGarvey led a movement among company owners to establish agreed-upon wage levels. This, he reasoned with them, would end the practice of employers trying to outbid one another for employees' services. He established training sessions to demonstrate to farm-based peasants how to become industrial workers and encouraged lenders to establish lines of credit for his workers. He even provided health care for anyone injured on the job. The system might appear to be an enlightened one, but it clearly established employers' control over their workers. Labourers were to be better educated, but it was an education that would benefit management.

Even though he was clearly in the business of making profits for himself and his fellow shareholders, McGarvey had always been highly regarded by his employees, in no small part because of his contributions to the community and the paternalistic approach he usually took toward them. Besides building a school, a day care, an orphanage and chapels, financing Catholic nuns and donating stained glass windows to a Catholic church, he sometimes met with the employees in an effort to demonstrate he appreciated their efforts. Beneath the primarily Canadian management was a workforce of Polish farmers, Jews and Ruthinian peasants, with the groups usually maintaining a cautious distance from one another. These divisions, plus the fact the farm workers thought of themselves as independents who sold their labour by the day, mitigated against any efforts to organize them and the strong collectivist feelings that built up among the workers in Russia prior to the revolution never evolved in Galicia.

While there were several work stoppages among the wax workers in Galicia, strikes among the oil workers were much less frequent. Just two work stoppages in the oil fields could be considered significant: One brief one in 1900 was sparked by a ban on alcohol; another in 1904-05 resulted in the Austrian military being brought in to protect the Hungarian strike-breakers McGarvey introduced. Work continued and while the Karpath's profits sagged during the strike, they remained healthy.

Alcohol was a significant problem in the workplaces of Galicia. Working and living conditions were poor and alcohol was a cheap diversion for the tired, overworked employees. It was readily available at the workplace, too. When McGarvey and Bergheim arrived in Glinik Mariampolski in 1883, there was already a tavern on the site of the distillery there, operated by the Jewish businessman Zelig Bergmann. Bergmann also operated "a couple of oil wells" in nearby Lipinki, says his great-great grandson, Allen Bergman, of Toronto. Zelig's son, Berl, was also associated with the oil industry as a barrel contractor under the company name Bergmann Fess Handl.

Worker unrest and violence was much more prevalent, and politicized, farther east in Russia. Work disruptions and full strikes – as well as a national work stoppage – came frequently to the Russian oilfields after 1900 as communist leaders tutored workers to demand better pay and labour conditions.

International Growth

While McGarvey and Bergheim had holdings in many countries, Galicia remained the centre of the Galician Carpathian company and its petroleum resources, despite the mounting problems there. After hitting its peak in the early years of the twentieth century, Galician oil production began to stall and prices were disappointing. In a letter in June 1908 to Ernest Nicklos, the drilling manager for Anglo-Mexican Oil Fields in Mexico and the son of an old friend and colleague, McGarvey confided: "We are having bad times in oil. Our production is large (but) there is no price. We are shutting down most of our drilling. No use drilling when one can buy oil at 1.25 (per 100 kilos)."

There was further bad news in 1910 when the company's Vienna offices were destroyed by fire. But the company was unperturbed by the disaster. By this time it was too successful to spend much time fretting. The building was reconstructed as a five-storey office and Galician Carpathian moved right back in – this time making the shiny new edifice their official company headquarters.

Despite troubling times for oil, the company continued to grow, not only in oil production but in refining as well.

In the early days, refining of crude oil entailed distillation of the product into three "fractions": a light fraction that was gasoline which at the time was of no use; a medium fraction such as kerosene, which was much in demand for lighting fuel; and a heavy fraction from which lubricating oil was obtained. McGarvey was a leader in introducing new sophistication to these processes and his refined petroleum was regarded as the best in Europe.

But with the arrival of the automobile, the business was beginning to shift, at least in those parts of the world where cars were becoming more popular, such as Britain, the United States and sophisticated European cities such as Paris, Berlin and Vienna. In recognition of these changes and the likely impact they were probably going to have on the business of refining petroleum, in 1895 McGarvey took a leading role in the creation of a new joint stock company to build a giant new refinery named Apollo in Bratislava, Hungary, with the bulk of its feedstock to come from Galicia and Russia.

Demand continued to grow and by 1904-05, existing refining capacity was again unable to meet demand. McGarvey led a co-operative effort to increase refining, still under the same Apollo name, with a new facility in Vienna. Later, the largest refinery in Europe was constructed by this McGarvey-led co-operative, this time at the Adriatic Sea port of Trieste, which at the time was part of Austria-Hungary. Trieste was the empire's most important seaport and was close to the home of the Austro-Hungarian Imperial Navy at Pula.

Then around 1912, McGarvey brought additional refineries located in Budapest under the Karpath's umbrella, further cementing his control over the Austro-Hungarian industry.

William Henry McGarvey, Helena Wesolowski along with their children Fred, Mamie, Kate and Nellie McGarvey

A McGarvey family gathering at Mariampol. Clockwise from lower left: William, Eberhard and Mamie, unknown man, Kate, Fred, Helena and Edward McGarvey. (Courtesy David Banting)

The entranceway at Schloss Graschnitz was marked by two stone lions. (Courtesy David Banting)

Complete Canadian drilling rig with
sandpump reel
"System Perkins, Mac' Intosh & Perkins".

Side view.

Front view.

A drawing of the Canadian pole tool drilling system McGarvey created and then introduced to Europe. (from Perkins, MacIntosh and Perkins drilling equipment catalogue, courtesy Joan Darby)

Kopalnie nafty w Krygu, poczta Gorlice – Petroleumgruben in Kryg, Post Gorlice

McGarvey and Bergheim first struck Galician oil at Kryg in 1883. (Gorlice Regional Museum)

Galician Carpathian Petroleum Company advertisement published in Oil News magazine, January 1914.

MURDER OF JAS. M'GARVEY.

TALBOT BARNARD ALSO KILLED.

Story of Murderous Attack on House in Caucasus—Two of Robbers Caught, Third Shot Himself.

Canadian Associated Press Cable.

London, Feb. 27.—James MacGarvey, Oil Fields manager, and Talbot Barnard, who had recently returned from Canada, were both murdered at Grosney in the Caucasus by armed robbers, who attacked the house while MacGarvey, his wife, and Barnard were at supper.

The robbers intercepted a boy giving the alarm and killed him, also a watchman. They then attacked MacGravey, who was killed with Causasian knives. Bernard tried to carry Mrs. MacGarvey into safety, but was overtaken and murdered; the lady was only stunned.

The murderers then stabbed the cook and finally decamped with one hundred pounds in cash.

TWO NATIVES ARRESTED.

Two implicated natives were arrested, and a third shot himself. Cossacks are still scouring the country.

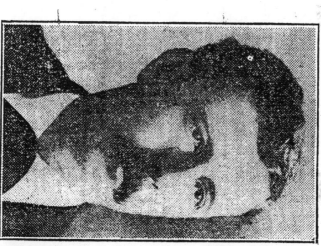

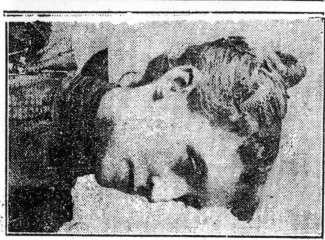

CANADIANS WHO WERE VICTIMS OF RUSSIAN MURDERERS.

On February 4, 1911, the Toronto Evening Telegram reported the murder of William's brother, James McGarvey, and the attack on his wife, Julia. (Oil Museum of Canada)

William and Helena McGarvey took a spacious apartment in this Vienna building when it was completed in 1897. (Gary May, 2007)

John Bergheim (third from right) arrived in Petrolia in 1879 to seek a partnership with William McGarvey (far right). The others are, standing from left: Cyrus Perkins, Alvin Townsend, John Martin, A. E. Slack, Eugene Yager and Neil Sinclair; seated from left: George McIntosh, George Fair and Angus McKay. (Lambton County Archives. The photo was published in Imperial Oil Review, Vol. XIV, No. 4, August/September 1930)

McGarvey is honoured by the Austrian Kaiser with the medal of the Iron Crown. (David Banting)

A transportable oil rig designed and produced by McGarvey's Glinik Mariampolski factory. The factory remains in operation today.

Rafinerya w Maryampolu

McGarvey's Glinik refinery about 1900. (Gorlice Regional Museum)

The Simmons & Woodward refinery site, co-financed by William McGarvey. (Courtesy Dave Hext)

McGarvey's Boryslaw properties were destroyed in the war. (Illustrirte Zeitung)

A portrait of William at home in Vienna, taken for the book, *Oil Fields of the Empire*. (Hathi Trust Digital Library, Ann Arbor, Michigan)

The last of William and Helena McGarvey's children, Fred McGarvey, sold the company. He died in 1963. (Courtesy Carol Chew)

CHAPTER 10

TO RUSSIA FOR CRUDE

In the latter half of the nineteenth century, the Nobel brothers created a huge industry in Baku that turned Russia into a major exporter and supplier of oil the world over. Now as the twentieth century dawned, Russia was the world's second-largest oil producing nation after the United States. It had made the Nobels even richer than they were before and when the Swedish-born brothers established their now-famous Nobel Prizes in 1901, a large share of the establishing fund came from Baku oil profits.

But that had happened under czarist rule and now in the early 1900s, that regime was creaking and cracking with age and the mismanagement of Czar Nicholas II.

Getting In On the Action

British companies, as well as that of William McGarvey and his British partner, John Bergheim, had missed the boat when they ceded leadership in Russia to the Nobels, known the world over as the Russian Rockefellers, and the later-arriving Rothschilds of France, whose specialty was transporting the oil by ship and by pipeline. Still, Western companies believed that with the continued wealth of the Russia oil fields, there was plenty yet to go around. In reaching this conclusion, they had not contemplated the devastating part politics would play in the country's future.

In the early 1900s, new oil strikes were made in Grosny, which sat in the northern Caucasus region, nearly five hundred kilometres north of the established Baku deposits. That put it closer, by about one hundred and sixty kilometres, to the key Black Sea port of Novorossiysk, a very important consideration for any newcomer enterprise. Russia produced far more oil than its agriculture-based economy could hope to consume, so the only thing that made the industry economical was the ability to export. Because of Russia's vast size and where in that mammoth land the oil was produced, pipelines and bulk tankers were essential to carry the crude from its source to the ports from where it could be shipped.

In 1901, Bergheim and McGarvey established a subsidiary of their Karpath operation in Russia – the Anglo-Terek Petroleum Company. Anglo-Terek conducted business in Grosny and was registered in London. To help get the refinery project up and running, McGarvey called upon an old Petrolia connection: Martin James Woodward. Woodward and McGarvey had operated one of the town's early refineries. Now, freshly back from Borneo where he had been engaged by the Shell Transportation Company to build a refinery, Woodward was asked to come to Russia for consultation and to get McGarvey's build started. This he did, finishing the project by 1906. Then Woodward was off again, this time to Chanute, Kansas, to become superintendent of the Kansas Co-operative Refining Company. He remained there until he died in 1912.

With Anglo-Terek up and running, McGarvey now needed a manager for the entire Russian operation. His brother, Albert, was already deeply engaged in Romania, so the obvious choice was their brother, James.

James was less than three years younger than William and had for many years been a trusted colleague. It had been James who came down to Petrolia from Wyoming to take control of the Mammoth Store while William devoted his full attention to building his early oil holdings there. During the 1870s, William disposed of his general store and James joined him fulltime in petroleum.

Also in the 1870s, an American cousin of the Michigan-born Helena McGarvey, Julia Maria Williams, left her Mount Clemens, Michigan home and came to live for a time with Helena and William in Petrolia, There she met James. James and Julia fell in love and married in 1879. They moved to St. Thomas, Ontario where their daughter, Helena Mary – named in honour of James' sister-in-law and known more popularly as Mamie –

was born in 1880. This made two cousins who were commonly known as Mamie – William's daughter, Mary, born in 1875, and her cousin – James's daughter, Helena Mary – born five years later.

James established his own business in St. Thomas and continued to list his profession as "oil operator" and "oil refiner." According to Frederick A. Fitzgerald, the first president of Imperial Oil, James owned a refinery in St. Thomas and developed his own oil properties there. While brother William opened and expanded operations in Europe, James worked on his own in Ontario but as the Galician Carpathian company grew larger and more successful, William persuaded him to relocate and give him a hand.

While it is not known exactly when he left for Europe, James clearly had a residence in England by 1896 when the Petrolia *Advertiser* indicated he and brother Albert had arrived back in Canada on July 2, 1896 "for a brief visit" from their work on the continent.

In 1901, James is listed as residing at 29 Waldeck Road, Ealing, England, and he has already made a name for himself. An advertisement in the *Nafta* business publication credits him with the creation of an underground oil storage stem that had been patented in Austria, Hungary and Russia. The ad invited inspection of the reservoirs, six of which it said were installed at the Karpath's refinery at Glinik Mariampolski. The tanks could be purchased or leased, with inquiries sent to James at 14 Great Winchester Street, London, an address deep in "The City."

But James had bigger things in his future. If the company was going to take on the huge job of setting up operations in Russia, it was decided a trusted lieutenant was required to oversee the operation. James was handed the task, taking over responsibility for the Russian fields operated by the Anglo-Terek and later the North Caucasus oil companies.

Success for James came quickly in Grosny. In 1904 he struck a "spouter" – the British term for gusher – that lasted a full two years, according to an article in *Oil and Gas* magazine on April 14, 1906.

McGarvey and Bergheim knew they would never reach the heights of success in Russia experienced by the Nobels, but were confident there was still plenty of money to be made there. Then, with Baku and Grosny well under development, new discoveries in the Maikop Valley in the Kuban province of southern Russia seemed to prove them correct. British capital began to flow into the Maikop region in dizzying amounts after 1905 and sixty new companies were organized, including Bergheim and McGarvey's International Maikop, mentioned in the Polish-language *Petroleum* magazine (No. 1, 1912, p. 26.)

The British fascination with the Maikop region, and their subsequent "invasion," was in no small part due to William McGarvey's advice. His partner, John Bergheim, introduced McGarvey to the influential British financier George Tweedy and the two immediately hit it off. McGarvey's skills as a petroleum engineer were legendary and Tweedy listened, absorbed in McGarvey's eloquent assessment of Maikop's petroleum riches. Tweedy responded by becoming a key developer of the British holdings there. "(McGarvey) was one of the great oil experts who supported Mr. George Tweedy in his belief in the future of the Maikop oil industry," reported the *Singapore Straits Times* of January 9, 1915. However, in fact it was McGarvey who convinced Tweedy of the region's petroleum riches.

Tweedy's personal papers, which now reside at the London Metropolitan Archives and are accessible online, make it clear how highly the wealthy financier valued McGarvey's technical expertise as he sought to evaluate the prospects for establishing a profitable enterprise in Maikop. On McGarvey's advice, Tweedy invested in a parcel of older companies that held the rights to what McGarvey felt were some promising plots there. In 1911, Tweedy and McGarvey established a co-operative corporate venture under the name Maikop Deep Drilling Company, as reported in *Oil News* magazine on December 5, 1914.

The previous year, McGarvey had demonstrated his own confidence in the future of the Maikop Valley by opening a drilling machinery factory at Ekaterinodar, a development that was hailed in *Petroleum* magazine (No. 1, p. 26) as evidence of the up-and-coming nature of the business there. The new factory was designed to supply the rapidly expanding Russian markets, with McGarvey's high hopes based on the sterling international reputation for the manufacturing of machinery his company had gained in Galicia.

Russia was going to be big business for the Karpath, and Mac believed that James needed to be a feet-on-the-ground manager for its oil fields there. James headed out from London to establish himself as director in

Grosny, the major city of Chechnya province. Work kept him in Russia for long periods of time while Julia and their daughter, Mamie, remained back in England. There was no telling how long James would need to be stationed in Russia and the couple agreed Julia and Mamie were better off enjoying the comforts of England rather than tackling the vagaries of the frontier existence they would face in Grosny. Mother and daughter enjoyed the security of the consummate Victorian family.

Some of Russia's provinces presented quite a different lifestyle from the one they were used to in Britain. Chechnya had come to be known as the czarist empire's Wild West, a place filled with bandits and desperadoes. Friction between the czar's ruling class and the local populations frequently broke out into violence.

The word "abrek" has a different meaning depending on who is expressing it. To the Chechen people, impoverished by the colonizing Russians and the invading Cossacks, it meant avenger. To those upon whom the abrek swooped down, it meant bandit and raider. Zelimkhan Gushmazukayev was an abrek, one who kept the colonizers and outside business owners on their toes. To the local populace, he came to be known as as a Chechen Robin Hood. Folk songs were written about him and his name is said to be given to young Chechen boys to this day.

It was into this environment that James McGarvey was sent to establish a company presence in the rich oil lands of the southwestern Russia territories. James was a debonair and even rakishly handsome man. Already in his sixties when he settled in to the job in Grosny, he remained so still, even as his handlebar moustache turned to grey and silver streaked his hair. More slender than his elder brother, William, who had slipped into a slight portliness in his later years, James continued to turn the head of many a Victorian lady.

When he arrived in Russia, James described the countryside and the lifestyle to his wife and daughter. The landscape around Grosny was ragged and empty, not at all like the green and leafy lanes of England, with its cheery cottages tucked among the emerald hills. Chechen summers were hot and dusty, the sun turning the grass brittle and brown. In winter when the winds howled, one dressed in furs and rode around in cutters. While winters were harsh, it was almost a relief when it snowed and covered the stark ground that was heavily pocked with oil wells and cluttered with ugly wooden rigs. A relief, that is, until the snow melted and transformed the land into a quagmire.

Julia preferred the comforts of life in England to the frontier existence of Grosny that James wrote about in his letters back home to her. He was, initially, fine with that arrangement. But over time James became lonely for Julia's company and urged her to pay a visit. Reluctant at first, she finally consented to venture forth in 1910. On September 13 of that year, Julia left her English home for the long trip; it was the first time she had ever set foot in Russia. Daughter Mamie, by this time married to the doctor, Percy Stanley Blaker, stayed at home. In a letter back to friends in England that November, Julia described the Grosny-area countryside and life there in fascinating detail.

The city of Grosny, she said, was situated in a valley that stretched about nine miles (fifteen kilometres) wide, along the foothills of the Caucasus Mountains. About 25,000 people lived in the city, a mix of European Russians, Armenians, native Jews, Persians, native Muslims and Cossacks. The Cossacks, she said, lived separately and governed themselves.

In the rainy season, she said, the mud was ankle deep since in the entire city there was just a single cobblestone street. Walking was not advised and so carriages became a necessary mode of transit.

Julia was enchanted by what she found. She described her fascination with the marketplace with its "wonderful variety of native peoples... Georgians, Tartars, Lezgins, Osetins and Chechens." There were eighty-two languages and dialects spoken, she said. While the Georgians were generally members of the Russian Orthodox religion, many of the locals were Muslims.

Julia went on to describe the Georgian man James hired to work in the house. "He wears on the street high boots way above the knees, a light fawn cloth coat arrangement. They are very fond of a good figure and are said to wear corsets so on a long waist is pleated a full skirt coming to the top of the boots, wears a black leather belt with lots of silver ornaments holding a revolver and a dagger." In Julia's eye, James' manservant posed a striking figure.

For Julia, her trip to the Caucasus was an unexpectedly pleasant adventure. She was impressed by the contrast between the rolling English countryside and the much more rugged landscape of the Grosny district. "On clear days one can see the mountains in the distance and it is a lovely sight covered with snow," she said.

Then, ominously, Julia confided to her friends that she was somewhat nervous about her safety in Grosny, "although there has never been any serious troubles, such as one reads about happening in (other parts of) Russia." Still, she said, "I always feel a little timid. In going back and forth from Grosny to the wells which are twelve or fourteen miles (nineteen to twenty-two kilometres), James always carries a revolver, but at the same time assures me there is absolutely no danger. I am always nervous at night and cannot help the feeling. I really could not live here all the time."

James was thankful that his location in Grosny kept him distanced – about four hundred and eighty kilometres – from the turmoil that had engulfed the Baku oilfields which had become, in no small way, the training ground for Russian revolutionaries. The chief socialist organizer there was a Georgian man named Joseph Djugashvili who went by the code name Koba and later became better known as Joseph Stalin. Stalin organized strikes and demonstrations that targeted the Rothschilds' holdings.

Still, the Chechen population despised the foreign oil drillers as much as they did the Russians, and these strong feelings were known to break out into violence, including train robberies, raids on private foreign-held companies and even murder.

With Galician oil having peaked and – apart from the Boryslaw-Tustanowice fields – dwindling, William McGarvey strongly believed his company's future rested in Russia. In 1910, Albert was pulled out of Romania and sent to work with James as the Karpath sought to shift its emphasis eastward. The McGarvey brothers recognized the dangers there. Albert told his wife, Lucinda Jane, that he wanted her to live with her sister and brother-in-law in London, Ontario during his assignment to Russia. If things didn't turn out, Albert would soon be back, he said. Lucinda later recounted that Albert's letters to her often referred to "the roughness and lawlessness of the country."

James felt differently. He had felt confident enough about the safety of his living arrangements that he had urged Julia to make the trip out. Grosny represented civilization and a city where he believed Julia could feel at home, at least in the short-run.

James McGarvey took ardently to the life he discovered in Grosny. He was clearly the nature-lover and adventurer among the three McGarvey brothers. An enthusiastic horseman, he acquired a fine stallion and travelled the territory he was responsible for on horseback, seated in the sling of a traditional Cossack saddle. In fact he rather fancied himself a Cossack-at-heart. Defining "Cossack" is not an easy thing. Cossacks, it is said, are "sensed" rather than defined. To be a Cossack is to belong to a community of shared traditions, culture and attitude toward one's duty and military service. It is a philosophy James eagerly embraced.

He even learned to ride "Cossack-style." This is a method that requires the rider to push back in the saddle and sit up higher on the animal. Control is maintained through the bridle and whip rather than by way of the stirrups, heels and toes, as is the case in the more popular cavalry riding style.

James McGarvey slipped into the job of overseeing the new company with a natural ease. He was as comfortable in the oil fields as he was in the office – perhaps more so. As manager, he was quite capable of undertaking any task he might ask a man under his supervision to do. Unlike his brother, William, who was something of a dandy and was years past contemplating a trip to the fields to conduct his work, James would exuberantly and without hesitation shove aside a native worker he didn't think was performing the job properly and show him how it was done. At any moment, James was prepared to thread two ends of pipe together, pack a steam pump or open a barrel of grease, jobs William never found much to his liking.

When Julia arrived in Grosny, she was readily impressed with the way her husband had taken to the task at hand. She learned he loved to recount details of his experiences in the field over dinner and, surprisingly even to herself, discovered she actually enjoyed listening to her husband's tales. James would come home, wash up and change into proper dinner attire. Julia relished his daily shoptalk over food.

As for their safety, James assured Julia everything was under control "Yes, I carry a revolver, but don't worry," he told her. "Everyone's too busy to get up to mischief during the day. The danger is only after darkness and by that time, we're all safe inside."

Sometimes James needed to spend a few days out of the office and closer to the oilfields, and for that he maintained another house that was just a half-hour's walk from the wells. Since he didn't need to be there all of the time, he let a trusted Polish couple live there, in exchange for boarding with them whenever it was necessary for him to stay in the fields.

As she became more acquainted with the country, Julia was curious about what life was like in other areas and agreed to join James on some of his trips to the fields he managed. That is where they found themselves in November when she wrote to her friends back in England. "We sometimes stay out a week at a time," she explained. But, she admitted, "I am more timid out here. In Grosny there are so many soldiers and mostly Cossacks, and they being pets of the government, they will shoot if necessary."

Julia stayed with James in Grosny much longer than she had planned. There was something enchanting about the place, she felt, quite a contrast to the English countryside she was used to, and she enjoyed once again being with her husband and sharing his life. James was, after all, 64 years old by this time and Julia would soon be 53. While they were both healthy, she knew their life together could not last forever. She seemed reluctant to bid him goodbye and return to England. From her arrival in September, Julia stayed through the fall and well into the winter.

Throughout the early winter months, relations between the locals on one side, and the government authorities and business operators on the other, further deteriorated.

James mentioned in one letter back to his sister Ellen Westland in London, Ontario "that owing to the threats made, he thought he might find it necessary to provide himself with a bodyguard," according to a newspaper account. He was finding Grosny a far different place than the peaceful existence he had known while working with William in Galicia. In another letter, James said "he found it necessary to have his properties guarded night and day, and that it was unsafe to venture out unarmed."

Amidst this growing environment of danger, the company received good news. William McGarvey wrote to his nephew, the dentist William S. Westland, in London, Ontario that James and Albert had struck a gusher at Grosny that promised incredible results and was bound to make them all even wealthier than they already were. In early 1911 while James stayed on to manage affairs in Grosny, Albert departed for England to provide details of the new strike to their fellow investors.

Julia continued to stay on with James. There was to be a special guest on the evening of February 22, 1911, and James and Julia looked forward to dressing for dinner and enjoying a glass of sherry with him. Talbot Barnard, an engineer and a trusted employee of James' company, had just returned from England. As dinner began, James and Julia listened intently as their guest began to catch them up on news from what they both now considered "home."

As was the case every evening, cook would roll a trolley from the kitchen into the dining room. He would serve, leave the dishes on the sideboard and roll the trolley back to the kitchen to prepare for delivery of the next course. The three dinner companions were finishing up the first course and anticipating cook's return when instead, three intruders burst through the door from the kitchen. James McGarvey sat in an armchair, his back to the kitchen doors.

Julia screamed. Before James had a chance to react, one of the burglars jammed his chair into the table, using its arms to pin him in. Unable to escape and defend himself, James was helpless as the intruder thrust a long knife through the back of his chair, piercing his body near the collarbone. James slumped forward.

As Barnard jumped from his seat, an intruder brought the butt of a pistol crashing down on his head and he fell, stunned, to the floor. Julia was flung to the floor as the men headed to the bedroom where they seemed to know the safe was located. They battered away at it with their rifles and any spare pipe they could lay their hands on. The invaders, unable to open the safe, lifted it and carried it away.

A report in the Toronto *Evening Telegram* on February 24 said, "the robbers intercepted a boy giving the alarm and killed him, also a watchman. They then attacked McGarvey, who was killed with Caucasian knifes. Barnard had been stunned by the blow."

Dazed and bloodied, Barnard shook off his grogginess, rose and tried to carry Julia to safety. But he had been severely weakened by the attack, and proved no match for the robbers. He was overtaken and the final murderous blow was struck. "The lady was only stunned," continued the newspaper report. "The murderers then stabbed the cook and finally decamped with one hundred pounds in cash."

The newspaper report said that the killers were three "natives" – a description used by Julia in her letter home to England. Two of them were arrested, while Cossack guards were scouring the frozen winter countryside for the third man, the newspaper said. He shot himself rather than succumb to capture.

Albert had been saved only by the fact he was in England on business. That is where he was when word came of the attack. He immediately sent a cablegram to Joseph W. Scandrett, the brother-in-law Lucinda lived with in London, Ontario. It stated: "James and engineer murdered in oil fields, Grozny. Julia wounded. Expected will recover. Albert."

A service for James was held in the chapel at Oilfields Hospital in Grosny and the body was sent to England. Later, his remains were reinterred in the cemetery where his parents were buried in London, Ontario. The murder of James McGarvey and Talbot Barnard was raised in the British House of Commons.

Julia was taken to hospital in Vladikavka, about one hundred kilometres from Grosny. She suffered no life-threatening injuries but her shoulder was permanently damaged. In September 1912, daughter Mamie Blaker travelled to the Continent to meet her mother and accompany her back home to Ealing. Julia continued to live in England until her death in 1950. She never returned to Russia and enjoyed a comfortable life on her generous survivor's pension from James's company. She travelled extensively by train in the 1920s and 1930s and was particularly fond of France's sunny South, especially resorts frequented by the "upper classes."

Later as a wealthy widow, Julia McGarvey basked in the attention of her many admirers, some of whom showered her with expensive gifts. One, an American diplomat who served in China, presented her with a sandalwood linen chest, carved with scenes of court life in ancient China. However neither he, nor any of her other gentleman friends, ever succeeded in convincing her to marry them.

David Ingleby, a great-grandson of Julia and James McGarvey and grandson of Helena "Mamie" Blaker, describes Julia as in possession of a "quaint nineteenth-century North American sense of humour" that forever instilled in him a fondness for the American humourist and author James Thurber. Ingleby, who now lives in Netherlands, also recalls Julia's ever-present walking stick.

"I remember my mother telling me that Julia stayed in Stockholm in the 1930s in an apartment belonging to Greta Garbo, in which the sheets were made of silk," said Ingleby. "I think she (Garbo) had something to do with the (American) diplomat."

Julia also maintained links to the family of William McGarvey and is listed in Fred and Madge's guestbook in England at Manor Farm House in 1944, her home address noted as being in Amersham, Buckinghamshire.

The question remained: who were the intruders and why was James McGarvey murdered? Was he targeted or was the break-in a random act?

James had assured Julia that Grosny was outside the mainstream of violence that plagued the oilfields of Baku. Nevertheless, Chechnya was still a violent society. As Julia wrote back in 1910, the countryside was filled with people from many backgrounds – including Georgians, Tartars, Lezgins, Osetins and Chechens – a cultural crossroads where the people were often in conflict with one another. The native people had one thing in common: they all disliked the ruling Russians and their duty-bound Cossack guards. They also resented the foreign-owned and operated oil companies. James was a wealthy man and keeper of the company payroll, undoubtedly seen as an easy target and quick source of money by any number of potential robbers.

Albert and Lucinda McGarvey's brother-in-law, J.W. Scandrett, told the *London* (Ontario) *Free Press*: "The natives have been exceedingly hostile to foreigners. It is an awful country. A man takes his life in his hands when he goes there. These men knew the risk."

Two days later, the London *Advertiser* identified the intruders as "a band of outlaws who under the leadership of Zelimkhan had been committing numerous depredations. ... On many occasions when pursued, they have found refuge in the mountains and have defied capture." Zelimkhan was finally felled by Russian soldiers and local police in 1913.

James's murder was a devastating personal blow to his family. And as manager of the Anglo-Terek and North Caucasus oilfields – fields that represented William McGarvey's great hopes for success in Russia – his death was also a staggering loss to the company. William had looked upon Russia as the company's next great frontier, a place that would more than compensate for Galicia as the oil fields there began to play out. Now, it seemed, his decision to expand there had cost his family dearly, and it was about to deal a further blow to his corporate empire.

A Literary Link

There is an intriguing side-story related to Mamie arriving to take her mother, Julia, back to England. Mamie's husband, Percy Stanley Blaker, was not able to join his wife on the trip to the Continent and instead sent his eighteen-year-old nephew, Richard Blaker, to escort her. Mamie was about thirty-one at the time. During the course of the trip, Richard and Mamie had an affair and she became pregnant. Never being one to beat around the bush, Mamie confessed all to her husband, Percy, and Percy, wishing to avoid family scandal, decided to hush the matter up. Percy Stanley Blaker acted as executor to James McGarvey's will.

Richard Blaker went on to become a writer and produced a novel based loosely on James McGarvey's adventures in the oil business from which his brother, William, the true petroleum baron, was expunged. *Here Lies A Most Beautiful Lady* was published in London in 1935 and became one of the year's best-sellers. There was also a sequel, *But Beauty Vanishes*. The books provide valuable insight into life in the Grosny oil lands of the era.

Counting on Russia

The murder of James McGarvey was the most devastating incident to occur in the first quarter-century that William's Karpath had been operating in Europe. But it was a harbinger of more to come.

James' assistant, Charles Wallen of Oil Springs, was chosen as a temporary operator of the fields, but a permanent replacement was not appointed until the next year. At that time, William's son, Fred, was appointed managing director of the whole Russian operation, as reported in *The Investors' Review*, Vol. XXX, July 6 to December 28, 1912. Fred McGarvey had been reported involved in the Russian operation as early as 1909 when he resigned from the Karpath's board of directors to take on more operational duties.

With James no longer available to call upon for help, William McGarvey himself travelled to Russia in 1912 to review company affairs and collect evidence of the huge new deposits of oil that had been discovered in the Maikop Valley during the previous year. William's own personal attention to the matter indicates just how crucial he believed Russia was to his company's well-being. At a time when Galicia's future as a supplier of oil was coming into question, McGarvey was keen to expand into Russia where he was of the strong belief petroleum was plentiful.

McGarvey established the Maikop Deep Drilling Company soon after James' murder. Its first big success came on property owned by McGarvey's International Maikup. Having drilled just over two thousand feet (six hundred and ten metres), oil was struck in copious amounts, *The Investors' Review* reported.

Mac McGarvey came away from his trip to Russia convinced that the company's future there was bright. But another unexpected death was about to leave yet another huge gap in the McGarvey empire.

CHAPTER 11

'HIGH HONOURS AND DECORATIONS'

U nder William McGarvey's firm leadership, the Karpath became so widely known and respected at home in Austria-Hungary that it was as frequently called simply the Austrian Oil Company and the National Oil Company as by its registered name of the Galizische Karpathen Petroleum Aktiengesellschaft.

Mac McGarvey was known as the man behind the achievements. Prior to his arrival, the petroleum business in Eastern Europe had been conducted in a highly unsophisticated manner: if the collection of crude oil even progressed to what could be loosely termed "drilling," it was often the purview of a local blacksmith. McGarvey introduced workshops onsite at all the wells, and went into mass production of oil. It was McGarvey who was primarily responsible for the mechanization of Eastern Europe's oilfields.

McGarvey was highly regarded by his peers. Besides holding office as head of the Karpath, he served as vice-president of the National Petroleum Society for much of the time he worked in the Galician fields. This was an unheard-of honour for a non-native Austrian or Pole.

McGarvey's was a household name in Austria-Hungary. But his fame extended much farther, beyond the borders of his adopted country.

When J. D. Henry wrote *Oil Fields of the Empire: A Survey of British Imperial Petroleum Questions*, he asked Mac McGarvey to write the prefatory notes. The book, published in 1910, included a comprehensive technical description of oilfields to be found in what at the time were considered two important potential sources of petroleum readily available to the British Empire: Trinidad and Newfoundland. Newfoundland did not pan out until its offshore resources were exploited many years later, but Trinidad would rapidly become an important source of oil for several decades. In part McGarvey wrote:

> The development of the petroleum industry today provides the means for the satisfaction of the desire, which has existed among mankind from time immemorial, for more light, greater power, and accelerated motion.
>
> It has only taken half a century to produce petroleum in sufficient quantities to warrant the almost unlimited investment of capital and establish the business on a firm commercial basis; in this comparatively short space of time oil has become a necessity to the whole civilized world; in the business of producing, transporting and refining, millions of money have been invested and hundreds of thousands of men find well-paid employment; and we now have organisations which for boldness of conception and the courage displayed in their materialization are not surpassed, and perhaps not equalled, in any of the world's great industries.

It is no accident that McGarvey was chosen to comment for the book's foreword and no small honour that he was. No one in the entire Austro-Hungarian Empire, and few if any in the broader world, were more knowledgeable about all aspects of the petroleum industry than William Henry McGarvey. Austria's emperor, Kaiser Franz Josef, had himself recognized the importance of oil and the opportunities that presented themselves when he visited Galicia back in 1880. It was his direct orders that led to amending the laws of the land in a manner that enabled McGarvey to introduce an efficient industry, based on Canadian drilling techniques, that could exploit Galicia's oil resources and make himself a wildly successful entrepreneur.

Knighthood Bestowed

McGarvey grew into the most important oil industrialist in the Austrian empire, a fact that was recognized by the emperor himself who bestowed "high honours and decorations" upon him. On November 30, 1908,

McGarvey was ushered into the realm of Austria-Hungary's Imperial Order of the Iron Crown (Kaiserlicher Orden der Eisernen Krone). The honour conferred automatic hereditary ennoblement, with the lower knighthood rank of "Ritter" bestowed upon him and a medal awarded him that a strict protocol dictated was to be worn on the left chest.

Portrait photographs taken of McGarvey at the time of his investiture into the Order of the Iron Crown depict a man brimming with pride and pleasure at the honour bestowed. He was the picture of a mature and debonair gentleman of considerable means, confident and cultured. His walrus mustache was a shade or two darker than his full head of pure white hair. While it had been a decade earlier, at the time of Helena's death, when McGarvey first began to be known in Petrolia as the "Petroleum King of Austria," there was now no doubt that it was a title well deserved. None other than the Kaiser himself had confirmed it. But not only was he Austria's petroleum king, McGarvey was the king of Canada's Foreign Drillers.

Despite the personal honours that had come his way, the murder of his brother, James, had not only been a devastating shock to William and his family, it had also shaken the company. Now, William McGarvey was about to suffer another terrible loss.

The End Of A Partnership

The man responsible for convincing William McGarvey to take a chance on Europe was born of humble beginnings in the Middle East, was educated in England, and used his inquisitive scientific mind to build a personal fortune. John Bergheim became more than just Mac's business partner – the two of them became trusted friends, known affectionately to one another, as well as to their colleagues and families, as "Mac and Johnny."

Within two years of Bergheim's 1879 visit to Petrolia, McGarvey and Bergheim had linked up in Hanover and created the Continental Oil Company. Progress there was slow, but once they accepted the challenge from Stanislaw Szczepanowski to continue on to Galicia, it was a new day. After they began drilling there in 1883, success quickly followed.

Bergheim maintained a London business address and in 1882 is listed as a civil engineer of Bergheim & Company at the fashionable Laurence Pountney Hill in London. It is an address that signalled his success – that he had arrived. Over the next few years the Bergheims moved a number of times to ever-better London neighbourhoods and for a while in the 1890s they spent a great deal of time in Vienna. It was during those years on the Continent that Bergheim created a stir among his friends and colleagues when he was swindled out of $100,000. For the already-wealthy Bergheim, the loss was no big concern – it was the public embarrassment that caused him great pain.

By that time, John and Clara Bergheim were living a very fashionable lifestyle and frequently entertained in regal style. Their Vienna house was known as a gathering centre for the city's social elite, a place where scholars, university professors, artists and financial barons alike came to visit.

Both of them missed England, however, and in 1898 they were back permanently, having purchased and moved to a mansion in the stylish northwest London neighbourhood of Belsize Park. It is still an upper-crust address to this day. The home they moved in to, now demolished, was situated on Belsize Lane and was aptly named Belsize Court.

While he was ambitious in business, Bergheim was also adamant that he maintain a healthy balance between those business concerns and his personal hobbies. His sharp scientist's mind required other outlets. His intellect and skills led him into the field of bacteriological studies and he kept a personal laboratory at his spacious home. He studied insects and how they spread disease. He devoted his garden to the development of rare plants and fruits.

He was also an avid photographer and experimented with techniques that he felt more accurately conveyed the essence of a person than a typical portrait ever could. Bergheim was the co-creator of the Dallmeyer-Bergheim portrait lense, a soft-focus lense that earned him the nickname "The Smudger." To some, his pictures were "just some blurry images," but to Bergheim, they were human studies that delved into a person's true spirit.

An early member of Britain's groundbreaking Linked Ring Brotherhood photographers group, John Bergheim's photography never achieved the critical acclaim enjoyed by his brother Peter. However, one portrait done in Vienna in 1895 of an exotic dancer, cloaked in a gauzy veil that covered just one breast, did succeed in causing a stir. Titled *Bajadere*, it appears to be Bergheim's only venture into the field of what was undoubtedly considered in his era to be pretty risqué.

Patron of the Arts

In London, the wealthy Bergheims were able to enjoy the privileged social life available to them in a world-class city. Bergheim developed an appreciation for the arts, and especially fine music, at an early age. In the 1870s, he joined the London Wagner Society to promote the great German composer's works. Bergheim served in a number of positions with the society, including treasurer.

When a young classical pianist named Arthur Rubinstein went to London in 1911 as a self-described "poor struggling musician," he was discovered by John and Clara. Rubinstein described their home and his friendship with them in his autobiography: "At the angle of a short street called Belsize Park (actually, Lane), a drive-in courtyard led to their house, a large but unpretentious three-storey building which stood by itself."

Rubinstein recalled the night of their first meeting, a recital at Bechstein Hall (renamed Wigmore Hall during the First World War), after which the Bergheims came backstage to introduce themselves. They invited him to dinner at Belsize Court and sent a car to pick him up. Rubinstein wrote this description of his first visit:

Two maids opened the door and took my coat and hat. One of them preceded me into the living room on the first floor, opened the doors, and announced loudly: 'Mr. Arthur Rubinstein.' There were several guests. Mr. Bergheim received me enthusiastically and introduced me, to my annoyance, as the "young genius." A short man in his seventies (actually his sixties), he had sharp grey eyes, which were bloodshot, constantly bulging with excitement, and a well-shaped but unmistakably Jewish nose (there's that Jewish reference again.) Mrs. Clara Bergheim, not much younger and no taller than her husband, was slim and neat, her grey hair dressed *a la* Queen

Mary. She was wearing thick-lensed glasses and had a tendency to blush so violently that even her nose turned red.

Their guests were interesting: among them were Sir Edmund Davis, one of the well-known Jewish millionaires to have made their fortune in South Africa; Ralph Peto, a young very good-looking gentleman, and his wife, a tall, lovely brunette; a niece of the duchess of Rutland and a cousin of Lady Marjory and lady Diana Manners, two famous English beauties; Sir George Henschel, a noted concert singer and the first conductor of the Boston Symphony Orchestra, and his daughter, Helen, a promising soprano.

The young musician's first experience at Belsize offers a revealing glimpse into the Bergheims' lifestyle and entertaining habits. He went on to describe dinner at a table "adorned with exquisite orchids in different shapes and colours, and the food was in the best English style. At the end of dinner, the host produced a few bunches of huge black grapes ... 'From my own hothouse,' he said proudly."

After dinner as was the custom of the day, the ladies left the room and the gentlemen remained behind for the serving of port. Bergheim showed his male guests out into the garden where he led them to a long row of greenhouses. " 'Here is where I raise my orchids and grow my fruits', he said, and gave us a long lecture on the merits of hothouses."

Eventually, Clara returned with the women and all of the guests gathered in the living room. "Mr. Bergheim took me aside and begged me to play. 'We have a fine, well-tuned Bechstein,' he said.

"I began with the *Liebestod* from *Tristan*, followed by my own concert arrangement of the *Walkurenritt*, two of my sure-fire hits. And the impact was overwhelming. I can't remember when my playing pleased a small group of people more."

Bergheim insisted on pressing a "small fee" into Rubinstein's palm, twenty-five pounds. To a struggling young musician, the sum was enormous and much-appreciated. Soon afterwards there was another invitation to dinner and the poor starving artist enthusiastically accepted, surmising there would be another payment involved. From then on, "Whenever I played (for them), I received the usual cheque of twenty-five pounds."

Afterwards, whenever his funds dwindled, Rubinstein contacted the Bergheims for another invitation. He was often a guest at their luncheons.

Bergheim's wealth enabled him to become a generous patron of the arts. He told Rubinstein he would "'take your career in England into my own hands, and you must stay with us.' I was deeply touched. I came to love this old man."

An Oil Tycoon In His Own Right

Over the course of his career, Bergheim was a partner – often with McGarvey – in several petroleum companies and while he never rivalled the Nobels and Rockefeller, he did enjoy a worldwide reach. He served as chairman of the Societé Francaise de Pétrole, the Nigerian Bitumen Corporation, International Maikop Ltd. in Russia, and Anglo-Mexican & Tampico Oil Ltd. in Mexico. He was director of the AG Petroleum Industry in Nuremberg, the Oesterreichische Petroleum-Industrie AG, the Russian Kuban Industrial and Petroleum Co. and Ekaterinodar, the drilling tool company he and McGarvey founded in Russia.

Before the British Parliament established a Royal Commission on the subject, Bergheim was one of the leaders in the push to adopt liquid oil fuel for British shipping and began efforts to find petroleum supplies within the British Isles. The venture proved unsuccessful and it was only with the discovery of the North Sea resources many years later that Britain was able to produce its own petroleum in large quantities.

During his career, Bergheim was also engaged in petroleum activities – either on his own or with McGarvey – in Croatia, Romania, the Russian Caucasus region, India, Egypt, Algeria, Central and West Africa, the Caribbean Islands and the Middle East.

While he maintained London as his residence, Bergheim was a well-travelled man, frequently visiting places around the world where his various companies did business. He was also known as a man of science, with an inquisitive mind, ability to size up a problem and quickly propose a solution.

One such example of his science-based intelligence occurred during one of the trips Bergheim took with McGarvey to Galicia. The two men stopped at the home of a peasant worker employed by their oil firm. The worker complained of not having felt well and being unable to eat. Bergheim was seized with the determination to discover why. He gazed around the man's humble home and was drawn to his stove, and the pot in which the man brewed his tea. Bergheim peeked inside. Finding the interior of the pot coated in tannins from the tea, Bergheim instructed him to clean it out and brew a fresh pot every time rather than simply adding water to the pot as had been his recent habit. After following Bergheim's instructions, the man reported to have immediately felt much improved.

(In more recent times, studies have found tannic acid in large doses to be linked to stomach irritation, nausea, vomiting and even liver damage. There are also hints that tannins are associated with an increased incidence of developing nose or throat cancer.)

It was during Britain's broad search for secure oil supplies prior to the First World War when Bergheim paid particular attention to the West African colony of Nigeria. There were obvious advantages to obtaining oil from a friendly British colony rather than from the Middle East where there were constant upheavals and competition from the Turks. Bergheim took the lead in 1906 and with the support of the British Admiralty, convinced the Colonial Office as well as the government of Southern Nigeria that petroleum could be exploited there. He established the Nigeria Bitumen Corporation and organized a monopoly on prospecting rights by buying up all drilling licences.

Nigeria's legislation was rewritten to accommodate Bergheim and he enjoyed a monopoly for the next six years. The company was registered in London and traded on the stock exchange there. Nigeria Bitumen was given a loan to support exploration and between 1908 and 1912 the corporation dug about fifteen wells at a cost of 143,000 British pounds. The future looked incredibly bright.

Life At Home

While he and Clara had no children of their own, John doted on his niece, Margaret Fanny Salome Bergheim, daughter of his younger brother, Peter. Peter Bergheim and his wife, Martha Sophia (Lindsay) Bergheim, died within two years of one another – in 1885 and 1887. Margaret was just ten years old when her mother died and John and Clara took on responsibility for her care. The couple was pleased when the young woman everyone called Madge decided to marry Fred McGarvey in 1901.

In fact Madge and Fred's first daughter, Leila Helena Margaret, was born at Belsize Court in August 1902. Living with Fred in Glinik Mariampolski, the young woman had begun to think of "going home" as her due-date approached. There is a photo of Madge, holding baby Leila tenderly in her arms, taken at the Bergheims' house. With no children of their own, the Bergheims were delighted at the prospects of hosting the birth of their almost-granddaughter and pampering their dear Madge.

John Bergheim was at the height of his career as a petroleum financier and promoter when he and Clara sailed to the Mediterranean, stopping at Gibraltar, in 1910, and then to South America during the winter of 1911-12. Sailing from Buenos Aires, the couple arrived back at Southampton on April 20.

A cablegram from Ernest Nicklos arrived at the Bergheims' on September 6, 1912, advising Johnny of a big new petroleum strike at his Anglo-Mexican Oil Fields Ltd., a subsidiary of the Anglo-Mexican & Tampico Oil Ltd. company he had founded. The couple was elated at the news and chatted excitedly about the prospects as they set out the next day in their chauffeur-driven car. They were heading down the Ripley Road not far from their Belsize home when their driver, Joseph Saxby, attempted to pass a vehicle in front of them. In an instant, a horse-drawn cart appeared coming in the opposite direction and Saxby swerved to miss it. A wheel of the Bergheims' car struck an embankment and it overturned.

In the days before seatbelts, Bergheim was thrown from the car and as he lay on the roadway the man and woman in the other vehicle drove away without even stopping to see if they could help. John Bergheim suffered a fractured skull and died in Surrey County Hospital three days later. Clara and Saxby escaped with minor injuries.

So Bergheim's career was cut short. He had been phenomenally successful in the petroleum field but his success fell far short of those he chased – Rockefeller and the Nobels. Nevertheless, the experience in

Nigeria demonstrates just how significant a force John Bergheim really was. Before his death, Bergheim had been a tireless proponent of Nigerian oil at a time when many others believed it was too risky a venture. Despite the doubts of others, he had succeeded in getting the exploration process going and financed by the British government. Once he died, there was no one left to carry the ball and according to an article in *The Times* on June 24, 1913, the search for oil there ended in mid-1913. The search would not be resumed for the next quarter-century.

There is a chilling, macabre aspect to Bergheim's death, one that haunted Arthur Rubinstein for the rest of his life. Just before the fatal crash, Rubinstein had attended a dinner gathering at Belsize and played Chopin's *Funeral March*. He made it clear to Bergheim that he did not want to play it, and ultimately performed it only under protest, saying he was superstitious about its potential effect. Bergheim, the man of science with no time for such foolish superstition, had laughed it off and insisted. Rubinstein played.

Rubinstein recalled he was in Ukraine when news came of the fatal car crash that had taken the life of his friend and benefactor. "The dear old gentleman," he wrote. "I cried like a child, feeling guilty for having played the ominous *March*. It was horrible to think of it, but I wrote a long letter to Mrs. Bergheim."

John's son-in-law, Fred McGarvey, had been named one of the executors to his will – Clara being the other – and oversaw Bergheim's wishes that the bulk of his estate go to his wife. The probate record for his will indicates he left his widow the tidy sum of 155,621 British pounds, a figure that would translate to well over twenty million dollars today. Other significant amounts went to his nieces and nephews.

William McGarvey had not only lost a business partner, he had lost the man whom, it could be argued, was more responsible than anyone else for helping him to create his company and obtain his fortune. The two men had hit it off immediately upon being introduced back in Petrolia that day in 1879. Bergheim had convinced William that success lay in the oil fields of Europe. William genuinely liked the man but he had not been immediately persuaded that the offer he was being made was the right one for him. Still engaged in Canadian oil as an oil well owner, driller and refiner, he was also considering a career in politics. What was best for him and what was best for his family?

It is interesting to speculate what route William McGarvey might have taken had circumstances turned out differently for him and had Bergheim not been so persuasive in his offer. What if he and Bergheim had not hit it off, or if they had never met? In Petrolia, Mac was for several years a low-level politician, serving as a councillor, reeve and mayor. He had been chosen Lambton County's warden. Unexpectedly, the local Conservative party had nominated him to challenge the incumbent Liberal for the provincial seat and he only narrowly lost an election that should not have been that close. It was close only because of the personal appeal of William Henry McGarvey.

Then there had been the contract from the Dominion Geological Survey to explore for resources in the Northwest, an exploration that showed some promise but was not in itself immediately successful. The timing had been wrong.

So by the autumn of 1880, William had been back in Petrolia after that exploration and was finishing the final months as a town councillor. He had disposed of his share of the general store and was full-time into the petroleum business. He thinks about his future. He is encouraged by many close associates to take the leap into politics and, as a supporter of Sir John A. Macdonald's National Policy, an opponent of the Liberals' policy of Reciprocity – or free trade – with the Americans. And then there is John Simeon Bergheim and his tantalizing offer of a partnership in Europe. Finally, he opts to listen to Bergheim's advice: Europe it will be.

And now three decades later, in 1912, the man – the dear friend – who had proved to be more influential in his life than anyone else, was dead.

The dream partnership of Mac and Johnny was no more.

Clara Bergheim

Clara Bergheim remained in touch with Arthur Rubinstein and contacted him during a visit she made to Madge and Fred McGarvey in Vienna a short time after her husband's death. Clara told the pianist she was well aware how Johnny had intended to help his career and she planned to follow through on those wishes.

Rubinstein was invited to Fred and Madge McGarvey's "large, comfortable apartment on the Arenberg Platz," which he discovered was two houses away from Polish pianist, composer and teacher Leopold Godowsky, whom he knew well. He soon learned the McGarveys were musical and shared a deep passion for the piano. "I was instantly at ease with them," he said.

That night, in a reflection of his father's lesson on giving back to the community, Fred added to Clara's contribution to the Poland-born Rubinstein, explaining, "My dear fellow, Poland helped me to my good fortune, and you simply gave me a chance to reciprocate."

Rubinstein visited Clara in England at Christmas in 1915 and despite the wartime rations, she proved able to serve a fat turkey and plum pudding flambé. After the war, Rubinstein was back for a visit and it seemed nothing had changed at Belsize. "When I asked her about wartime in England she reduced the conflagration to a domestic difficulty. 'It was hard to get tea and sugar and other things I can't think of. It was becoming difficult to heat the hothouses,'" she added.

Clara found life lonely without her husband and after the war she took a cruise to Mexico, a favourite haunt the couple had shared. It was a voyage of nostalgia, one in which she thought of the grand times she had spent with her beloved Johnny. During the trip, she met another passenger, Joseph Fletcher Toomer. The two fell in love and they were married back in London on October 7, 1920. Clara could not wait to convey the whole story to her good friend, Arthur Rubinstein.

She lived until 1929 and continued to reside with her new husband at Belsize Court.

CHAPTER 12

FOR GOD AND COUNTRY

John Bergheim's sudden death naturally came as a shock to his business partner and old friend, William McGarvey. Contacted in Vienna with the news, Mac made immediate plans to attend Johnny's funeral and Fred said he wished to accompany his father to London.

Father and son attended the service. Afterwards, as they turned and walked away from the gravesite, the pair was approached by a man the elder McGarvey recognized immediately: Charles Baker, Bergheim's most trusted aide on his coveted Nigerian oil project. McGarvey had spent many hours with Bergheim and Baker, discussing the prospects for establishing a flourishing petroleum business in the West African colony.

McGarvey introduced Baker to son Fred. Then Baker leaned in closely to McGarvey and in a low voice said: "I have an important matter I would like to discuss with you, sir. It must be in the utmost confidence, however. Could we meet someplace in private?" Baker placed his lips to Mac's ear and whispered in a conspiratorial tone befitting a James Bond novel: "Mr. McGarvey, your country requires your services."

On Matters Of Security

Nearly two and a half years earlier, on April 4, 1910, William McGarvey had prepared remarks for an upcoming book authored by the renowned petroleum expert, J.D. Henry. As one of the world's foremost experts and a veteran of nearly half a century in petroleum, Mac was a natural to have been chosen for the task. It was with a clear-eyed view of future events that he wrote about the crucial role he fully believed petroleum would play in world affairs. "I feel strongly that the future safety and security of the (British) Empire depend in no small degree on our securing within the colonies and dominions a large and reliable supply of petroleum for use in the warships of the Empire," he wrote.

"Safety and security," Mac had written. Four years before war broke out, William McGarvey was concerning himself with the weighty issues that would determine the course of history. He "strongly" believed that those who recognized and settled those matters would prevail in whatever troubles the future would bring. He was of the firm opinion that petroleum would play a key role in determining world events.

McGarvey's perspective was one that aligned him with Admiral John Arbuthnot Fisher, who had been Britain's First Sea Lord from 1904-1910. After stepping down from that post, Fisher, the self-styled "oil maniac," spent the next few years advocating for Britain to switch its naval fleet to oil-powered locomotion. He warned that Germany was far ahead of Britain in developing petroleum diesel engines for the purpose of propulsion. When Winston Churchill was appointed First Lord of the Admiralty in November 1911 and therefore the cabinet minister in charge of the navy, he appointed Fisher as his adviser.

Fisher knew naval technology was changing quickly and was determined Britain would not be left behind. In 1900, the coal-powered steam turbine was still driving the world's warships and, to a smaller degree, the smaller merchant ships. But by 1908, the diesel engine began to take hold of the market. The internal combustion engine used heavier fractions of oil rather than gasoline and motor spirit and it was beginning to be used in submarines and small surface craft. The wrinkle came from the fact that when "large power" was required, the coal-fired-steam turbines still had no rival. Coal remained king in the ships of war. Destroyers, cruisers and battleships were too much for the diesel technology of the era. But Germany recognized the benefits of oil and was working hard to develop the oil-fired turbine-driven engine for primary propulsion in its major fighting ships. Fisher saw what lay ahead and it frightened him. Britain was not keeping pace with Germany and must act quickly if it wanted to maintain its mastery of the seas.

Fisher was a man of grand dreams. He once advocated an underground "sea" in England that could be filled with oil, with lines running to the ocean so that it could be used to fuel the fleet. He feared Germany was far ahead of Britain, with plans under way for a petroleum-fuelled battle cruiser. He also feared a coming war with Germany and believed it was crucial for Britain to be properly prepared.

No sooner had Churchill been installed as the minister responsible for the navy when Fisher was writing him about the benefits of operating the naval fleet on oil. On December 10, 1911, Fisher wrote: "When a cargo steamer can save seventy-eight percent in fuel and gain thirty percent in cargo space by the adoption of internal combustion propulsion and practically get rid of (coal) stokers and engineers, it is obvious what a prodigious change is at our doors with oil!"

Agreed, said Churchill, but the problem is that Britain is not an oil-rich nation. Where could the oil be obtained? A flurry of letters were exchanged by the two men and on May 26, 1912, Churchill wrote to Fisher: "Find us oil in sufficient quantities and at a reasonable price in peace, and without interruption in war, make us feel that we can count on it and swim on it; guarantee its supplies and reserves and you will have added another to those silent victories of peace...."

Churchill had come to understand well the advantages of petroleum-based fuel to propel Britain's battleships: better speed, a wider range of travel and lower cargo weight. In other words, it was clearly more efficient than coal. But the full government needed to be convinced, a task that would not be easy with the labour movement and the coal industry coming down hard in opposition. Britain was rich in coal and dependent upon others for oil. Creating arguments for oil would be a delicate task.

On July 31, 1912, Churchill received cabinet approval to create the Royal Commission on Fuel and Engines, "to report on the means of supply and storage of liquid fuel in peace and war, and its application to warship engines, whether indirectly or by internal combustion." To give the commission the status he knew would be needed to get its findings and recommendations passed in parliament, he appointed the oil maniac himself, Admiral Fisher, as its head.

Sailing To Victory On A Secure Sea Of Oil

Fisher was given full freedom to choose whomever he wanted to serve on the committee and invite to give evidence. He selected Bergheim as an adviser – "the main adviser," according to an obituary. But Bergheim's unexpected death that September put an end to those prospects, just as Fisher was preparing to get the commission under way, so he began to consider Bergheim's long-standing partner, William Henry McGarvey. Mac's credentials were well known and widely respected. But McGarvey was in Vienna. In the event of war with Germany, where might his loyalties lie? Fisher wondered.

Could war be possible? For many years, Churchill had not been worried about such a question, but his thinking abruptly changed in July 1911, when the German gunboat *Panther* sailed into Morocco's port of Agadir. Germany intended to demonstrate it was going to join Britain and France in capturing a piece of the African continent and all of the economic and political benefits that came from its exploitation. With that single act, Churchill instantly reached the conclusion that Germany was becoming a threat.

Hard on the heels of the *Panther* episode, in 1912 a German book began making the rounds in opinion-makers' circles across the Continent. *Germany and the Next War*, by General Friedrich von Bernhardi, seemed to be predicting war between Germany and Britain. Bernhardi glorified Germany's past wartime efforts, chastised those who would weaken the national resolve and deemed his countrymen "the ruling people of the Continent by the power of their arms and the loftiness of their ideas." It was an alarming warning to Britain.

While the thought of war remained unlikely in the minds of most people, those in positions of power were watching with increasing alarm at the signs that were building around them. In that same year, Fisher warned Churchill that owing to Britain's apathy, Germany was sprinting ahead with the development of the internal combustion engine and feared that a German battle cruiser was "under weigh."

(Ironically, Churchill's argument for oil fuel for the navy could have been dramatically advanced if he had revealed what only a handful of people knew at the time: that the British-built *Titanic* would probably not have sunk if its engines had been diesel-powered. The massive "unsinkable" passenger liner went to the bottom of the Atlantic off the Newfoundland coast within months of the *Panther* episode. Its sinking was hastened because of the fire that started in the coal and weakened a crucial bulkhead, according to testimony at an inquiry. The widely held belief, now set firmly in *Titanic* lore, was that iceberg damage was responsible for the ship's demise. However, that was, in Trumpian language, "fake news," a story encouraged by the British government. Certainly the ship had struck an iceberg, which caused an enormous gash in its hull. But the gash alone was not sufficient to have caused the quick sinking of the giant ship and the loss of so many lives. Rescue ships had not had the luxury of time to arrive on the scene and save more passengers because the coal fire had hastened its sinking. The truth was that the iceberg damage was less important a factor in the large number of deaths than the coal fire. British authorities feared that if they had admitted as much, panicked passengers would abandon the White Star Line and other British liners in favour of German and American ones that were already powered by diesel fuel.)

McGarvey was an enthusiastic cheerleader for oil power, as per his strong words in *Oil Fields of the Empire* about securing a reliable empire-based supply of petroleum for warships. In that book, he explained that the potential resources of the British Empire had been ignored for many years because it had been easy to access the huge resources of the United States and Russia. "We did not think seriously about colonial oil field development." It was time for Britain to think in those terms for its own security, he said. McGarvey continued:

> The object of this work on colonial oil is to draw the attention of British people, the British (g)overnment, the (g)overnments of the colonies to the immense deposits of petroleum within the border of the Empire. I sincerely hope that it will assist the fast-spreading movement in favour of the provision of an adequate all-British oil fuel supply and making of the Empire reasonably independent of the production of foreign countries.

It was the clearest indication yet of McGarvey's belief that the British Empire needed to secure reliable supplies of oil that were not dependent on other non-Empire nations. Because of those words, Fisher was fairly confident that McGarvey would be onside with Britain in the event of war. There was ample evidence McGarvey valued his Canadian roots by virtue of the many times he spoke of his love for his homeland. He had written a letter to Ernest Nicklos, the son of Charles Nicklos, one of his most valued managers, when the younger man was working in Mexico in 1908. Of Nicklos' fellow Canadians working with him in Mexico McGarvey wrote: "please tell them from me that they must uphold the honour of our Canada."

Even though he had lived in Austria for many years, McGarvey still spoke fondly of Canada whenever the opportunity arose, including on the occasion of his seventieth birthday and when friends and colleagues feted him and Helena at their twenty-fifth anniversary celebration.

But how seriously did McGarvey take the threat of war between Germany and Britain? If he had any inkling of trouble on the horizon between the two nations, it must have pained him considerably and caused him great worry. He was, after all, a British subject yet Austria – Germany's ally and a nation to which it was linked by race, language and culture – had been his adopted land since he moved to Galicia in the 1880s. Besides his frequent remarks about his love for the people of Galicia, William also was known to express strong respect for the Austrian Kaiser. In his June 1908 letter to Ernest Nicklos, McGarvey wrote about the festivities in Vienna marking the sixtieth anniversary of Franz Josef's reign.

"It was a grand sight," McGarvey said. "Took over three hours to pass, all the different nationalities were represented in their national costume. Galicia made a fine display with riders in Polish costume besides all the other officers."

Then later that year, the Austrian Kaiser had awarded McGarvey the Order of the Iron Crown. McGarvey enjoyed a strong emotional attachment to Austria and its leader. With the shifting European allegiances driving a wedge between the familial relationship once enjoyed between the British and Austrian royal families, McGarvey found himself in a terrible conflict. What would he do?

Clandestine Hearings Begin

Hearings of the British Royal Commission were to begin on September 24, 1912. Among those who joined Admiral Fisher on the commission roster was Sir Thomas Boverton Redwood, at the time considered Britain's foremost resident authority on petroleum. When a list of prospective witnesses was drawn up, Redwood and Fisher were instrumental in ensuring that Bill McGarvey was among them. The problem was, with the growing international tensions between Britain and Germany, they knew McGarvey would find himself in a dicey position and they were unsure what efforts to take to approach him. Bergheim's unexpected death provided the commission with the opportunity it needed to seek his help. With McGarvey in London for the funeral, Bergheim's right-hand man, John Baker, was dispatched to make the clandestine approach.

"Mr. McGarvey, your country requires your services," Baker had said.

Once explanations were made, William and Fred McGarvey agreed to visit the Office of the British Admiralty during their stay in London and share their thoughts. On September 17, a week before the commission was scheduled to commence its work, the two men went to Admiralty House where they joined Baker in the office of F.W. Black, the Admiralty's director of navy contracts. Black assured McGarvey that the commission's reports would all be marked "subject to the provisions of the Official Secrets Act," that they would each be stamped "secret" and that they would never be presented to parliament. The testimony, including whatever remarks the McGarveys should choose to present on that day, would not be made public and the findings of the commission would be used to advise the government in setting the future course of British policy. The nation's security hung in the balance.

The McGarveys — father and son — required no convincing about the significance of the commission's findings and recommendations. Then, assured their words would never get back to Vienna, the McGarveys looked at one another and nodded. Fred McGarvey then told Black: "it is an open secret (in Vienna) that the German government have their arrangements in case of war for a supply of petroleum from Galicia and Ro(u)mania." William nodded.

Fred's fateful words reached the eyes of the commission members in a statement presented on October 15. Germany was indeed preparing for war; everyone in Vienna apparently knew that. And in that event Galicia, certainly, as a part of the Austro-Hungarian Empire, would clearly be within the purview of the Germans. But Romania? Britain had been relying on Romanian oil in the event of war. The McGarveys' message was a red flag, an unnerving reminder of Britain's vulnerability. The commission acted quickly. On November 27, 1912, after just two months of testimony, it issued an interim emergency report to the British cabinet.

"We are of the opinion even at this early stage we should clearly set forth some points of pressing interest gravely affecting the great question of our naval supremacy," the commission said. It continued that evidence had been collected on "various" potential sources of petroleum for British ships and further investigation was required. In the meantime, the committee stated, it was essential to begin establishing adequate reserves, given that unlike coal, "oil fuel does not deteriorate by storage."

During his meeting at the Admiralty, William McGarvey went on to speak at length about his own background and experiences, and about how he had become known for his expertise in deep-well drilling which was credited with opening up the industry not only in Eastern Europe, but around the world. His late partner, John Bergheim, had often sought his advice as developments proceeded in Nigeria. In his statement, McGarvey pressed hard for continued efforts in the West African country where, he believed, all the signs – including extensive asphalt beds – pointed to an excellent potential.

He said while neither his company, nor he personally, held any financial interests in Nigeria, "I took a great interest in the developments. It is also our business to keep posted on what is being done in other petroleum mines throughout the world." In other words, McGarvey was saying that when he recommended further work in Nigeria, he understood where that country stood with respect to others, and that he had no personal stake in saying so.

Yet while all of the signs for excellent oil recovery in Nigeria were good, McGarvey cautioned, only actual drilling could prove the existence of profitable resources.

There have been times when I thought I had mastered the theory of petroleum deposits. Later, however, my theories have been upset by some new developments, until at last I have come to the conclusion, based upon experience, that the same law which has always existed, will exist until the end of time, and is unalterable, viz., that nature indicates where her treasures may be found, but that she does not give them up without a due expenditure of work, energy, perseverance, and courage. I consider it would be almost a crime not to continue the drilling of the two wells as deep as possible.

His statement to the Admiralty official revealed something interesting about McGarvey's own beliefs. He was never a strongly religious man and his referencing of "nature" rather than God is further evidence of this. While he lacked the formal education of Bergheim and son Fred, McGarvey's experiences in the oil fields of Canada and Europe had taught him a great deal about the science of petroleum; he would never allow his Methodist upbringing to take control of his certainty in the superiority of science. He was a "lucky" man and a man of great skill. He was never a sentimentally religious man.

Churchill and Fisher thought it crucial to get the commission's first report in the hands of the government as soon as possible so as to convince it to approve the task of converting the fleet. The McGarveys' revelation that Germany had "arrangements" in place to guarantee access to Romanian oil was the impetus and crucial push needed to sway government opinion. Germany meant business and Britain had no time to waste if it wanted to keep pace and retain its mastery of the seas.

Having issued its emergency interim report, the commission went back to business, collecting evidence on where Britain could obtain the petroleum resources necessary to fight a war. Subsequent reports were issued on February 28, 1913 and February 10, 1914 – just six months before Britain declared war on Germany. As the McGarveys were promised, none of the testimony was released to parliament and remained locked up until 1964.

The McGarveys' testimony on Romanian oil had been crucial. While nothing specific of what was said was known outside of a small circle of the British government at the time, Canadian writer Victor Lauriston (under the pen-name William E. Park) revealed the impact they had had. "When the British Admiralty had under consideration the introduction of oil as fuel for the navy, he (William) was called upon for expert advice and his recommendations largely governed the adoption of this improvement," Lauriston wrote in an article for *The Oil and Gas Journal* published on December 17, 1914. Lauriston's source for this conclusion was Fred McGarvey, with whom he had corresponded immediately after William's death less than three weeks earlier. Fred judiciously omitted his own part in the matter. He was, after all, still a resident of Vienna and needed to be guarded in expressing his political views.

However, the McGarveys were not sufficiently persuasive to convince the British government to press on with exploration in Nigeria as they had hoped. That country did not become a major petroleum producer until the 1950s.

In the meantime, by 1914 the British Admiralty, buoyed by the commission's findings, entered the oil business itself when it took over the Anglo-Persian Oil Company and turned its attention to the Middle East. Anglo-Persian Oil evolved into British Petroleum, later known simply as BP.

In opting to concentrate on Persian (Iranian) oil rather than that of Nigeria, Britain had cast its lot and set the stage for a bloody encounter with Germany and the Ottoman Turks in the Middle East. Britain was confident its control of the Suez Canal would make Persia the preferred choice over Nigeria for oil. It is arguable now that Nigeria might have been the safer choice and had the government opted for a West African supply rather than Persia, as McGarvey advised, it might have avoided a great deal of spilled blood in the war that was about to commence.

Had his advice been heeded, William McGarvey might have changed the face of the First World War, and hastened the development of West African oil.

Dabbling In The Canadian Oil Sands

Despite the recent downturn in oil prices and production in its home fields in Galicia, the Karpath had grown in astonishing fashion in the past years.

By the time McGarvey gave his statement to the royal commission, the Galician Carpathian firm employed 2,000 workers. Related companies such as those operating in Russia and Romania employed thousands more. But despite his nationality, McGarvey's Galician Carpathian Petroleum was not a British company; it was an Austrian company, and international tensions were on the rise between Britain and Germany. Austria was undeniably Germany's close ally.

After the commission finished its work, proponents of oil took little time to gather forces to press for the modernization of the British navy, with officials searching for oil around the world, including Canada and Newfoundland, the latter at the time being a British colony rather than a Canadian province.

R.D. Noble wrote for the *Oil and Gas Journal* on September 25, 1913 about the potential for Canadian crude. Noting the growing dependence on crude for navigation of the seas and the air as well as surface travel, Noble pointed to the obvious problem, that Britain possessed few domestic resources. "(T)he question of supplying oil to the British government in sufficient quantities from British territory is now of paramount importance to the empire," he wrote.

> People look to Canada for a solution of this problem because for over a half century Canada has made herself famous for petroleum operations, and the Canadian system of drilling is known all over the world, and Canadian drillers are employed with great success in both the hemispheres today and Canadian tools are being manufactured, both in Petrolia and Manchester and elsewhere, by Canadians and supplied to the world's oil fields. It is therefore to the experienced pioneers of this great industry that people look for counsel and advice ...

Noble implored Canadian experts to scour the country for oil resources that could be utilized by the British navy.

A month before his plea, the Dominion Conservation Commission joined the campaign for Canadian oil and used the opportunity to advocate for development of the Athabaska oil sands in the country's isolated Northwest. Here is an account of that campaign that appeared in the *Chatham News* on August 21, 1913:

If Canada becomes a base of supply for fuel oil for the British Admiralty, in furtherance of its scheme for operating warships by oil instead of coal, the tar sands of the Athabaska River in the Canadian West will be the principal source of supply, according to the opinion of James Whyte, deputy chairman of the Dominion Conservation Commission of Ottawa.

'If the tar sands of the Athabaska mean anything,' declared Mr. Whyte, when interviewed, 'it is that below them are quantities of petroleum. On three occasions wells have been sunk, but this was always done on a wrong principle. The boring was not of sufficient size. It is wholly probable that if the examinations were made under proper conditions(,) the supply would be forthcoming in paying quantities. We are endeavoring to interest capitalists in the proper development of these deposits. The oil in the Eastern (Ontario) wells is too valuable as an illuminant to be used for fuel.'

Whyte said the British Admiralty was aware it had a tough job "to convince the cautious Englishman that they have not been led by the always impulsive first lord (Hon. Winston Churchill) to overlook grave complications in the great naval adventure, for the change from coal to oil is nothing less." Britain had plenty of coal, and little oil. A proper system of security for cross-ocean shipping of petroleum would need to be established, continued Whyte.

He went on to say Germany was in better shape with regard to oil supplies, only having to tap into the great supplies that existed in Romania. Whyte's words were prophetic but perhaps not for the reasons he assumed. The fight for Romanian oil would become a fierce one.

It is indicative of McGarvey's far-sightedness and penchant for a good gamble that he was one of the early investors in the Athabaska oil sands.

Today Canada's oil sands are well known the world over as potentially Canada's largest source of petroleum. They are the result of a mixture of sand, clay, water and bitumen, which combined to create a tar-like form of petroleum. (Note the use of "tar sands" in the early reports mentioned here. That earlier term has been gradually replaced with the more environmentally acceptable "oil sands".)

Peter Pond of the North West Company was likely the first European to set eyes on the Athabaska tar sands in 1778. The first government-sponsored survey of the tar sands dates to 1875. Then in 1888 Robert Bell, then director of the Geological Survey of Canada, reported to parliament: "The evidence ... points to the existence in the Athabasca and Mackenzie valleys of the most extensive petroleum field in America, if not the world."

That attracted the attention in 1897 of a German-born man named Alfred von Hammerstein. Hammerstein fancied himself to be of a certain noble lineage and preferred calling himself "Count" von Hammerstein. The title, while carrying little real substance in his case, sounded impressive to nobility-loving anglophiles in Canada and added gravitas to his credentials. According to the Canadian Petroleum Hall of Fame in Calgary, there is evidence that Hammerstein may have originally been more interested in Klondike gold but somewhere along the line he became diverted to what is now northeastern Alberta and what he believed to be its "black flowing gold" instead.

In 1903, Hammerstein brought drilling equipment, supplies and men to the region and three years later formed the Athabaska Petroleum Syndicate. McGarvey had met Hammerstein in Germany and was drawn to the prospects of a new supply of petroleum in the far reaches of his homeland. (It had been McGarvey, after all, who travelled to Saskatchewan on behalf of the Geological Survey back in 1880 in search of resources.)

According to Calgary author Joyce Hunt who has researched the Athabaska oil sands history: "(Hammerstein) did travel to Petrolia to buy equipment that he shipped to the tar sands ca. 1910." It is logical to believe that Hammerstein was directed to Petrolia by his co-investor, William McGarvey.

The worldwide search for reliable sources of petroleum was heating up. In the latter days of peace before the First World War commenced, McGarvey's investment in Hammerstein's syndicate was reported in *Family Herald* magazine on August 26, 1914 under the headline: "Canadian Controls Great Oil Area." The article said in part: "Mr. William H. M(a)cGarvey, of Vienna, Austria, whose name has been associated with the Austro-German syndicate said to have acquired control through Count von Hammerstein of great oil areas about Fort McMurray in Northern Alberta, is a Canadian by birth and education, and in fact up to thirty-three years or so ago he was well known in political and industrial circles in the Dominion."

Nothing much ever came of Hammerstein's exploration work – like many others, he was unsuccessful in attempts to extract oil from the sands. A few years before he died in 1941, he attempted to offload his Athabaska properties onto both Imperial Oil and Royal Dutch Shell, but neither was interested. It would be many decades before technology was successful in extracting the petroleum. William McGarvey never earned a dime from them.

Nor would the Athabaska oil sands ever be of any help to the British navy as they prepared for war.

CHAPTER 13

'THIS STRESSFUL TIME'

William McGarvey was at the zenith of his power, his influence and his prestige as preparations were made to mark his seventieth birthday on November 27, 1913. A grand celebration was held for him at the Hotel Metropole in Vienna with family, friends and colleagues invited to honour him and recognize an exemplary life.

The National Petroleum Society journal *Nafta* ran a glowing account of the affair in which it lauded his ability to adapt to his adopted country. He clearly loves his chosen homeland, the journal said, and never shirks his responsibilities to his community. Even though he never learned the Polish language, he is highly popular among the natives because he assimilated well into his new society, the report said. In this regard he serves as a model to other foreign-born capitalists who came only to make money without giving anything back.

"We value his ability to adapt to our traditions and expectations. It all comes from his basic character: he is a good man and good people prefer to accommodate others and live in peace. McGarvey is highly respected in his industry as evidenced by the enormous number of congratulatory messages received from other oil circles."

McGarvey responded to the article with a letter to the publication in which he declared his "passion" for Galicia and Austria. "It's something I will always carry in my heart. I consider it my duty to repay the debt that I owe this country."

While he was moved by the outpouring of affection and respect his birthday celebration elicited, there was undoubtedly a touch of sadness for McGarvey too, when he thought about how his first wife, Helena, would not be there to share in the accolades, an honour she richly deserved. Helena had been a key player in the early days when William and the Karpath were just getting established. Her guidance and wisdom helped enormously as he strove to fit in to Galician society.

A formal photo of the birthday gathering shows William sitting front and centre amidst the opulence and splendour of the hotel's ballroom. Seated two to his left is his son, Fred, generally seen as the heir apparent. The internationally renowned London-based journal *Oil News* published the photo on February 7, 1914.

Mac's First Car

Gasoline had always been a "fraction" of the oil distillation process but it had not always been a useful one. Siegfried Marcus experimented with gasoline-powered locomotion as early as 1864 but the internal combustion engine remained nothing more than the stuff of experimentation until 1885, when Karl Benz developed his petrol- or gasoline-powered "motorwagen." Germany remained at the forefront of development of the horseless carriage for a number of years.

In Britain, Henry Royce built his first motorcar in 1904, the same year he met the acquaintance of a London automobile dealer named Charles Rolls. In March 1906, the pair created the Rolls-Royce motorcar company. The next year, the company's Silver Ghost was declared the best car in the world after a gruelling test in which it travelled twenty-seven times between London and Glasgow over frequently hideous road surfaces.

In 1913, just six months after his friend and business partner was killed in a car accident, William McGarvey joined the modern era of personal transportation when he purchased a Rolls-Royce Phantom from the company's Vienna dealership. McGarvey was immediately thrilled and wrote to the Rolls-Royce corporation: "Regarding the automobile I recently received from your company. It is a pleasure for me to inform you that I am very much pleased in every respect with the same. In terms of reliability, silence and impeccable operation in every respect, the car responds with total excellence from the very start. I would be happy to allow you to use my remarks as you feel is appropriate."

The company did just that, running McGarvey's testimonial in the German-language *Reichspost* newspaper of Vienna. William's son, Fred, seemed also to have been impressed. He bought his own Rolls in October. Fred explained it was those road tests in England that sold him on the vehicle for its reliability and its luxury.

Unfortunately, Fred's driving experience was not without mishap. He and Madge were out for a jaunt with their brother-in-law, Kate's husband, Erik Jurié, in May 1914, when their driver struck a bread cart on the streets of Vienna. The cart's operator suffered a fracture to the skull, although the car's passengers were unhurt.

Within months of Fred's automobile incident, Europe would be caught up in senseless warfare — warfare powered by the very petroleum products from which the family firm had earned its wealth.

Storm Clouds

Respected British oil expert Boverton Redwood undertook a detailed inspection of the Galician fields in 1914, the results of which provide an interesting snapshot of the petroleum-drilling business at the outset of war. He found that at that moment in time, there were 1,595 producing wells. Of those, nine hundred and fourteen were pumped by way of steam power, six hundred and twenty with gas power, eighteen were free-flowing and forty-three were still hand-pumped. He also found signs of trouble: while attempts were being made to expand the McGarvey-controlled Boryslaw field, he said, fields in western Galicia were substantially curtailed due to the onset of war.

Galicia's place in oil was slipping while farther south on the other side of the Carpathian Mountains, Romania was becoming an important oil supplier. Austrian and German military authorities, alarmed by reduced oil flows in Galicia, considered their options for expansion there, while Germany moved to sew up a greater level of control of Romanian oil in the event it was ever needed. It appeared ever more likely it would be needed.

While the Karpath enjoyed a foothold in Romania, with William's brother, Albert, having previously played a lead role there, the company had never been a significant force in that country. After all, Austrian Galicia had been performing well and Russia had recently become a far more important cog in the company wheel.

Soon, however, everything was about to change in ways William McGarvey could never imagine.

Austria-Hungary: The End Of An Era

War comes, sometimes by surprise, sometimes by design and sometimes by accident. There are elements of all three in the seeds of the Great War of 1914 which, later when these things became so frequent they were assigned numbers, would be dubbed the First World War or World War One. William McGarvey played a significant role in preparing for war – by design as well as by accident – but when it came, it proved to be not only terribly destructive to his companies, but more than likely a significant trigger in his own death. The war also proved that while Standard Oil was large and diverse enough to withstand the upheaval, the Canadian's relatively small independent enterprise was not.

While it is rarely thought of in this regard, World War I was the first major war fought over oil. Years before the superpowers in our modern world felt the need to gain dominance in the Middle East, Turkey, Germany, Austria, the British Empire, France and the United States went to war in no insignificant way over their thirst for petroleum and their desire to maintain secure supplies. The arms race, the colonial-era fight for dominance of empires, competing ideologies: these were all reasons that led to the international tensions that were set alight when a crazed Serbian nationalist shot and killed the Crown Prince of Austria. But strip away the details and the fact is that Germany's desire to supplant Britain as the chief naval power was central to the fighting. And Germany would never be able to gain dominance, nor would Britain be able to maintain it, without adequate supplies of oil to fuel their machines of war.

The similarities to our modern era are striking and they don't end with the importance of oil. Just as we are seeing today, for more than a decade before the 1914 assassination of the Austro-Hungarian Crown prince, terrorism had caused humankind to wonder just what was going on and where it would end. Starting with the 1901 assassination in Buffalo of United States president William McKinley, railways were being blown up and bombs were thrown onto the floors of stock exchanges. Terrorism was a fact of life for many places across the globe.

By 1914, Austria-Hungary had been united for a very long time. American historian Enno E. Kraehe credits a combination of factors for the empire surviving for as long as it did: its army, its bureaucracy, the Catholic church, and a genuine loyalty to the long-reigning Emperor Franz Josef. Those factors began to come apart after Austria annexed Bosnia and Hercegovina in 1908 and the independence movement commenced its rise in the Balkan states. Then, in the twilight of its influence, Austria took a step too far. After the assassination on June 28, 1914 of Archduke Franz Ferdinand, heir to the Austrian throne, Austria-Hungary issued an ultimatum that it could not back up.

With Germany's professed support, Austria-Hungary demanded that Serbia allow the authorities in Vienna to hold their own inquiry into the assassination. It further insisted the Serbs put a stop to all anti-Austrian propaganda and root out the terrorist cell that was responsible for the assassination. Serbia was given forty-eight hours to respond. Austria was fully confident that Serbia could not — or would not — comply. War, they fully expected, would be inevitable, and it was a war the Austrians actually welcomed.

Meanwhile, Germany and Britain moved closer to war as 1914 proceeded. Where did that leave McGarvey and the other Canadian Foreign Drillers and their families? Vienna itself boasted a population of several hundred British subjects – Canadians and Britons – and there was an Anglo-American Society of which McGarvey had served several times as president. As alarm rose among their membership, McGarvey decided to take action. With war looking more and more likely, on August 2, 1914, he called a press conference of Vienna's English-speaking journalists and released the text of a letter he had sent to the British foreign minister, Sir Edward Grey.

The letter urged calm in the midst of "the severe crisis that threatens peace in Europe." Austria-Hungary's "United Nations" of citizens are a peaceful group, the letter said. "The firm hope of the English citizens living in Vienna is for the neutrality of England at this crucial moment. In the spirit of genuine friendship, and with the best of intentions at this stressful time, we wish to point out that England may remember His Majesty the Emperor of Austria (Franz Josef) has always distinguished himself to England. We are grateful in the memory of his friendly attitude toward England when England waged war against the Boers."

What McGarvey and the rest of the Anglo-Viennese populace did not know was that events behind the scenes had moved far ahead of where they could have guessed. The chances for turning back were dimming. Grey saw the defence of France against German aggression as a key component of British foreign policy. As such, by the time of the McGarvey letter, Grey had already entered into an agreement with France and Russia, with each guaranteeing to come to the aid of the other in the event of war. Grey conducted this diplomatic procedure behind closed doors and not even Germany was aware of it. By this action, Grey assured that the existence of that agreement could never be used as a deterrent to German aggression. It has been argued that had Britain publicly declared early support for France, Germany would likely have convinced Austria–Hungary to settle with Serbia rather than go to war. Instead, Germany convinced the Austrians a quick war was winnable. Alternatively, if Britain had made it clear they would remain neutral in the event of war, France and Russia would not likely have been as aggressive as they were in pursuing a fight with Germany and Austria.

The hope in Berlin and Vienna was that the ultimatum issued to the Serbs would cause a short and decisive conflict, that Austria would be able to crush the Serbian insurrection before Russia had time to act, and that peace and victory would come quickly. In that event, there would be no Balkan insurrection. That serious miscalculation, and the inability of the leaders at the time to put a stop to the escalation, saw Russia, allied with the Serbs as well as Britain and France, send its troops pouring over the border into Galicia where they headed straight for the working centre of William Henry McGarvey's corporate empire.

As a source of oil, Galicia was becoming less important to Germany than in the past. Galician oil production peaked in 1909 at 10.3 million barrels although, while it fell steadily thereafter, it remained significant, according to *The Oil Weekly* magazine of January 20, 1923. With Galician supplies falling, Germany had come to count on imports from the United States. In the event of war, Germany knew oil supplies that needed to be brought across the Atlantic Ocean would be vulnerable. Romanian oil seemed the most immediate logical short-term replacement.

Romania was becoming more important to the world of oil production and by 1910, it had begun to eclipse Galicia. In 1913, Romanian production peaked at 13.6 million barrels. Germany had moved decisively to tie up access to Romanian oil, as Fred and William McGarvey had told the British Royal Commission on fuel and oil supply.

Meanwhile, Austria remained almost entirely dependent on its own Galician oil. Add to that the importance of maintaining its territorial integrity, and it became clear the Dual Monarchy needed to do all it could to protect Galicia.

The Russian Invasion

In 1914, McGarvey's Glinik Refinery remained one of the largest in the world. It consisted of four boilers for crude oil distillation, plus eight petroleum-based oil distillation and coking boilers and three vacuum distillation boilers. The refuse from this latter unit was turned into asphalt. There had been several modernizations and upgrades over the years, including one after a fire in 1896 in the paraffin department. Then in 1909, a redistillation department was constructed, consisting of eight boilers for converting paraffin into spindle oils and machine oils. A refining department processed a range of finished oils to supply the changing and maturing marketplace.

Then came the Russians. McGarvey's main refinery and his oil wells were obvious targets for the Russian invasion and when war was declared in August 1914, they struck quickly. By mid-September, the czar's forces occupied the Boryslaw-Tustanowice region of Galicia, including McGarvey's wells and factories there. The Galician fields were not nearly as important to the Russians as they were to Germany and Austria. Russia had its own industry and besides, the Russian military was not nearly as mechanized, and therefore not as dependent on oil, as their opponents were. But Russia was determined to cut them out of Galician oil.

The effect of the Russian invasion was quickly noted in America. "One of the most important points about the Russian conquest of Galicia," wrote the *New York Times* on September 13, 1914, "is the fact that Germany is now completely deprived of sources of supply of petroleum and naphtha products, of which almost the entire yield in Galicia annually was taken by Germany (This was true only if Austria was included in the greater German 'nation'). As the Germans are waging this war mainly on a mechanical basis, this loss of motive power for automobiles, aeroplanes and dirigibles must tell heavily on their effectiveness."

It is interesting to note that the *Times* writer apparently was unaware of the arrangements Germany had made to access Romanian oil, a fact the McGarveys had warned a British Royal Commission about nearly two years earlier.

A Canadian Family's Experience

With war enveloping the Eastern Front, the Canadian Foreign Drillers found themselves in the midst of the chaos.

Jake Perkins and Charles Nicklos left Petrolia as part of the Canadian contingents that came to Galicia to work for William McGarvey. With them came their wives, Jennie and Jessie, and children and over time, their sons began working in the business as well. Besides his work with McGarvey, Perkins joined with his brother Cyrus, and Cyrus's brother-in-law, George MacIntosh, to create the Galician Boring Tool Works company at Stryj. Later, the Canadian trio opened a branch in St. Albans, England, which Cyrus's son, Charles, managed.

The Perkins and Nicklos families had been friends since arriving in Galicia in the mid-1880s and were officially united in marriage when Jake and Jennie's daughter, Olive Perkins, married Ernest Nicklos, son of Charles and Jessie. Ernest, seeing his future in the newly developed Mexican oil fields, had moved his family to Tampico in 1911, where he tended to his new duties with a company headed by John Bergheim, the Anglo-Mexican & Tampico Oil Company.

With talk of war beginning to circulate across Europe, in May 1914 Charles Nicklos, who had built and managed oil fields and refineries for

McGarvey, decided to up stakes in Krosno and move his family back to North America. Rather than returning to Petrolia, Charles and Jessie headed to Wisconsin where they established a dairy farm. The Perkins family remained in their Galician home at Humniska, close to where the Nickloses had lived in Krosno, and about 75 kilometres east of Glinik Mariampolski. The Perkinses remained confident in peace and lamented the loss of their old friends and inlaws, the Nickloses.

Most of the other Canadian Foreign Drillers believed Charles and Jessie Nicklos had been too hasty in their departure, that they were being alarmist about the prospects of war and its impact on the oil patch. All seemed calm as the summer of 1914 commenced. The Perkins family gathered for a reunion that included daughter Olive and her young children, Winifred and Gordon, who were visiting from America. Then came the assassination in Sarajevo and Vienna's ultimatum.

Still, it was hard for the Canadian oil workers and their families to believe their idyllic situation would end. Surely cooler heads would prevail, they thought, as the Perkins family reunion continued. They played tennis on the courts Jake had built, and sipped iced tea in the garden. Jake enjoyed quality time with his grandchildren and smiled as little Olive would shout "ballo, horse!" to his favourite steed. Jake Perkins seemed so confident there would be no trouble that he wrote to his son-in-law in Mexico that if political instability and violence continued in that country, he and Jennie would be pleased to keep Olive and the children until it passed.

Later that summer, the Russians invaded Galicia and the Perkins family began to understand their predicament. In early September, Jake sent his family to live with relatives farther west in Bielitz where he felt they would be safer. Jake stayed behind with eldest son Herbert to secure the family home and shut down their wells. Then with word the Russian army was approaching, Jake and Herbert buried as many of the family valuables as they could. They wrapped the silver, then rolled up the oriental rugs and hid them inside empty drilling casings which they then sank into the wells. Then they headed west to join the rest of the family in Bielitz.

The next three months proved a hellish existence for the family. The youngest Perkins son, Eddie, had been attending school in Canada before coming for the summertime reunion, and decided he had better head back to classes. Austrian authorities stopped him before he'd gotten far and tossed him into an internment camp at Kautzen, Austria. Eddie Perkins was, after all, a foreign national of military age, from a country with which Austria was now at war. Olive headed out with her children, aged two-and-a-half years and two months, and somehow, despite the fact civilian train travel had been halted, made her way to the Austrian port of Trieste, where she caught a ship to New York. Olive's account of her experience would remain brief and vague for the rest of her life.

According to her granddaughter, Joan Darby of Pittsburgh: "Although Dado (Olive) never related the story to me in great detail, she told me a very kind man helped her when she was in great need, and she never forgot his kindness. She said to me: 'They say that everyone meets Jesus once in their lifetime, and that was my time.'"

Overcome By Worry

William McGarvey marked his seventy-first birthday on November 24, 1914, and despite the worries of war, he and Eleanor decided to throw a quiet dinner party at their Vienna home. It would be held that Friday, the 27th. A select group of old friends, including Jake Perkins and fellow Canadian George MacIntosh, William's children, and company officials Wladyslaw Dlugosz, Josef Grzybowski and August Gorayski, were invited. It is likely that as Jake Perkins and William McGarvey spoke, concerns over Eddie Perkins's wellbeing at Kautzen were discussed.

News from the Russian front had not been good in the past few weeks. The battles during September had been devastating to the Austrians as the superior Russian numbers pushed them back to the west. McGarvey received detailed updates on his properties in and around Mariampol and had been advised the damage was extensive. Production at the refinery and machinery factory had been halted, as had new oil field work.

For McGarvey and the other Canadians who were caught up in the fighting, the emotional toll was just as bad as the financial one. They had come to Europe as Canadians and as British subjects, and had embraced Austria as their second home. They had been well received by the Austrians and in McGarvey's case, even decorated by the emperor for his contributions to the nation and for making Galicia a petroleum powerhouse. The Canadians were very good at building a business and making money. Now, McGarvey and the others were helpless to act as they watched the Russians destroy all they had built. What made it all the more painful is the knowledge that Canada, the country from which they had come, was at war with the Austrians and the Germans, and allied with the Russians.

In the proceeding months, McGarvey had tried to put politics aside as best he could. In Vienna where he was long known for his generosity, in the early days of the war he established a fund to help care for Austria's injured soldiers. It was as close to "business as usual" as he could manage. There were newspaper accounts in the Viennese and Polish press throughout late summer and the autumn months about large donations made by both William and his son, Fred, to various charitable organizations, including a Widows and Orphans fund and the Austrian branch of the Red Cross. In this way, William could carry on his sense of duty to his community and prove his loyalty to Austria, without betraying the British and Canadian cause. It would serve to assure the Austrian authorities there was no cause to question his actions.

While McGarvey had suffered from poor health in the months leading up to the dinner party, by all accounts he was his old charming self that evening, engaging his guests in conversation and recalling old friendships and pleasurable moments in a long and illustrious lifetime and career. He even gave a short speech. After dinner, however, he told his wife, Eleanor, that he was feeling tired and thought he had better head off to bed.

"A bit of indigestion," he told her. "I'm sure that's all."

It was about 9 o'clock. Eleanor thought little of it and kissed her husband goodnight. William seemed to be sleeping soundly when Eleanor later slipped into bed beside him.

In the morning, Eleanor found William unresponsive. She summoned the doctor and called Fred. The doctor concluded William had died from a heart attack soon after turning in for the night. Fred took control of the situation. He told friends and family that undoubtedly the emotional strain of William's wartime losses and the split loyalties under which he was forced by the realities of international politics to endure, had played a significant part in his death. Fred wrote back to relatives in Canada on December 5:

> It is my sad duty to inform you that my beloved father died on the 27th (November). He had been ill for some months but we did not think until quite lately that his days might be numbered. We had celebrated his birthday last Friday by a small dinner party. He retired to bed, early, and died suddenly, without a struggle, owing to heart failure, at about half past nine in the evening. Undoubtedly the sad times prevailing in the greater part of the world at the present moment hastened his end.

William himself might well have had a premonition of his pending death in recent weeks. It was just November 10 that he visited the offices of his Vienna lawyer, Joseph de Griez, to update and finalize his last will and testament. The will reveals he still owned a home in Petrolia as well as several properties in London, Ontario and Winnipeg. Those property holdings also reveal more evidence of McGarvey's generosity.

The Petrolia home was inhabited by Mary Daniels, the widow of former McGarvey employee James Daniels. She lived there rent-free and McGarvey stipulated those arrangements were to continue until her death. At that time, the house was to be sold and the proceeds donated to the Petrolia hospital. One of the London homes McGarvey owned was the residence of his sister and brother-in-law, Ellen and Dr. George Westland. As well, some of his Winnipeg property was to be sold and a bequest given to his niece there, Helena Vanalstyne.

The Galician Carpathian Petroleum Company announced the death of its president in *Petroleum*, the official publication of the industry: "His passing was sudden and gentle. We have lost a reliable, faithful friend, whose noble character has secured him a lasting place in our memory."

An obituary in *The Oil and Gas Journal* of Tulsa/Chatham said this:

> That the strain of war, involving both Britain and Canada, his native country, and Austria, the country of his adoption, had much to do with his death is generally believed. Furthermore, his oil properties in Galicia, Austria, have been the storm centre of many battles, one village – Mariampole – which he founded having been wiped out in the Russian

invasion. Many of his holdings were in the vicinity of Krakow, where fighting is now taking place, his refineries must have suffered severely, and relatives in Canada believe that his losses were enormous.

Estimates of McGarvey's wealth at the time of his death refer vaguely to it being "in the millions" – a great deal of money at the time.

Stories circulated in wartime Canada that McGarvey had been "under suspicion" by the Austrians and their German allies because of his Canadian origins and British links. One even had it that he had been "interned" by the authorities. It is perhaps natural that such rumours would be born from the suspicious environment of wartime but in fact no such internment ever occurred and if the authorities were suspicious of McGarvey's actions, there is no evidence to suggest it. Perhaps the war muted the laudatory obituaries but the fact that a Canadian businessman's death was even mentioned in the German-language newspapers and other publications of the day speaks eloquently of the high regard in which he was held by those of his adopted country.

"The most prominent personality in the Austrian petroleum industry," said the German-language *Petroleum* magazine. "One of the leading figures ... a self-made man in the best sense of the word. He was long the entire soul of the company."

Wiener Zeitung lauded McGarvey for his "endless energy and his magnificent knowledge of drilling techniques." He was highly respected in Viennese society for his "kind character and his fine philanthropy," it said.

Zeitschrift des Internationalen Vereines der Bohringenieure und Bohrtechniker said: "The petroleum industry of Galicia, of which a great part is his accomplishment, will always remember him." *Zeitschrift* continued with a glance ahead to what it hoped would be better days: "His son F. J. M(a)cGarvey, who in earlier times already had a stake in the company, will now follow in his footsteps and lead the company in the future. After the liberation of Galicia from the Russian invasion, he will find there an extensive field of operations. Here he will find the opportunity to prove that he is the genuine son of this eminent father."

English-language publications also lauded him, with *Oil News* magazine on December 5 hailing him as "the doyen of the petroleum technologists and a very popular man," and "(t)he most prominent figure in European oil since the Nobels."

A few years later, on June 16, 1921, the Petrolia *Advertiser* looked back on his life and remarked: "Next to Sir Boverton Redwood, McGarvey was counted the world's greatest petroleum technologist."

On the same day the Vienna newspapers carried news of William's death, they were also filled with reports from the war: battles continued in West Galicia and the town of Czernowitz had fallen to the invading Russians.

Evidence of the untenable situation McGarvey found himself in between the British and the Austrians came when the Viennese newspaper *Der Morgen Wiener Montagblatt* in its obituary referenced his letter to the British foreign minister, Sir Edward Grey. The newspaper wrote: "McGarvey made his opposition to England's ignominious attitude no secret and was one of the first to protest the English repudiation of peace."

In the heat of wartime, the Austrian newspaper's sentiments are understandable, but as a proud and loyal subject of the British Empire, Mac would have found the publication's twisted interpretation of his words painful to hear. In fact, McGarvey and the other expats in Vienna had not "protested" Britain's "repudiation of peace," but only made an appeal for cooler heads to prevail.

The funeral service was held at the McGarvey residence at 2 Gusshausstrasse and William was buried in the Protestant section of the Central Cemetery of Vienna next to his first wife, Helena. Among the attendees at the service were Princess Hanna of Liechtenstein, a representative of Austria's imperial family, members of the Austrian, German and Polish nobility, cabinet ministers, parliamentarians and local politicians, artists, industrialists and other business leaders.

Hours after Jake Perkins attended his great old friend's funeral, Austrian authorities swept down and took him into custody. As British subjects, Jake and Jennie were now under suspicion. They were told they would escape the fate of their own son, Eddie, and would not be interned, but that for the foreseeable future they would be placed under house arrest in Vienna. The following May, and undoubtedly on account of his illustrious father's lofty reputation, Eddie was released from custody on the undertaking that he would live, under house arrest, with his parents.

For many in Galicia, Austrian military authorities' suspicions of collaboration with the Russians proved far deadlier. Many suspected of treason were brought before military tribunals and court-martialled. Some were executed. Estimates of the number of these executions ranged from several hundred to the thousands. There is no evidence any of the Canadian oil workers were among them.

However, many deemed to be unreliable were arrested and either sent to internment camps or, like Jake and Jenny Perkins, placed under house arrest. It is possible McGarvey could have faced the same treatment had he lived, although the fact his son, Fred, remained free in Vienna suggests that their social standing, and their generous contributions to charitable causes related to Austrian war veterans and their families, would have been enough to keep him free.

CHAPTER 14

CAUGHT IN THE MIDDLE

From mid-November 1914 until early May 1915, Mac McGarvey's Glinik Mariampolski refinery and factory in West Galicia were often caught up in the midst of the fighting. British oil expert Boverton Redwood reported that oil production was greatly curtailed "and in places brought to a complete standstill ... when the adjacent territory became the theatre of conflict between the Russian and Austrian armies."

The Russians did allow some fieldwork to resume for the collection of crude when they took over, but the refineries were nearly completely shut down. By May 1915, there was a stockpile of six million barrels when the Russian line was later broken by the joint German-Austrian counter-offensive. As they retreated, the Russians set fire to "a considerable part of the petroleum stored in the East Galician fields," said Boverton Redwood. Quoting the *Frankfort Gazette*, Redwood said that of three hundred and nineteen wells in the Tustanowice region of East Galicia, now the centre of the Karpath's crude production, two hundred and twenty-nine were destroyed and 2.3 million barrels of crude were burned when the Russian army retreated.

Further on-the-ground descriptions of the mayhem came from reports written by the priest, Bronislaw Swieykowski, who was serving at the time as mayor of Gorlice. His description of the situation is recorded in *The Days of Terror In Gorlice* (published Krakow 1919). According to Swieykowski, Russian artillery fired ceaselessly into the city and the McGarvey refinery, causing several fires to break out. The worst, he said, was at the refinery and lasted three days. The Russian attack on the refinery and the nearby city park intensified from February 27 to March 1, 1915.

McGarvey's paraffin factory caught fire on March 31 and the refinery burned through to April 25. Mortars were fired into the oil tanks, stoking the flames, and the Russians began a house-to-house gorilla campaign. The entire city of Gorlice was left in rubble, the incoming missiles now from both sides igniting refinery facilities and oil tanks that earlier had been spared.

On May 2, the 82nd division of the 41st reserve German corps arrived under General Francis. As dawn broke, seven hundred German and Austrian cannon opened fire, with 700,000 missiles launched over the course of the next four hours. At the centre of the fighting, a ghastly blue flame hung over the oil wells but when it was over, the Germans had taken back the Karpath's Glinik Mariampolski refinery.

A Heavy Toll On The Foreign Drillers

Many long-time Canadian oil men and their families were caught up in the strife. Typical of their experiences was that of George MacIntosh and his son, Carl. Carl lived with his wife, Frieda, and children Ralph and Molly, in Kraznica, a pretty village at the foot of the Carpathian Mountains near Boryslaw, when war was declared on July 28, 1914. Frieda's Austrian brother was immediately called up to the army and stationed at Sambor. Carl paid a visit to take him some clothing and only upon his return home did he start to think about the risk he had taken. As a Canadian and a British subject, Carl MacIntosh was now considered an enemy alien. Luckily, his trip ended without incident.

One day, Frieda took Molly and Ralph for a walk down the road near their home and watched as soldiers rushed to catch trains that would take them to battle.

"The weeks that were passing were terrifying," said Frieda, "as so many rumors were coming through. Like killing people ... and robbing. We decided to run for the mountains." That proved a mistake. They should have gone to a city where organized protection existed. "In small villages, it is left to the mercy of bad characters. To see the running people on their way to Hungary was a terrible sight. Women, children, cows, dogs, cats, chickens, bedding and other things they could take on a wagon from their homes. One cannot forget the frightened faces."

There was little reprieve when the Germans and Austrians recaptured the region. While at first they felt some relief, Carl MacIntosh and other Canadians then found themselves under suspicion and threat from the military. Some were interned or – like Carl's father, George, who operated the Perkins, MacIntosh & Perkins drill tools manufacturing company in Stryj – placed under house arrest by the Austrians. It was time, Carl decided, to escape Galicia while they could. They headed east into Russia, gambling it would be safer to stay among Britain's allies. On the way, they witnessed thousands of wounded Austrian soldiers being brought back from the front. They heard cannon fire and bombs exploding nearby. Carl and Frieda learned later that the Austrian army had come to their home and looted it. A few days afterwards, the Russians overwhelmed the region again, and took whatever was left.

Carl and Frieda's experience was typical of many of the Canadian Foreign Driller families who were caught in the midst of the fighting. In March 1915, a report was prepared for the British cabinet based on eyewitness accounts of early wartime events in Galicia. "British subjects," it said, which would include Canadians, "were registered but not interfered with." When the Russians arrived, they pillaged homes in Boryslaw. When the owners complained to the Russian commander, he told them such matters were out of his control.

"The English people then moved in a body to a small village in the mountains and stayed there for a month whilst things quieted down. Stray bands of Russians visited them and helped themselves to blankets and clothes."

The Russians then sent a "punitive expedition" into Boryslaw and Drohobycz, with soldiers ransacking the shops and burning the principal buildings. British refugees fled to Dembrowa where, with the assistance of an Englishman who was married to a Russian woman, they pleaded their case and were "little troubled." The Russians left "after receiving gifts of food." The Russian military then opened soup kitchens and worked with the local oil workers to reopen shut-in and damaged wells.

It was the opinion of the British source that the Russians preferred continuing their battles in the mountains where snow was "breast-deep" and frosts were severe, because the "wretchedly clad Austrians" were ill-equipped to fight there. "The Austrians are in rags," continued the report. "Their long great-coats have been torn away at the bottom in strips to bind round the legs and feet. Generally, they wear boards on their feet, their boots having been worn out long ago."

The source said the Russian Red Cross had been of considerable assistance to the British residents. "On the night following a battle, all the wounded are brought in and all the dead buried. The Austrian Red Cross seems non-existent."

"The country is settling down to the ordinary round of work. The trains are largely used for the conveyance of materials for the troops, but there are a few trains per day for civilians. No one is allowed to leave Galicia without a permit. There is still a considerable number of English people at Boryslaw." The Russians had apparently allowed the informant to leave because he told authorities he planned to join the army and fight the Austrian-German alliance.

The fierce battle at Gorlice proved the importance of the oil industry to the war's conduct. In their retreat, the Russians had set fire to all that they could in order to keep the oil out of enemy hands. Then the Austrian army, after receiving German help in recovering the wells and refineries, tried immediately to resume the industry's activity. McGarvey's refinery was placed under military supervision and as a result there is no record of the plant's operation during this time. It is known, though, that in May 1915, steps were taken to restore production at McGarvey's Gorlice installations. Drilling began to restore damaged wells and to accommodate the crucial need for production at a time when the railways were required to move troops, a sixty-five-kilometre-long pipeline was built between the state-run refinery at Drohobycz – which was quickly repaired after surprisingly light war damage – and Chyrow. Finally, after months of upheaval and a growing demand for crude to operate the German and Austrian war machines, the Boryslaw-Tustanowice oil fields were able to supply the refineries at Lviv (also known as Lemberg) in East Galicia. McGarvey's key Glimar refinery at Mariampol, however, remained in ruins.

Throughout 1916, Fred McGarvey led efforts to restore full production at the company installations in Galicia, with oil output gaining between 1915 and 1916 by about forty percent before it began to drop again with the resumption of strife there. Explained Boverton Redwood: "The dependence of the German and Austrian military authorities on the Galician oil fields until late in 1916 for the greater supply of their motor fuels and lubricating oils resulted in a high level market for crude oil in all the Galician districts that served as a decided spur to activity in drilling throughout 1916."

The story was similar in Romania, where "fields were first held by the Allies but were lost to the Germans in November 1916," said a report in *The Oil Weekly* on January 20, 1923. "Before retreating, (Allied) troops plugged and filled all the holes with junk of all sorts and burned the oil in all the tanks. As soon as the Germans captured the fields their experts worked unremittingly to restore some of the production."

Romanian production, crucial to the German military, fell throughout the war years. By 1917, it was down to 2.7 million barrels before recovering to 8.7 million during the last year of the war when the industry was partially rebuilt.

While Carl and Frieda MacIntosh fled to Russia, many of the Canadian workers simply left the Eastern European fields entirely and took up work elsewhere. The *Sarnia Observer* reported on July 7, 1915: "Many of the Petrolea drillers who were in foreign fields but were forced to come home on account of the war, are signing contracts and leaving again to resume their work. Burma, Egypt, Persia and Venezuela are the destination of those who have signed up recently."

There were exceptions, those who chose to remain in the country they had called home for up to three decades. Among them were Jake and Jennie Perkins. By the summer of 1915, with the Russians having been driven back east, they received word that their Humniska home had avoided damage. It had been saved because it was used as the headquarters of a Russian general. A pet parrot had survived the invasion too, and when Jake and Jennie were able to return, they discovered the parrot had even picked up some Russian phrases in the interim. Son Herbert fared less well: his home in nearby Rowne had been burned to the ground and the garden was covered in hastily dug Russian graves. The stench of death was everywhere, Herbert said.

The Perkinses had been under house arrest in Vienna for several months and Jake was eager to get back to work at his oil production company. Despite the support of Fred McGarvey and the government petroleum office in Krakow, Austrian authorities resisted throughout most of 1915. Finally, with the Russians on the run and the Austrian imperial military authorities in dire need of petroleum to operate the war machinery, the green light was given for Jake to return home and once again take up his business. His relief was evident in a letter Jake wrote in November 1915 to his daughter and son-in-law in Mexico: "I was many times afraid I would break down completely and lose my senses. Then I got permission to return to my business and pleased to inform you, I am feeling first-class again." Austria's and Germany's high demand for oil kept Jake busy throughout the following year.

In Mariampol, however, the Russians were back in control by the summer of 1916, cutting off the Karpath's refinery and factory. They remained in control of the region until the anti-czar revolution resulted in the troops being recalled to their homeland.

Canadian-born workers such as Jake Perkins tried to remain aloof from the politics of war. They had come to the country to earn a living and produce oil. As best they could, they shut their minds to thoughts of how it was being utilized by the competing armies.

Yet Galicia remained a key factor in the war effort. By 1917, the Allies were convinced that depriving Germany and Austria of petroleum was the surest way to guarantee victory. *Sinclair's Magazine*, as reported in the *New York Times* on July 15, 1917, said: "Give oil to Germany and you prolong the war; take it away and you hasten the end." With Galicia providing half of the Axis' oil supply, taking it away from them would be as devastating as denying them ammunition, said the *Times*.

In little more than a half century, oil had proved what a valuable commodity it could be. In that time it had progressed from a rough, unsophisticated business to one of the world's foremost industries, and one considered well worth fighting over, regardless of the human cost. Few of oil's principal actors had played a more significant part in that transformation than William Henry McGarvey.

A Son Takes Command

Frederick James McGarvey was the clear favourite to take over the Galician Carpathian petroleum empire after his father died. He had been William's obvious choice for many years and had been carefully groomed, taking ever more responsibility in a series of moves. He had played a significant part in the company's expansion into Russia, perhaps to the chagrin of William's younger brother, Albert, who was never more than a high-ranking employee of William's company. Then, with William's death in November 1914, Fred stepped in. The board of directors hastily met and appointed Fred McGarvey the company's new general manager. When the German army pushed the Russians out of Galicia, Fred took charge of the rebuilding process and got the company back into production. He and wife Madge continued to live in Vienna throughout the war years.

Four hard years of war and his torn loyalties took a terrible toll on Fred and once the fighting stopped, he took charge of the search to find someone to buy him and the other major shareholders out. He led negotiations that resulted in the purchase of the Karpath by the French corporation, the Dabrowa Oil Company. We can imagine the sadness with which Fred McGarvey presided over the final board of directors meeting of the Galician Carpathian Petroleum Company that day in 1920. Two years later on January 13, 1922, the Karpath shut its doors for good.

Revolution In Russia And The McGarvey Family Feud

During and immediately after the war years, the picture within the bounds of Russia was equally chaotic. With James and William both now gone and William's son, Fred, chosen to lead the company in Vienna, the McGarvey company's fortunes in Russia were in the hands of Mac's younger brother, Albert.

There was never any hint that the McGarvey brothers were "created equal." The Galician Carpathian Petroleum Company was not a partnership of brothers. In the early days, James and Albert were both treated as employees of the corporation and compensated as such, although in Russia they acted with considerable independence and were well rewarded for their success. When William wrote his will just days before his death, he left a sizeable bequest of real estate to his sister, Ellen Westland, and a cash sum to the daughter of his other sister, the late Mary Vanalstyne. Mary had died two years earlier in Winnipeg. Albert was the only other sibling still alive and there is no mention of him in the will.

Even though he had been given responsibility to direct the Russian operations, in many ways, Albert seemed to be treated as a second-class member of the family. In fact, he is wiped right out of the family tree that was created by William's granddaughter, Molly. What did Albert do to deserve such treatment? If there was a family feud, where did it begin?

Of the three brothers who took up the business of oil, Albert, the youngest among them, seemed in many ways the least successful. William was the brains behind the company and James was the brawn. Fred was the heir apparent. In the early years, Albert was the "go-fer": he was the one sent back home to Petrolia to round up new employees to keep the family enterprise well supplied with skilled oil craftsmen and technicians.

That is not to suggest that Albert's part in the company was insignificant. After the deaths of James and William, Albert continued to exert considerable influence in the business of oil. Born in 1851 at Huntingdon, Albert was just six when Edward and Sarah moved the family to London and nine when they relocated to Wyoming and opened the general store. Albert lived in Wyoming at the time of the 1871 census and was still there 10 years later. When his parents left Wyoming to return to London, Albert stayed behind as operator of the family general store and oil wells. It was Albert who was in charge when the store ran into financial difficulties in the late 1870s and, with creditors in hot pursuit, it had to be refinanced, likely with financial help from big brother Mac. And it seemed in the early years, Albert who was in charge when his father got into trouble with Canada's Department of Inland Revenue for non-payment of taxes.

Albert stood five-foot-five, the average height of a man in that era. He had clear blue eyes. He married the American-born Lucinda Jane Taylor on November 13, 1878 in Wyoming, with his elder brothers, William and James, listed as witnesses. The couple had no children.

A newspaper story in Petrolia's *Petroleum Advertiser* in January 1879 indicates Albert was about to take on a term as a Wyoming town councillor.

He did not stay long because in the early 1880s, Albert wrapped up the Wyoming and area business and prepared to join William as an employee of the new European oil enterprise. With William busy setting up shop in Hanover and then Galicia, and planning for expansion into Romania, it fell to Albert to act as the hiring agent and go-between. He made several trips between Petrolia and Europe. In November 1885, Albert was ensconced at the Tecumseh House hotel in Petrolia, accepting applications for drillers and rig builders interested in joining the McGarvey company in Eastern Europe. Interviews were conducted and once the hires were made and contracts signed, Albert accompanied the men to Europe and got them settled, then set up in the family business.

Albert was back in Petrolia the following summer and on July 20, 1886, he left again, this time for Romania, with a contingent of Canadians – Robert McKaig, William Hopkins, David Slack and James Ward – for the oil fields there. The *Petrolia Advertiser* remarked: "They are getting a regular army of Canadian drillers in that country, and if a secession wave was to strike that province we fancy the Canadian element would nearly predominate."

Albert would live overseas for most of the next 35 years. He owned a property in England where Lucinda often lived, although they occasionally returned to Canada for business and, in Lucinda's case, for extended visits. According to the *Petrolia Advertiser*, Lucinda was in town in May 1890 and stayed for an entire year. That same news story indicated Albert was "in company with his brother, W. H. McGarvey, who is doing an immense oil trade in (Galicia)."

In 1901, Albert went to Russia to help his brother, James, establish the Northern Caucasus Oil Company in Grosny. Its headquarters was in London, England. Over the coming years, Albert purchased considerable holdings on behalf of the company in Russia and maintained his estate in England where Lucinda lived. By 1906 at the age of 55, he was described on a ship's manifest as having grey hair.

After James's murder in February 1911, Albert took over as Northern Caucasus company managing director. Despite the unrest, Grosny oil production was booming and was now challenging its longer-established southern neighbour, Baku, for supremacy among Russian oil fields.

Albert was insistent Lucinda not accompany him to Russia due to the danger and, knowing he would be away from England for some time, insisted she go to live with her sister and brother-in-law in London, Ontario. Albert remained in charge at Grosny until his retirement and departure from Russia in 1921, although he was often away.

Albert made frequent trips back to Britain and Canada. In 1915 during the war, he visited London, Ontario and was mentioned in a local newspaper. "Prominent in the Russian oil industry," said the headline. He told the reporter that 1,500 of his employees in Russia had been called in to that country's service to help fight the war. He said the fervent belief in Russia was that the Allies would succeed against Germany and Austria.

After a brief visit, Albert went back to Grosny to maintain the Northern Caucasus Oil operation as best he could in the face of the acute labour shortage that came from the demands of wartime. According to an abstract from the London Metropolitan Archives on the Anglo-Maikop Group, operations of some of the Russian companies had to be curtailed during the war due to a scarcity of labour, and some were suspended until after the war. In 1915, however, Albert helped in the formation of the Russo-English Maikop Petroleum and Trading Company that was designed to hold all of the group's Russian properties and keep as many of them as possible in operation.

In 1916, Albert returned to Canada for a visit before once more heading back to his duties at Grosny. He and the other oil company managers knew there would be plenty of demand for their precious product during the pursuit of victory, if they could only keep enough employees to maintain their operation.

Then came 1917, a cataclysmic year for Russia. When war began in 1914, Czarist Russia had entered as an ally of Britain and France, but Czar Nicholas' regime collapsed and he resigned on March 1, 1917. (The following year, on July 18, the czar and his family were murdered on order from Vladimir Lenin.) A provisional government was formed under George Lvov and a soldiers' committee was established to demand peace. The Russian Revolution broke out on November 8, 1917 and a day later, the victorious Bolsheviks seized Grosny. The new regime was determined to pull Russia out of the war and in March 1918, with the Bolsheviks firmly in power, Russia gave up considerable territory previously held by the czar, including Ukraine and the Caucasus region. Grosny and the Caucasus province in which it was located were thrown into chaos.

Before the war, when he took over the Northern Caucasus company from his slain brother, Albert had selected Charles Wallen of Oil Springs as his right-hand man and manager, the position he himself had held under James' leadership. With this promotion Wallen, who had once served as a lesser aide to James McGarvey, enjoyed a comfortable existence in a manager's house at Grosny with his wife, Florence, and children Elaine and Charles Jr. The household was also made up of an English nurse, an Irish governess for the children, Cossack guards, a valet, coachman, cook and a houseboy.

Throughout 1917 the Russian workers, emboldened by the rise of the Bolsheviks, began to seize control of oil companies, including the Northern Caucasus, and demanded managers work for the same wage as the rest of their workers. Just ahead of the takeovers, Albert McGarvey escaped with as much of the company's money and records as he could gather and fled to Britain, leaving Charles Wallen in charge.

Wallen wrote in a letter to the Petrolia *Advertiser* that was published January 17, 1918, that on the previous December 1, "Tartans" – in fact he was referring to the Turkish ethnic Tatars – set fire to several oil wells and killed several McGarvey workers before being driven off by soldiers and local residents.

In January 1918, the revolutionary government began the process of nationalizing the oil industry, without offering compensation to owners. When the Bolsheviks seized control, "Mr. Wallen was forced to remain as manager of the field, but his salary was reduced to the same as that received by his Bolshevik office boy," according to an interview Wallen gave the *London Free Press* for an article published on February 15, 1919.

Rumors of kidnappings and murders spread throughout the community and roving bands of drunken insurgents attacked the Wallen home, slashing the furniture in their search for cash. The Cossack guards the company had hired to protect McGarvey's oil fields proved incapable of maintaining order.

Wallen told the *Free Press* that local "boys of twelve and old men of eighty, armed and crazed with lust of destruction and killing, menaced the lives and property of everyone." Bandits carted away anything of value they could find, including the Wallens' private property. When they left, the looters opened up the wells and set them on fire.

Carl MacIntosh, having escaped what he thought was the worst of the fighting in Galicia, eventually found a position with the McGarvey companies in Grosny as a manager under Wallen. When they first arrived, Carl and his family felt relieved to be out of the fighting and happy with their home that stood on a hill overlooking Mount Kazbek. "In the spring, tulips, peonies and other flowers grow on the hills," said Frieda MacIntosh.

But they quickly discovered the troubles they had left in Galicia had simply moved with them to Russia. Lawlessness was on the increase as a result of the general political upheaval that was sweeping the country. At Grosny, the MacIntoshes went to bed only after all of the windows were shut tight and secured with shutters and iron bars. Later, after a dispute with his boss, Charles Wallen, MacIntosh left the McGarvey company entirely and lived for a while in Kiev before the family made their final dash to England.

Days before Christmas 1917, the Wallens reached the same conclusion — they must escape. They could take no more of the threats and violence that dogged them at Grosny. No longer knowing the whereabouts of company director Albert McGarvey, they scraped together what belongings and cash they could and fled. With a complete breakdown in order, none of the Canadian families could ever be sure which side to trust. Anarchists and revolutionaries set wells on fire and the acrid smoke that billowed up from them turned day into night. Charles Wallen's brother, Edwin, remained behind and Charles later learned he had converted to Bolshevism. After a long and circuitous journey that took them to the Caspian Sea, the Volga River and then the Barents Sea and Scotland's Orkney Islands, the Wallens finally made it to London, England, where they waited out the rest of the war.

Albert McGarvey spent the worst part of the troubles back in Britain and Canada. In 1918, in the latter days of the war and in the hope that the anti-Communist White Army would soon seize control of the Caucasus region, Albert is listed as a passenger on the White Star Lines *Lapland*, when the ship left New York for Liverpool. Albert returned to the company headquarters in London and then, in the belief the peace that would be beneficial to his company was in sight, went back to the Caucasus to pick up the pieces and get the company operating again. But there was no peace and the region changed hands several times before the Soviets took control in 1920.

With the Soviet revolutionaries taking over the foreign-controlled oil industry, Albert McGarvey left Grosny and headed back to London, Ontario for a visit, perhaps to pave the way for his pending retirement. Just a year later, at the age of 70 and still in good health, Albert decided it was time to leave the business. He moved back permanently to London, to the Richmond Street residence of Lucinda's sister and brother-in-law, Mr. and Mrs. Joseph Scandrett. Lucinda had already spent much of the past few years there.

In 1922, Albert sailed to England to tie up loose business ends, staying at the Hotel Russell on Russell Square in London. Despite his retirement, he is still listed as an oil operator. He returned home to Canada but he and Lucinda would have only a short time remaining together. Lucinda died from breast cancer on September 12, 1923.

Albert stayed on with his brother-in-law – Lucinda's sister had died a few years before – and on January 11, 1925, he and Scandrett paid a visit to a friend, A.R. Cairncross. The men were to have lunch and discuss the weighty issues of the day. During the course of lunch, Albert suffered a heart seizure and died almost immediately. Probate records filed at the Middlesex County offices in London indicated property valued at 32,296 pounds, 2 shillings, 1 pence, which translates into about half a million dollars today.

During this whole time – the war years and afterwards – Albert appears to have had little contact with his nephew, Fred, who was pulling together the remaining pieces of the family petroleum empire to prepare for sale, or with other family members. We can only guess as to why Albert did not associate with the rest of the family after the war. In the early years of the family business, he had been entrusted with the job of hiring Petrolians to fill the many positions requiring expert oil men in Europe. After James' murder, Albert took on the leadership role with the Russian branch of the company. Yet despite his business that kept him in Russia for the rest of his career, his name never appears in Fred and Madge's guest registry in either Galicia or Vienna. Travel records indicate Albert frequently crossed the Atlantic after that time in connection with his Northern Caucasus oil company position, with limited family interaction.

In fact the only record of a meeting that involved both Fred McGarvey and his Uncle Albert came as the Anglo-Terek company was being wrapped up. Fred and Albert are listed as attending the final meeting of the board on November 19, 1924, at the old company headquarters in London. It was just two months before Albert's death in London, Ontario.

Adding to the Albert McGarvey mystery and a suggestion, perhaps, of a family feud, is the fact that Fred's daughter, Molly, the keeper of the family genealogy record, eliminated Albert completely from the family tree she created. All of this points to a falling-out between Albert and Fred and, perhaps, between Albert and his brother William. In two obituaries for Albert published in the two London, Ontario newspapers in 1925, there was only a brief mention of William – and it erroneously indicated he was still alive – and no mention of James or Fred at all. Was there some hostility between Fred and his Uncle Albert? Might it have been caused in part by Fred taking on a far more significant role with the Russian companies and, eventually, with the entire Karpath empire – at Albert's expense? Might it also be connected to William omitting Albert entirely from his will? And might Fred have blamed Albert for the total loss of company assets in Russia?

Years later, in 1959, Fred McGarvey seems to have tried to gloss over the feud in a letter he wrote to the London-based editor of the *Petroleum Times*, R.B. Rogers. He did not differentiate between the achievements of William's brothers, Albert and James, and said only that the youngest of the McGarvey trio of brothers had "lost everything he possessed in Russia as the result of the First World War." (Actually, it was because of the rise of Communism and the confiscation of foreign industries.) The fact remains, Albert is expunged from any account of regular family affairs.

A few years later, oil operators made at least one attempt to make peace with the Soviets. A co-operative of owners of the Anglo-Maikop group tried to persuade them to allow the restoration of work, but this failed. With the Soviets having expropriated all foreign oil holdings, Fred McGarvey later said all of the Karpath company's "very considerable investments" in Russia and the newly established Soviet Union ended up being "a dead loss."

The McGarveys' holdings there were ultimately brought down by the fighting and politics of the Russian Revolution.

McGarvey's Empire Of Oil Reaches Its Conclusion

The sale of the Galician Carpathian corporation by Fred McGarvey did not immediately end the family's association with the petroleum world. Outside of the Karpath's immediate holdings, Fred, William and the Karpath had owned several other corporate entities, the largest of which was the Apollo refinery at Pressburg (later renamed Bratislava), near Vienna. Fred was now approaching fifty years of age and was a very wealthy man. Wartime and post-war rebuilding had taken its toll on him and it was time, he decided, to get rid of the rest of his holdings. The Pressburg refinery was sold to an American interest and was later taken over by the Nazi regime. It was bombed by the allies in 1944. The lesser holdings were sold off to a variety of buyers during the 1920s.

Now, it could be said, the McGarvey empire had reached its close. In exchange, Fred, Mamie and Kate McGarvey had been left with a great deal of money.

In 1928, the Dabrowa Oil Company, which had negotiated with Fred McGarvey for the purchase of the Galician Carpathian, joined with Societé Francaise des Pétroles – of which John Bergheim had once been chairman – and two other smaller companies, to bring Galician Carpathian into the fold of the newly created Pétroles-Premier-Malopolska. Established in Boryslaw, the new company produced forty percent of all of the oil consumed in Poland. In 1939, the Glimar refinery was taken over by Poland's German occupiers and after the war when the Soviet Union took control of Poland, the refinery was nationalized.

One of the finest tributes to William McGarvey's career came, two decades after his death, from the French company that had purchased the

Karpath and incorporated it into its own holdings. Malopolska officials said the Karpath was the most valuable of its acquisitions and the pearl in its holdings. "Such is the legacy of the business of the great industrialist, William McGarvey," wrote Dr. Stefan Bartoszewicz in an article titled "Memories from the oil industry" and published in the industry journal *Nafta* on February 25, 1934.

In the 1990s with the demise of the Soviet Union and the Eastern Bloc, Glimar was re-etablished as an independent free-market company. Modernization during the early 2000s saw the demolition of several of the old McGarvey-era buildings. In 2011, a Canadian company, Glimar Hudson Oil, took over and for a brief moment, ownership of the flagship refinery had come full-circle, back into Canadian hands.

The refinery was later closed permanently. The tools factory continued operation and exists today as Narzedzia I Urzadzenia Wiertnicze Glinik (NiUW Glinik).

CHAPTER 15

A PRIVILEGED LIFESTYLE

Thanks to Fred McGarvey's skillful handling of negotiations for the sale of his assets in the Karpath and its associated companies, he and his two sisters enjoyed privileged lifestyles, as did Fred's daughters. Then, as Hitler's influence spread throughout Europe, the unwanted shadow of politics began again to affect the McGarvey family's destiny.

Family Gatherings

As Edward, the family patriarch, had once said in a letter to relatives, the McGarvey family was well spread out. In Canada, Edward and Sarah spent their final years in London, as did one of their sons, the other having moved to Massachusetts. Edward's brother's family members were in Saskatchewan and Alliston, Ontario. Sons William, James and Albert and their families were spread throughout Europe. Daughters Ellen and Mary were in London and Winnipeg.

Mary, the eldest of Edward and Sarah's children, married Andrew Sidney Vanalstyne of London, Ontario, on August 28, 1866. The couple moved to Winnipeg and had two children – daughter Ella "Helena" Vanalstyne – whom William remembered in his will with a bequest of $3,000 CDN – and a son, Edward Sydney Vanalstyne. Mary died in 1912.

William's second sister, Ellen, married George Philip Westland of London, Ontario, in 1872. George, a homeopathic doctor, was 16 years Ellen's senior. The couple had three children: Frank, Mabel and

William Sydney. Ellen was sixty-seven when she died in 1917 from gastric carcinoma. As noted earlier, the Westlands lived in a home that was one of several London properties that William owned. Clearly, his penchant for diversification had stretched beyond his oil business into real estate.

Just three of William's five children survived him. His eldest daughter, Mamie, lived at Schloss Graschnitz from the time she married Count Zeppelin in 1895 until her death in 1962. She had no children and she was, in the way a relative once described her, an enthusiastic farmer.

In her later years, "she was stone deaf," said a niece, Patricia Lindsay, "due to a mistake by a specialist." Details of that "mistake" are now lost to history.

For about fifteen years, Mamie was joined at Schloss Graschnitz by her sister, Kate, who had been widowed sometime around the end of the First World War and moved down from Vienna to be with the countess. Kate and her husband, Erik Jurié von Lavandal, did not have any children, although family members say she relished her role as aunt and elder cousin, shepherding her various nieces, nephews and "cousins-once-removed" around and showing off the sights in Vienna. Kate died January 28, 1934 at Schloss Graschnitz.

Distance dictated that even for a family as prosperous as theirs, reunions were few. But there were notable gatherings that occasionally brought some of them together for family celebrations. On the first Christmas after their marriage in 1901, Fred and Madge opened their Glinik Mariampolski home to Mamie and Eberhard von Zeppelin and sister Kate, who, not yet married, was living alone in Vienna. There were also other visitors –William's sister Ellen Westland, and her daughter, Mabel, from London, Ontario. The group stayed until after the New Year. Ellen and Mabel had arrived in Austria that summer and spent time at Countess Mamie's Graz castle, before making the trip with the Zeppelins to Mariampol.

Then at Christmastime in 1904, there was another gathering at Glinik Mariampolski. Mamie and Ebert travelled from Schloss Graschnitz to spend the holidays with Fred and Madge. Adding to the merriment was the arrival from Winnipeg of "Auntie Mary Vanalstyne", William's sister, along with her daughter, Helena, named for her aunt.

The Good Life In Austria

"I never knew the old Vienna before the war, with its Strauss music, its glamour and easy charm."

Thus opened the classic film, *The Third Man*, and its words spoken by the narrator over scenes from the war-ravaged but still beautiful city.

The narrator of *The Third Man* might not have known Vienna before the war – the Second World War, that is – but Fred and Madge McGarvey, as well as their daughters, Molly and Leila, certainly did. Vienna became, more than any other city, the hometown of the bulk of the McGarvey clan. As a cultural and business hub, it had attracted Helena and William and as their children grew up, they too were mesmerized by its allure.

Fred and Madge moved there permanently in February 1910, leaving Mariampol as a holiday getaway near the bucolic Carpathian Mountains. While there was a certain sadness in leaving "the dear old house" that William and Helena had built overlooking the Carpathians, at the edge of the refinery and factory property in Mariampol, the life they were about to commence in Vienna more than made up for it. They found a comfortable city home at Arenberg Ringstrasse 16, where they remained until the second half of 1938.

Fred was an avid horseman and while at Mariampol, he loved to take visitors out riding through the park that surrounded his residence, then up into the Galician countryside. It was a pastime he did not plan to give up after he moved to Vienna. The McGarveys maintained their own riding horses at the Spanish Riding School Stables in that city. Mamie's Schloss Graschnitz estate offered another grand riding experience, enveloped as it was by the pastoral hills and Graz Mountains, part of the Central Alps.

Family members visited the countess frequently and she kept a set of apartments specifically for Fred, Madge and the girls at the sprawling Graschnitz Castle, situated outside St. Marien, north of Graz in the district of Murztal and the province of Styria.

"As with a lot of the family," said their niece, Patricia Lindsay, Fred and Madge "would spend summer holidays at Graschnitz," usually with their daughters. The surrounding hilly countryside afforded the family excellent opportunities to explore by horseback, she said.

One winter, Fred and Madge visited Madge's younger brother, Peter Bergheim, at his home in England and planned fox-hunting outings with the Bicester Hounds organization. "It was an exceptionally frosty winter and they hardly had any hunting at all," said Peter's daughter, Patricia. The couple loved England and often visited.

Fred was a keen fly-fisherman and enjoyed catching the trout that inhabited the streams around his family's country estate in Austria. He was also an eager guide to the best trout fishing for anyone else who happened by.

Fred and Madge enjoyed the superlative Viennese ambiance in the latter years of the city's Golden Age. They stayed through the First World War when the city suffered deprivation from embargoes but no physical damage, and then through the years between the wars. They thrived in its confident sophistication and stunning Imperial City charm. Their luxurious apartment on the Arenberg Ringstrasse placed them squarely in the midst of the beautiful city where they would live for nearly three decades.

Their elder daughter, Leila, had been born in 1902 while her mother was staying at the Bergheims' Belsize Park home in London. Molly was born four years later in Vienna. Her parents had travelled there from Mariampol to ensure access to the finest medical care. The sisters enjoyed a privileged upbringing and were, respectively, aged eight and four when their parents moved the family to Vienna. They attended fine schools there and learned to appreciate all the culture and entertainment the city had to offer.

Leila enrolled in university in Vienna and then decided in 1932 that she would move back to Britain, the country where she had been born. She found a place at Harrington Gardens in the Royal Borough of Kensington and Chelsea, a wealthy municipality that encompasses such neighbourhoods as Notting Hill, Knightsbridge, Chelsea and Central and South Kensington. Three years after her arrival, Leila rented rooms at 44 Cresswell Place, just down the street from the mystery writer Agatha Christie Mallowan and her husband, Max. With her strong knowledge of German, Leila McGarvey also worked as a translator.

Molly studied voice in Vienna and performed as a classically trained soprano there. Among her belongings are programs for concerts she was featured in at the Vienna Concert Hall and the Vienna Opera House.

Occasionally, her performances would be accompanied by the Vienna Symphony Orchestra.

Molly's first significant performance on an important stage came at the age of twenty-three in autumn 1929. The critics raved. "The young singer made a brilliant debut," wrote critic Paul Bechert. The next spring, Bechert heard Molly perform again and said, "when she came back with her Liederabend, she furnished evidence not only of increased stage assurance, but also of a higher artistic polish. She gave a difficult program and gave it splendidly, with perfect diction, excellent voice control and vivid interpretative powers."

On October 18, 1935, Molly was given top billing at the New Styrian Song Recital in Vienna, perhaps the most important concert of her career. A newspaper reviewer lauded her as "…a concert singer of the highest quality. I have seldom encountered a better trained soprano…a most agreeable surprise." In reference to her performance of a particularly difficult vocal composition, the reviewer said it was "sung by Molly McGarvey superbly, both from a technical and musical point of view."

Molly became well-known and much loved in Vienna as a semi-professional singer, her specialty being "lieder," a type of German art song from the Romantic period that was highly emotional and expressive, with strong lyrical melodies and rich harmony. Among the most famous composers of lieder were Franz Schubert, Robert Schumann, Johannes Brahms, Hugo Wolf and Richard Strauss.

Dubbed the "Viennese nightingale," Molly felt she was good enough to undertake the challenging performance of opera. It would be a demanding course, but she was thrilled by the prospects. When she told her father, Fred forbade his daughter, however beautiful her voice, from pursuing a professional career on the stage.

It would be the first of two significant decisions Fred McGarvey made on behalf of his younger daughter that critically affected her life. The other would come a few years later on matters of the heart.

Fred McGarvey's reasoning for "forbidding" his daughter to sing professional opera remains unknown. He could have been scandalized at the prospects of Molly entering a career as a professional entertainer. Born into a middle-class Canadian Victorian household, educated as an engineer and a scientist, old-fashioned and autocratic, perhaps he did not wish to see a "performer" in his family.

Or perhaps Fred feared the impact failure on the opera stage might have on his daughter. Up to that point, her reviews had been excellent, but opera required a special talent, one perhaps Fred feared his daughter did not possess. Regardless of his reason, Fred made it clear there would be no career in opera for Molly.

There were further recitals for the Viennese nightingale but she would not progress beyond the semi-professional and her Austrian career would not last much longer. "She had given successful recitals in (Vienna), but the war put paid to any possible career," said a friend of Molly's from Oxford who came to know her well, George Stuart.

Neither Leila nor Molly ever married, although Molly is said to have had a fiancé who was killed during the Second World War. He was the only love of her life. Just as he prevented a professional singing career in Vienna, her father did not "permit" Molly to marry the man she loved, says David Banting. "He was German or Austrian. She had set her heart on him in Vienna." Whether Fred felt the man was not good enough for Molly, or perhaps he was already married, is now unclear. "Molly adored her father and was in later life volubly adoring of his memory," says Banting. "But I always suspected she was also very angry with him."

Beyond that, Banting says he knows little of Molly's mysterious relationship but always felt she lived "a life of some long-ago private disappointments." Yet she was remembered for her immense charm, style and generous hospitality and was a woman of "great gifts and vitality, with the dignity and privacy of a world that is now past," he said.

Molly simply did not speak of the matter of that lost love. Friend George Stuart could only say: "sadly, her fiancé was killed in the war and she never married."

Also living in Vienna, Eleanor, William's second wife, maintained close links with the family of her late husband. While she spent quite a bit of time in her native England, she never returned there permanently.

Eleanor was far closer in age to the children – Fred, Mamie and Kate – than she had been to her husband, William. And while the children might at first have been excused for being suspicious of her motives in marrying their wealthy father, they were, in short order, won over by her charm and sincerity. The children saw clearly that "dear Nora and Papa" were deeply in love and enjoyed the rich social life that Vienna provided.

Eleanor paid a visit to Fred and Madge in Vienna in May 1932, just before Leila left the city to commence a new life on her own in London. Eleanor was still only fifty-five years old but there is something about her signature that suggests a far older person. The strong and confident pen strokes she exhibited in earlier years had been reduced to a signature that was shaky and hesitant, hinting of a palsied or tremorous hand. While signing her name "Eleanora," a name she often signed in the various family guestbooks, she was frequently referred to as "Nora" by family members. She was also a frequent visitor to the Schloss where she, Mamie and Kate got along famously.

Nora later reverted to her maiden surname of Hamilton after a humiliating experience in a Vienna courtroom in 1929. Through testimony at the sensational murder trial of Colonel Felix Gartner, described as a handsome grey-haired ex-officer with Austria's Imperial Habsburg Dragoons, it was revealed that the former Nora McGarvey, the "rich English widow" of the "petroleum magnate," had been married to the accused for seventeen days. A newspaper account reported Gartner told the court Nora had refused to let him into their house on their wedding night. Gartner was furious, and claimed Nora had forced him to travel second-class when they took the train to Cannes, while she rode in first class. At the hotel, she booked them separate rooms. After the trial and stung by the publicity, Nora dropped both the Gartner and McGarvey names that had been so embarrassingly linked to the scandal and reverted to Eleanora Hamilton.

Just before the Second World War, Eleanor left Austria and moved to Geneva, Switzerland. She remained an enthusiastic traveller and in 1948 she is listed as a visitor to Fred and Madge's Manor Farm House in Oxfordshire, England. She spent her last days in Geneva.

Mamie's Country Castle

Schloss Graschnitz, the estate William purchased for Mamie and Eberhard von Zeppelin when they married in 1895, became a place of refuge for the whole family and remains today as a sort of memorial to the oil baron's life. It is the place William sent Helena to in 1898 when she was feeling poorly and the place where she died soon afterwards. It is also the place William frequently took Nora, after they met in 1905. It remained in the family for nearly seven decades and exists today as a riding school.

Countess Mamie von Zeppelin kept a guestbook at the castle and over the years the names of many a guest appeared, visitors from across Europe and North America. Occasionally the names were accompanied by remarks about their stay. Before she and William McGarvey married, Eleanor Hamilton joined him at Schloss Graschnitz and on August 22, 1905, she wrote as they departed: "The kindly welcome and pleasant days we have spent in Graschnitz shall ever remain a pleasant memory and in leaving we express our wish that the pleasant intercourse begun may continue through life."

On January 1, 1906, Nora was back as Mrs. McGarvey and wrote in the guestbook: "Nora and Papa (William) thank dear Ebert and Mamie for the very happy Christmas and New Years which they have passed in dear old Graschnitz. It has been a very happy time indeed and one which will be long remembered." Apparently even Nora referred to William as "Papa."

On another of their trips, William himself wrote eloquently about the beauty of the estate, the town of Graz and the mountains that surrounded them. It was autumn in 1908, a day he described as "glorious," without a cloud in the sky. The variegated colours of the woods entranced him and inspired him to describe the picture as one that could never be captured by any painter. He and Nora rode over the hills in a "Roman chariot," one he said was copied after "the famous Ben Hur." William always had an affinity for the classics, as evidenced back in Petrolia so many years before, when he had entertained onstage at the Oil Exchange Hall by reciting from Hamlet's Horatio.

"Dear Mamie walked out as usual (and) ran over the fields," he continued. Her favourite pair of dogs came along "to protect us...Sorry to leave the enchanted view."

The Roman chariot — likely a small horse-drawn cart or trap — was used again in August 1912 by William and Eleanor, with Mamie accompanying them on one of her white ponies.

There are other references to a "mountain fortress" not far from the castle, a rustic cabin the family would hike to when they wanted to enjoy the clean mountain air.

Nora continued to make frequent visits to the castle after William's death and in one remark dated February 1916, she thanked Mamie for bringing "sunshine into my life again. Thanks for all your kindness and attention."

After the Great War, in 1921, Fred and Madge's daughters, Helen and Molly, spent their summer holiday at Graschnitz, one of many to come. Helen turned nineteen during her stay and at the end of her visit wrote: "I have never spent such a lovely summer holidays. Thank you ever so much, Aunt Mamie, for all your kindness to me." Added Molly: "Am looking forward to coming again next year."

Nora returned in 1931 after what she called a "long time of absence" and referred to "dear beloved Graschnitz, the old place of so many happy recollections."

She returned again after Kate's death in 1934 and spent more than three months with Mamie that summer. When she departed, she wrote: "I leave with a sad heart. The memory of our dear Kate, who I miss so much, is ever with me."

Fred and Madge paid a visit in January 1935 and Madge wrote: "We have come and gone so often, yet our feelings remain the same. We love coming and hate to go away, however long we stay."

On July 18, 1939, after their last visit before the war, Fred's remarks are particularly poignant: "A perfect and happy visit, (over) all too soon, but an everlasting memory accompanied by the constant wish that we may soon be together again." They would soon be separated by a long war.

Nora, who paid a visit in August 1938, wrote that she was "leaving with a sad heart for Switzerland." She would not return to Graschnitz for ten years. It would be twenty years later, in 1958, when she penned her final words from Mamie's estate, but the sentiment was always the same: "(Five) happy weeks spent in dear Graschnitz surrounded by so much kindness and wonderful hospitality. Dear Mamie looked so after my diet, God bless her for all her kind deeds, heart full of thanks."

Meanwhile, as the 1930s progressed, the McGarvey family grew ever more uneasy about the political situation that they feared was beginning to encircle them in its tightening grasp.

Escape From The Nazis

The Anschluss came to Austria on March 12, 1938. It changed everything. Anschluss refers to the annexation of Austria into Nazi Germany. It occurred the moment Hitler marched German soldiers into Vienna and annexed Austria into the greater German Reich, an act that was welcomed by not only Austrian Nazis but by a large portion of the rest of the population too. With nationalist anti-Semitic sentiment rampant, anyone with any potential connection to Jewishness began to fear for their future in Austria. Fred and Madge feared that Madge's and daughter Molly's "Bergheim" heritage might label them as Jewish. After all, it seems now almost certain that Madge's grandfather, Melville Peter Bergheim, had been born Jewish in Prussia and later converted to Christianity when he went to Jerusalem.

In Hitler's increasingly paranoid society, perhaps even Mamie could be under suspicion, due to the Zeppelins' past links to Jews. As for Leila, she was already living in England and safe, for the moment, from the Nazis' grasp.

As a result, Fred commissioned the services of the Stokes and Cox agency of London to provide evidence they did not have any Jewish background. The Stokes and Cox partnership was established by Ethel Stokes and Mary Cox. Each had her own personal link to the McGarvey family and each was eager to help out as the political climate in Austria and Germany degenerated throughout the 1930s under Hitler's National Socialism.

Mary Cox was a friend of Countess Mamie von Zeppelin and often visited her at Schloss Graschnitz. Ethel Stokes was a friend of Fred McGarvey. She had transferred her financial affairs to Fred's care, confident in his investment acumen. In 1938, it was Fred's turn to ask Stokes for help. Could she help him collect the necessary documentation to submit to the authorities to obtain an Aryan certificate, clearing the family members of any question of having Jewish heritage?

In Nazi Germany, Aryan certificates were documents certifying that a person was a member of the Aryan race. Beginning in April 1933, they were required of all employees and officials in Germany's public sector, including education. They were also required in order to become a citizen of Germany. After the Anschluss, Austrian citizens began to realize they too would require Aryan certificates to ensure their safety.

"Lesser" certificates required a total of seven birth and baptismal documents for the applicant as well as their parents and grandparents, plus three marriage certificates for parents and grandparents. "Greater" certificates, essential before inheriting land and for the privilege of joining the Nazi party, required the tracing of the family pedigree back to 1800 (1750 if one wished to be chosen an SS officer). Applicants needed to prove "none of their paternal nor their maternal ancestors had Jewish or coloured blood."

With so many applications already in the pipeline, progress on the McGarvey file was slow. In the meantime, Stokes needed a reciprocal favour from Fred. She asked him to help another friend obtain a visa to leave Austria. It got Fred thinking: with the political climate as it was, might it be time for him to obtain visas for his own family members as well? Should he be leaving the country that had been so good to him and the place he had known as home since he was twelve years old?

Fred's search for evidence of the family's background is a chilling reminder of the black cloud of Nazism that shrouded Europe and which would eventually draw the world into war for a second time in a quarter-century. However, there was one positive outcome from Fred McGarvey's search: he and Ethel Stokes uncovered a great deal of family history that informed future generations and was in no small way responsible for enabling the writing of this book. For instance, Fred learned much about William and Helena's ancestors in Ireland, Canada, the United States and Poland, and even uncovered the Petrolia gravesite of his baby brother, William Edward, and Helena's brother, Charles. The genealogical work Fred accumulated was passed on to his younger daughter, Molly, who became the keeper of the family records.

In the previous century, fears of being identified as Jewish had so worried John Simeon Bergheim that for years after moving to Britain he claimed to have been born in Germany rather than Jerusalem. In later years, a portion of the Bergheim family adopted the surname "Lindsay," borrowing it from another branch to which they were connected by marriage. But that had been a different time and a different place. The Nazis were now actively depriving Jews of their basic rights.

Mamie's last visit to her brother at his Vienna home took place from March 10 to March 21, 1938. During her visit, German troops marched in and Austria was swallowed whole by Hitler's Greater German Reich.

Fred, Madge and Mamie watched with alarm as many of their fellow Austrians welcomed Hitler, accompanied by a 4,000-man bodyguard, into their country. On March 15, they listened nervously as the Fuhrer addressed a cheering crowd of 200,000 at Vienna's Heldenplatz where he told them: "Not as tyrants have we come, but as liberators." Fred, Madge and Mamie were not convinced.

With the Nazis gaining further power in Germany and a growing level of support for the movement in Austria, Fred and Madge decided it was best to take daughter Molly and flee to England. A distant American cousin and friend, Beth Chew, learned later from Molly the family "were being investigated and harassed." Fred had seen it all before: during the Great War, he had watched his father's oil empire crushed and was forced to pick up the pieces, paste them together as best as he could and sell it off. It had been a sad time for Fred and he was loath to go through such an experience again.

Fred's sister Mamie was determined to hold out. Austria was where her home was, she said. Her father had bought it for her and had defended it successfully in her divorce proceedings with the philandering Count Ebert. She had stayed during the Great War. She would never let it go. Besides, she had begun recently to let out rooms at the castle to holidayers. She would not be alone.

It must have been a sad parting on March 21, perhaps with entreaties from Fred and Madge for Mamie to change her mind and come with them. She would hear nothing of it. She would stay. Then, having bid her brother and his wife and daughter *auf wiedersehen*, Mamie headed to the train station and left Vienna for what she hoped would be the safety of her Graz country estate.

After Mamie's departure, there were five further visits to Fred and Madge McGarvey's Vienna home recorded in the guestbook over the course of the summer. The last, dated August 22, suggests a departure for England in late August or early September. The guestbook, which they had begun in Mariampol and then taken with them to their new home in Vienna, was now closed.

The McGarveys fit in well with British society and Madge had quite a number of relatives there who could vouch for them. Fred, Madge and Molly moved in with one of those relatives, Madge's sister, Georgina (Bergheim) and her husband, Percy Banting, in Guildford, Surrey. The McGarveys were now quite far removed from the frontier democracy within which William's generation had grown up and built a company. England was their emotional homeland and the logical place to which they must escape if "escape" was what they must do. And as wealthy British subjects living in Austria, they enjoyed much more freedom to flee the continent than did the vast majority of potential refugees – Jews and non-Jews – who looked longingly across the Channel.

However, there were still matters that needed to be addressed, including issues of currency exchange, which became an immediate concern for the couple. Within days of Hitler annexing Austria, regulations were passed requiring citizens to declare and "offer to the Reich" all non-German securities, currency and other forms of wealth. After months of legal battles, Fred was finally freed of obligations to the Reich and, under close supervision by envoys of the Nazi regime, packed his household effects and had them shipped to England. They remained in storage for the next year.

In January 1939, soon after arriving in Britain, Fred and Madge took a trip through Rome to North Africa and spent several months in the Algerian capital of Algiers, and the neighbouring Morocco. In late July, and with tensions on the Continent rising, all seemed quite stable at least in Austria under Hitler's seemingly protective wing. Fred, Madge and their daughters felt safe enough to pay a final visit to Austria and spent time at Schloss Graschnitz with the countess. Issues of politics were discussed and perhaps the family began to wonder whether all might yet be well. In August and before returning to England, the McGarveys took a side trip to Switzerland where they visited Nora. But the political situation had deteriorated. In Zurich, said Fred, they were advised against continuing their journey through France by car. "After unavoidable delays, (we) reached England a week before the outbreak of war."

Years later, Fred McGarvey revealed that he had not intended to spend the rest of his life in Britain after escaping Austria and Nazism. In an ancestoral memoir he penned in 1961, Fred explained that British foreign currency exchange regulations prevented him from transferring the bulk of his wealth to his native Canada, where he had planned to resettle. Under the circumstances, the best course of action would be to remain in Britain and protect his sizable fortune.

Once finally accommodating themselves to a permanent life there, Fred and Madge went house hunting and came upon "a charming little manor house at Old Headington, near Oxford," said their niece, Patricia Lindsay. Manor Farm House sat on the Dunstan Road in Headington, just outside the city of Oxford. The property had ceased being farmed in the 1920s and Manor Farm was turned into a lovely private home, one of those charming abodes that still speckle the English countryside. The previous owner, Richard Hartley Rose-Innes, had been a surgeon who bought the property in 1933 and added two wings. After contracting tuberculosis, Rose-Innes went to live in South Africa and the property was put up for sale.

Fred and Madge loved the place immediately. There was a garden and an orchard, with outbuildings and a field. Fred took easily to the life of a gentleman farmer and raised goats, a pastime he came to love.

"We lived not all that far away, so saw quite a lot of them," said Patricia Lindsay. "Aunt Madge had eye trouble and had several cataract operations." After losing all of her sight in one eye, Madge lost most of the sight in the other and became entirely dependent on Fred.

Patricia Lindsay recalled that her "Uncle Fred had a great head of white hair and remained very active. He was delighted when I spent a year in Hungary and then learned Polish. He wanted to talk Polish with me, but (since he was) extremely deaf by then, it wasn't easy."

"Yes, he was very strong and active," added Patricia's sister, Sonia. "He was of medium height. I remember he had a Canadian accent. Madge was gentle and kindly, pretty and slender."

Through it all, they seemed quite successful in moving much of their money out of Austria and into a British bank.

"Certainly he was well enough off in England," says David Banting, "buying the Manor House in Headington, Oxford, and later leaving Molly with considerable money of her own."

As they eased into life in England and with Europe now fully preparing for war, it took the McGarveys little time to recognize they had done the right thing in leaving, and their fears grew for Mamie's safety at Schloss Graschnitz.

On September 1, 1939, German troops invaded Poland. On September 3, Britain and France declared war on Germany. On September 10, Canada declared war on Germany.

At Manor Farm house in Oxfordshire, Madge and Fred started a new guestbook.

CHAPTER 16

ANOTHER WARTIME

The First World War shattered the empire established by the king of Canada's Foreign Drillers, William Henry McGarvey. The Second World War dealt a staggering blow to his descendants, but they were determined to persevere. They had inherited Papa's fighting spirit, a spirit that was about to be put to the test.

Britain: In The Home Guard

Having chosen to live on opposite sides of the wall that divided the world between the chief combatants, Britain and Greater Germany, Fred and Mamie, the last two remaining children of William and Helena McGarvey, were unable to keep in touch during the war years. Each carried on with life in their own way.

As he was now in his mid-sixties, Fred was too old to serve in the military, but did his part for the war effort by joining Britain's Home Guard, created in early 1940 as the country's "last line of defence" in the event of a German invasion of the island nation. He served until mid-1943.

Mamie stayed on at Schloss Graschnitz and did her best to maintain the property which she kept and maintained not only for herself, but as a sort of memorial to Papa.

Fred's two daughters would be William McGarvey's last direct descendants. Having left her singing career behind in Vienna, Molly did not attempt to pursue it on the professional stage in England. Instead, she performed volunteer work during the war years and frequently entertained British troops through ENSA (Entertainments National Service Association). Whether the professional stage might have been seen by Fred to be beneath Molly's station, or whether he secretly believed her to be not talented enough to succeed, Fred agreed to tolerate a voluntary vocation of entertaining the servicemen and women, just as the beloved songstress Vera Lynn did. Perhaps seeing the King's own daughter and heir to the throne, Princess Elizabeth, serve as a driver and mechanic for Britain's Auxiliary Territorial Service was sufficient to sway him.

Leila and Molly were highly proficient in the German language and both obtained wartime employment in Britain as German-English translators.

Austria: A Countess's Story

Mamie continued to farm her property in Nazi-occupied Austria. Unfortunately, however, that property was set in a prime location for German troops. An anti-aircraft gun and six cannon were placed on the hill above Schloss Graschnitz and glared down menacingly at the countess's estate. Hundreds of German soldiers – and eventually Russian prisoners of war – were housed there in wooden barracks. Under command of the military, their meals were cooked in the castle courtyard and carried up on mules. The hill was the same one that members of the McGarvey family had climbed countless times to enjoy the fresh air and the view, a hill that now served a sinister purpose.

To make way for the barracks and open up lines of sight, "all the beautiful trees were cut down, some ancient oaks, and the whole place was honeycombed with deep trenches," Mamie later said. "When an enemy plane appeared, the shooting that went on was terrible. All the (estate's) roofs and windows were ruined. We could get no glass and had to stop them up with boards and cardboard."

Yet despite those challenges, Mamie fared surprisingly well in the Austrian countryside during the years under Nazi occupation, far better than she would have had she lived in Vienna. Many aspects of life continued normally in the countryside. Occasionally, when it was safe, her friend, Clara, would come down from her Vienna apartment to pay a short visit.

Her good friends and neighbours, the Nechelheimers, were regular Sunday guests. While supplies of tea were scarce, Mamie always made sure to set aside enough to serve during their weekly visits. The Nechelheimer home, Schloss Nechelheim, sat just north of St. Marien, about two kilometres from Mamie's Graschnitz, and she paid them frequent return visits. But if Mamie escaped the war years fairly unscathed, save for the loss of trees, some damage to the buildings and the inevitable shortages of staples, the aftermath is what would leave her reeling.

With the war reaching its conclusion, Mamie was finally able to renew contact with her brother and his family. In March 1945, with Nazi Germany back on its heels and two months before the European war officially ended, a letter arrived from Fred that had been posted four months earlier. Of course Fred and Madge were eager to hear how their sister and sister-in-law was making out in occupied Austria, and how she had survived for the past six horrific years. When finally she was able to respond, the story Mamie told was a harrowing one.

Initially, she had been unable to respond, but an English squadron leader's arrival on July 24 filled her with hope of renewed contact. The squadron leader was an Oxford native who said he knew the village of Headington well and offered to deliver her letter. "I have missed you sadly all these long years," Mamie wrote Fred on July 29.

Since the actual wartime experience had been relatively benign for Mamie and her neighbours, they were not prepared for what was to come after their "liberation." She wrote that on April 1, word arrived that it would be the Soviets, and not the hoped-for British, who would be first to arrive in St. Marien to occupy Murztal province. The populace immediately began to "make preparations" by hiding away their valuables as best they could, Mamie said. They worked hard for a week, then rumors circulated that the British were coming closer and "we quite counted on their coming here before the Russians, and many people brought things out from their hiding places. I unfortunately did also. Then on May 8 the news reached us that the Russians were in Murzzuschlag and on the following day they marched into Marein."

Mamie then began to tell the horrible tale of the brief Soviet occupation.

"All was quiet until the afternoon and we were told that plundering was not allowed. Towards evening a wild horde of plunderers, men and women, suddenly came down on me. I was suddenly surrounded by a gang of terrible creatures led by two (Soviet) uniformed men. In a few minutes everything was torn open and they took the first picking of things. They expected to find great riches and not finding much, they threatened me with a revolver pointed at me to show the hiding places. I gave up part of my jewels and some silver which I had at hand.

"The gang was all over the house, opening all cupboards. What was not unlocked was smashed open. After they left, late into the evening we hid what we could. Especially (Mamie's servant) Agnes helped. She had been here some weeks – she managed to get out of Vienna just before the Russians entered – hid some of your things," Mamie told Fred. "The next morning the plundering went on. There were thousands of Russian work people, and French too. They came in groups with armed men in uniform with guns to protect them and help them steal. It went on for over a week, night and day. It became so dangerous for me and I saw that I could do nothing to save things. I was threatened so badly to tell where I had hidden things."

Mamie hid in the dining room of Fred's castle apartment with her maids and two other families who had sought refuge at the Schloss. Mobs rushed in and out as they pleased, taking whatever they wished, leaving only the frightened residents' mattresses and bedclothes behind.

Who were these looters who came with the support of the Soviet "liberators"? While Mamie's descriptions are vague, it appears as though a great number of them were local people who were perhaps in dire need and jealous of the better-off and noble families. She referred to some of them being of French and Polish background. Later, she mentioned that the authorities led searches of area homes in attempts to recover some of the stolen merchandise. The actions of often-drunken soldiers in Soviet military uniforms – including rape and looting – proved a black eye for Moscow and were eventually met with severe consequences for the known perpetrators.

Being strongly advised to leave her home, Mamie donned a disguise ("Frau Winter's modest country shawl," she said) to hide her identity and fled with a small group of neighbours to a shooting lodge in the mountains where friends had been holed up for weeks. The friends were gone by the time they arrived. The group stayed a week, often leaving the hunting lodge and hiding in the nearby forest when danger approached.

After a week they chanced a return home, only to find the Schloss in a sad state. "Everything had been turned up in the house and every cupboard opened and emptied out. Not much furniture was damaged, though."

Mamie explained the depth of anger that was now directed against many of the Austrians who had been perceived as collaborating with the Nazis. Many of her friends were among those now targeted. Those of French and Polish background were turning their wrath on some of the locals, she said.

"I lived in the dining room of the Kellerhaus, as it was too dangerous to stay in the main house, the wild hordes kept coming in day and night. But I commenced to try to make order. Then the whole place was seized for hospital, and in three hours everything had to be emptied out. I rescued what furniture I could and what I could not rescue was thrown out of the window – what the hospital people said they did not need. They would not let me go in the house any more to rescue things."

As Soviet military patients began to arrive, they sat "all over and on the nice chairs and sofas with their dirty feet and clothes. We kept on carrying furniture and the staff kept grabbing the things out of our hands, saying they needed them.

"I do not ever remember running so fast and working so hard as in those few hours. I was trying to rescue the little that had been left to me, small pieces of furniture and dishes. I looked out of the window and saw in the courtyard those two nice leather chairs of Kate's (their late sister) being stripped for the leather and bit of horsehair, and then chopped up and taken away to burn. I found afterwards the ruins with many other pieces of furniture that had shared the same fate."

Mamie had volunteered the courtyard of the Schloss to harbour local homeless families. Now the Soviets ordered everyone living in the courtyard to leave. Quickly, Mamie made arrangements to house the displaced local families in other buildings on her property. Each of the cottages and buildings had been given names. Three families were put in Lechnerhaus, three in the Forsthaus, another man in a room at Leichtfried.

She herself seemed on the verge of having to share a mansarde or attic room at Leichtfried. "So I asked Ernest (Nechelheimer) to put Agnes and me up. He and Nini have been most kind to us. We share one room and I am very grateful to them." But even as she and Agnes arrived at Schloss Nechelheim by horse-drawn wagon, a tearful Nini greeted them with the news that they, too, had been robbed of most of their belongings. Luckily, said Mamie, she and Agnes had brought a carriage rug, an old eiderdown blanket and a few of Fred's horse blankets with them.

"I asked Agnes if ever when she mended your horse blankets, the idea had come to her that some day she would be glad to use them as sheets."

While the Soviets were there, at times there had been four hundred hospital patients housed in the castle proper. Mamie rejoiced when she was told they would be moving out and on July 22 the Soviets were gone, six days after her seventieth birthday. So was most of the furniture, and what remained was in sad condition.

"It will be long before the place is habitable again," she said. In many parts of the schloss, barely a window was left intact.

The Kellerhaus, which Fred's family always used when they paid a visit, was spared most of the damage as it had been used as the Soviet officers' quarters. "I am arranging a few rooms to live there and will be using your kitchen for the present," Mamie told Fred. She explained one of the locals had been using it, an option she felt better than the alternative in which a family of six would have been occupying it. "Your furniture I stored in the bedroom and bathroom before the Russians came and I put notices on the doors, saying the contents were the property of a British subject. It helped some, but the rooms were opened and a lot of things taken out."

Mamie was already eagerly anticipating and planning for Fred and Madge to pay their inaugural post-war visit. "I can arrange your rooms again and make you comfortable – unfortunately without your carpets. The Russians stole all the carpets. I had stored them under the terrace and found all intact when I returned from the country. The plunderers had pulled them all out but (a servant) put them back. They had got wet and I thought it better to bring them up and store in your bedroom. But the hospital people took them away from me while we were carrying them up. They stole more and did more damage than the plunderers before."

Earlier in the war, Mamie had packed away Fred and Madge's linens and most of their clothes and put them in a spot where she thought they would be safe from bombs. They too went beneath the terrace before the Soviets came but they, too, were discovered and carted away by the thieves.

Most of Mamie's own clothing had been sent away for safekeeping but the plunderers got them too, she said. All that was left were some pillowcases, a pair of shoes and a few dresses. Few of Mamie's own possessions remained, but at least her old brown winter cloak and sable cape were salvaged. "These few things are now my sole possessions. These were my last hope and things I need so much, a fur coat, best shoes, typewriter, small pieces of jewelry I was so attached to. All gone. And there is very little hope of finding them."

Mamie had stayed away from the castle as much as possible while the Soviets were in residence. "Russians kept coming into the house, running all over, taking whatever they could find."

The post-war plundering of Austria was nowhere worse than in the Murztal, said Mamie. Vienna had not been hit as hard. "We are quite robbed out. No one has been spared." One family of friends had been forced to live with the village priest because they were left with nothing. "No one seems to have a mattress left, or a bed cover. I was quite alone to face all this wild horde," she said, noting her male staff had been "quite useless." One, a young Swiss property manager she'd hired a few months before, "was so terrified of the Russians that he disappeared to Switzerland, leaving only an adjunct, a poor invalid with one leg, to help me. But he was brave and did the best he could."

Mamie had run a good-sized farm operation before and during the war. Pigs, several cows, chickens, plus saddles and harness, the tractor and most of the wagons and all the smaller implements had been stolen by the looters. She was left with just six cows. "I have to commence quite new if I want to keep on farming." At present, there was no farming across the region, the Soviet military animals having mowed down the fields.

Mamie was disheartened. "I have had so much misfortune with *verwalters* (managers). There seems to be no one … decent and honest."

Mamie recounted the sense of distress and hopelessness that was sweeping the countryside around Schloss Graschnitz. "Many people committed suicide when the Russians came. Words cannot describe what we went through here. The last two months seem like a terrible nightmare."

She was, however, able to keep family documents and portraits intact. In proud recognition of her family's achievements, she saved one of William McGarvey's prized portraits hanging on a wall and placed a second behind a cupboard in anticipation of the day she would be rebuilding. Then she listed some of the other damage done. Brass doorknobs stolen, leaving it hard to open doors – if the doors survived. Many were simply smashed through. "Cupboards that I did not unlock for the plunderers were simply smashed up and ruined."

Bathtubs had been removed and one was found in the cow stable, another in the chicken yard and one in the laundry. The piano had been taken out to the garden where the soldiers used it for "dancing and theatricals," Mamie said.

Vienna was a "sad sight," she added, with much of it destroyed in the bombing. It has been estimated that more than one out of every five houses in the city were partially or completely destroyed and almost 87,000 flats were uninhabitable. Bridges, sewers, gas and water pipes were ripped apart. "The Nazis destroyed a lot before leaving."

It took little time after the Russians left the Graz area for Mamie and her neighbours to begin to rebuild. First, she said, the entire property needed to be cleaned and disinfected. In the meantime she stayed with friends and made daily trips to the castle to begin the long process. In total, it took ten women, three plumbers, some carpenters and various other workmen labouring three weeks to help Mamie make the repairs required. She hoped that in two or three months, Fred would be able to pay her a visit.

Although Austria had been annexed with the support of a large portion of the country's population, the Allies agreed it would be treated as the first victim of Nazi aggression and helped back to independent statehood. Under the occupation, the country was divided into four zones – British, American, French and Russian – as was Vienna. Areas occupied by the British and Americans fared far better than the province of Murztal. But happily for Murztal, it was the British who took control after the initial Soviet invasion.

While the area had undergone two months of the liberators' terror and plundering, said Mamie, now the Soviets were gone and "we are relieved at last and it is so good to see smiling faces again."

Despite the devastation, there was still plenty to celebrate. Ernest and Nini Nechelheimer had been great friends to Mamie for years and Mamie told Fred that just as they had the previous five years, the couple invited her to recognize her birthday – this was her 70th – with them. Clara had brought a strawberry-filled cake. Gifts were somehow found in the deprivation that marked life in post-war Austria and the table was decorated with candles and flowers and a large green paper "70."

A few of Countess Mamie's stolen items were recovered with the help of the local police authorities once the Soviet troops left. "A notice was put up that these things must be returned. Some have been brought back and are in keeping with the gendarmerie. But there is not much. I am going to have a few house searchings made with the help of the gendarmerie. It is very disagreeable, but that is the only way I can get back a few things."

Mamie presented Fred with a list of items she hoped he would bring with him when finally he was able to visit. Stockings ("I have only a few pairs of very thin old stockings"), material (but not tweed) for a warm skirt, and some soap. Tea would be nice, too, she added, since hers was several years old and she had only been able to use it sparingly, on Sundays. Dishtowels and dusters were also much in demand. "There seems no possibility of (buying anything local) here for the next months."

Mamie had welcomed the arrival of the British and now they were in control of the district, the locals began to breathe more easily. Arrangements were made for Mamie to put up five British officers and one hundred and fifty soldiers, a situation she found far more palatable than the Soviet military hospital with all the accompanying looting. The previous months were like a terrible dream, she said. "No one who has not witnessed all can realize to the full extent what we have gone through. Now we are safe under the English protection."

Mamie called in a local man to fix the doors, replace the locks and get the toilets running again before the British army arrived. "I am going to live in the Kellerhaus, in Helen's (Leila's) old room," she said.

The British army was also pitching in to get the castle up and running again. Mamie was looking forward to living back fulltime at Schloss Graschnitz. "I hope some of the English officers will give me some tea here."

Mamie referred to several locals who had already been imprisoned, their Nazi-sympathizer past now catching up to them. They were in prison in Graz, "for many years, I think."

As for her own relations with the Nazis, Mamie credited a local administrator named Strohback for exerting influence on her behalf and keeping her out of trouble during the war. While he was never a Nazi, she said, "he saved me from having bomb refugees in the house. I had only two families, but in dwellings outside – and they were enough trouble!"

During the war, Strohback had also helped her set up the dining and billiard rooms with beds, giving the appearance that they were available for use as a hospital when needed, thus avoiding further problems with the Nazi authorities. When this was done, little did she know that when the Soviets came, the castle would be turned into a real hospital.

Yet clearly Mamie was forced to keep a low profile during the ordeal of war. She mentioned one area woman who proved "much too grand a lady for the country" and the difficulties that arose as a result. Mamie had spent weeks working hard and struggling to return her home to a semblance of order. No one could accuse her of being "too grand a lady."

Mamie had kept two small dogs, fifteen-year-old siblings Grete and Blondy, but with the Soviets bringing a mass of confusion to the place, she feared for their safety. With the hunger and privation sweeping the countryside, they might fall easy prey to looters. Reluctantly, she had them euthanized. "It was a terrible decision but I thought it my duty towards the dear faithful little friends. They had been my faithful companions for years, and I would never have forgiven myself if anything had happened to them. Now they are sleeping their last sleep in the garden of Nechelheim (castle). I miss them very, very much."

Fred and Madge were greatly relieved to get the letters and hear that Mamie was safe. They knew they would be unable to make it to Austria that year, with civilian communications still in disarray. Britain itself was under heavy rations but with the help of donations from friends, they collected some of the items she pleaded for, put together a package and arranged to have it sent through the military. Thanks to British military officers, the much-anticipated package arrived on October 13. Mamie cried with joy.

"I cannot tell you how delighted I am with all the treasures you sent," she wrote later that same day. "The jacket to match the brown skirt, the skirt, and belt-ribbon to enlarge it. I have become much skinnier than I was." There was tea and soap as well as a dish towel, stockings and gloves.

In the interval, Mamie had recovered her fur cloak and typewriter, a trunk full of blankets, dish towels and papers. Fred and Madge assured Mamie she was welcome to use any of their belongings she could salvage and Mamie was delighted to report there were two fox boas, a white rabbit rug, some corsets, a hat and a dress of Leila's.

Winter would be bad, with no coal and little else available for heating purposes.

In early October, Mamie paid a visit to the nearby town of Bruck. "The shops are beginning to open up again but are very empty yet."

As Mamie wrote her letter, her friend Clara, who had been through so much with her, was making new curtains for the doors from an old piece of muslin. Most windows would go without curtains. Many didn't even have any glass left and would have to be boarded up against the coming winter cold.

When Fred and Madge replied to Mamie, they send news that Papa's second wife, Nora, was still alive in Switzerland, where she had fled just before the war, although not faring well. It seems Nora had broken her hipbone. "I have not had news from her since December (1944)," replied Mamie, and that only indirectly, from a Mrs. Wirtz with whom Nora was staying. Nora's belongings at Schloss Graschnitz, including clothing, furniture and photographs, had been looted by the Soviets, Mamie told her brother.

If the family at one time feared that Eleanor, who was much younger than William, might have been a gold-digger, their fears soon subsided and "dear Nora" became a valued member of the children's circle of friends. Over the years, she frequently visited Fred, Mamie and Fred's two daughters. In Mamie's will dated 1959, Nora is listed first among the beneficiaries. Her address is listed as the Geneva Hotel in Switzerland.

While Mamie longed to see her brother in person, she warned that travel was still perilous on the Continent. Many cars were windowless and not only would it be cold, there would be no food to be had along the way. It had taken the military sergeant who delivered her package nine days to travel from England, and Fred would not have access to the military stations the sergeant stopped at along the route. "I hope the trains will be better soon."

Democracy was returned to Austria in November but there was plenty of privation. The new chancellor, Leopold Figl, told Austrians: "I can't give you anything for Christmas. I can't give you candles for your Christmas tree – if you even have one. Not a single piece of bread, no coal, no decoration. We have nothing. I can only beg you: Have faith in this young Austria!"

Fred did finally make it to Schloss Graschnitz the following spring, alone. Later that year, a final box of Mamie's clothing was found, none the worse for wear except for some shoes. A few carpets were also found.

The British troops stayed at the castle three years until Mamie had the opportunity to lease space to the ministry of education for a school. When she told the commander the chance had arisen for her to lease her property and make some much-needed income, he arranged to have the remaining troops depart.

In a letter to a distant Canadian relative in 1950, Mamie sent along some photos and described the views of the castle and its surroundings. She no longer lived in much of the castle but described various parts of the place: the metre-deep walls of the original structure; the long wing with the dining room, billiards room and hunting room with all of its shooting trophies; and the library. The section containing the library, she said, was what she had rented to the education ministry.

This was the new reality and one that Mamie spent no time crying over. "So much was destroyed by the Russians that I could not furnish it all again," she explained. Besides, it would have required a lot of servants to operate, and the post-war servant shortage remained acute. There was also a housing shortage and had she not let the space out, she would have lost it anyway. "The beautiful rooms with the pretty floors would have been turned into kitchens and everything would have been ruined."

After the British left, Mamie restored one portion of the castle – the Kellerhaus where Fred and his family had spent their summers for many years – into an apartment for herself. "Dear Madge and Fred were so good in sending materials for the repairs, as there was nothing to be had here," Mamie wrote her relative.

Papa's legacy had been saved.

CHAPTER 17

THE LAST GENERATIONS

Madge's niece, Patricia Lindsay, paid a holiday visit to Mamie at Schloss Graschnitz during the time Patricia was studying in Hungary in 1948-49. Lindsay recalled Mamie met her at the Graz train station with the pony and trap, and drove the two of them back to the castle. Was it the same trap, perhaps, that Papa and Nora had set out in on their trek through the countryside so many years before?

The castle estate had required a great deal of restoration after the post-war damage. It took Mamie until spring 1953 before she was finished bringing the castle's farmland back to its original state, including the planting of grass and grain in a large field on the hill that had, not that long ago, been the site of German soldiers, guns and Soviet prisoners-of-war. All around there were pastures once more. While she received some financial assistance from the government, Mamie bore most of the expense herself.

With the war over, Madge and Fred greeted more guests to Manor Farm House in Oxfordshire. Nora paid her first post-war visit from Switzerland in 1948.

Mamie spent Christmas 1949 at Manor Farm, the first time in more than a decade she had enjoyed the holiday season with brother Fred and his family. She told her brother and sister-in-law she had never been alone for the holidays during the war years, however, with "kind neighbours" always close by and eager to share what little they had.

Excited by the prospects of Mamie's holiday visit, Fred cut a tree from his own garden to celebrate the festive occasion. The German tradition of Christmas trees was a significant part of celebrating the season for the McGarveys. Prior to leaving for England that year, Mamie gave trees to all of her farm workers and brought another up to Vienna to place on the graves of her father, William, and sister Kate. Graveside Christmas trees are the custom in Austria, she explained to a friend in America.

Mamie flew to London from Vienna. "With a half-hour stop in Zurich, the journey was supposed to take six hours," she said, "but we were longer on the way this time as it became necessary to change planes in Zurich. Anyway, much better than going by rail which takes about thirty-six hours."

As young girls, the Lindsay sisters, Sonia and Patricia, who had grown up near Manor Farm, recalled Christmas there as a time of great celebrations, with traditional trimmings and happy evenings spent around the grand piano, singing. Molly would present excerpts from operas and entertain them with her "Viennese nightingale" voice.

Leila would come down from London for the holidays. Back in the city, she utilized her fluent German to obtain a position as a translator for the British contingent at the Nuremberg Trials. The trials were held in Nuremberg, Germany between 1945 and 1949 for the prosecution of German military leaders and political officials, industrialists and financiers for crimes committed during the war.

Apparently inspired by her experience with the legal world, Leila decided to study law and enrolled at Oxford University. She was nearly fifty-two years old when she graduated in 1954, and was invested into the Honourable Society of the Inner Temple, one of the four Inns of Court or professional associations for barristers and judges in London. The "inn" is a professional body for barristers that provides legal training, selection and regulation. Afterwards, Leila practised as a London barrister. Dan Chew, the son of Leila and Molly's distant American cousin, Beth Chew, was seventeen when he accompanied his mother to the event and remembers the festive occasion, including a nine-course dinner with wine. "It was a very formal black tie event with liveried wait staff and many toasts." As a teenaged boy, Dan Chew was impressed by the "many fancy cars guests arrived in."

Leila's accomplishments are ever the more impressive when considering she had been stricken by tuberculosis as a child and developed a severe curvature of the spine. The family believed she caught tuberculosis from milk obtained from a diseased cow. For the rest of her life she required a cane, and eventually a wheelchair.

Fitted with a leg brace, her walk might have seemed "ungainly," said her cousin, David Banting, but she was absolute in her determination not to let her physical issues hold her back. Leila, whom many family members, including Banting, knew better as Helen, "insisted on travelling by bus to get around London and accepted no help," he said.

Madge did not make it to her daughter's investiture. In her later years, she was blind in one eye and severely vision-impaired in the other. Her general health started to fail about 1950 and she died in October 1952. Fred stayed on at Manor Farm and remained active, with the help of his Austria-born housekeeper, Emmi Gibson, and her British husband, George. Emmi had come to England with Fred and Madge back in 1938 and remained a loyal and much-loved servant.

Mamie visited her brother early in the spring of 1953 and on her return home, stopped off for a visit to Vienna, which was still under Allied occupation. Fred would be visiting her at the castle about the end of May and was looking forward to some fly-fishing and rest.

It was during that trip, and perhaps thinking of his own mortality, that Fred McGarvey stopped off in Vienna and went to the Protestant section of the Central Vienna Cemetery, where he stood at the gravesites of his father, mother and sisters Nellie and Kate. He had arranged for the remains of the four individuals to be disinterred, cremated and placed in separate urns to be shipped to England.

"He wanted the whole family to rest forever together," Beth Chew recalled Molly telling her. Chew, who had become a close friend of Molly's, added: "She said her father stood in the Vienna cemetery and watched each exhumation to make sure that the right graves were dug and that each set of remains was placed in its own container." While the whole procedure seems ghoulish now, it also speaks to the man's precise attention to detail and his determination to see the family together, again, in death.

The individually packaged ashes were sent to England and placed in a vault at the family gravesite at Headington, Oxfordshire. A grove of rose bushes was planted at the site.

After his wife's death, Fred travelled a great deal, often with his older daughter, Leila. After Leila's graduation from Oxford, in August 1954 father and daughter sailed first class on the *Empress of Australia* to Quebec City. The immigration records report mysteriously that when he arrived at the Port of Quebec, he was "not in possession of necessary travel documents." There is no further indication of what happened, but he was apparently allowed into the country because on September 28, they are recorded arriving back at Liverpool on the *Empress of Scotland*, having departed Montreal.

It would be Fred McGarvey's last trip home to his native Canada, the country to which he had originally planned to relocate after he escaped Austria. Currency exchange restrictions had prevented him from pursuing his fondest wish. Eight years later, in October 1962, Fred sounded a wistful tone as he wrote to a distant cousin, Orville Gamble, in Athelstan, Quebec, not far from where his father had been born: "I doubt that I will see Canada again."

In the winter of 1955, Fred and Leila holidayed on the Spanish island of Tenerife, arriving back home on March 12. Leila took a trip alone to New York City on the *Britannic*, in August 1960.

By the mid- to late-1950s, Mamie was growing ever more feeble, entirely deaf and ill, although she was able to make a final trip to visit Fred in England in 1962. Fred, whose hearing was severely impaired by this time, began to spend more time at the castle looking after Mamie and her affairs. On one of his visits, in 1959, Fred and Mamie were approached by an old friend of the countess, Georg Graf von Plettenberg, with an attractive offer. Sell Schloss Graschnitz to me, Plettenberg suggested, and I will let the countess remain for the rest of her days.

Mamie, Fred and his daughters were saddened at the prospects of Schloss Graschnitz slipping from the family's hands, but with Mamie growing increasingly feeble and the rest of the dwindling family in England, it made sense to sell. Fred's financial acumen never left him, however. He struck a deal with Plettenberg and a selling price of 7,650,000 pounds was agreed upon. Plettenberg initially handed over five million pounds

— the balance to be paid in 1962 — and moved in to the first floor of the Kellerhaus, the estate structure that had been the vacation abode for Fred, Madge and their daughters for many years.

The 1960s marked a cultural and social revolution for the western world, a time of tumult and division. Civil rights, the Vietnam War, flower power and psychedelia, and the turn-on, tune-in and drop-out counter-culture philosophy of Timothy Leary disrupted the post-war tranquility that had descended throughout the 1950s. It was a stark break from the genteel Victorian period that had given birth to the four generations of McGarveys who built an oil empire and then basked in its wealth.

The decade also marked the commencement of the family's final days. Within a short time, three of the remaining family members would die: Mamie, her brother Fred, and his daughter Leila.

Countess Mamie von Zeppelin was home at Schloss Graschnitz on November 7, 1962, when she fell and suffered a fracture to the ball and socket joint of her upper femur or thighbone. It is a difficult break to occur but when it does, the ball is disconnected from the rest of the femur. The important thing with what is called a "femoral neck fracture" is that the blood supply to the fractured portion of the bone is often damaged as well and if this happens, there is a good likelihood that it will never heal. Today, hip replacement is usually the best course of action.

Mamie was taken to hospital in Graz but due to her advanced age – she was now eighty-seven – the medical options were limited. She was immobilized to make her as comfortable as possible, and to allow whatever healing might occur to commence. The prognosis was not good. Fred was called to Mamie's hospital bedside and a Protestant rite was administered. Mamie died at the hospital on November 29, 1962. Her remains were cremated and Fred took them back to England for interment in the family gravesite at Headington.

Count Plettenberg took over the estate. For the first time in nearly seven decades, the castle that had provided refuge for three generations of McGarveys passed on to someone new. Plettenberg opened a riding school which was eventually taken over by his son, Christian Ducker-Plettenberg and his wife, Isabella. As a young boy, Christian had known Mamie and often played at the estate grounds.

It was just a year after Mamie's death when Fred suffered a coronary from complications of emphysema and on November 25, 1963, three days after the assassination of John F. Kennedy, he died, with daughter Leila at his Manor Farm House bedside. Molly left her place in London and moved out to the farm where she lived with her sister until Leila died the following April.

Now Fred and Leila were also interred at the family plot at Headington, next to Mamie, beneath the rose bushes.

Molly was now alone and the last descendant of William Henry and Helena McGarvey. With George and Emmi Gibson helping out – he with the gardening and she with the housekeeping – Molly remained at Manor Farm House but in 1968 she sold a portion of the property to a hospital corporation. The next year, the hospital sold the land to developers and a housing complex was built there. Molly never forgave them.

George Stuart, who for many years enjoyed a spiritual companionship with Molly, paid frequent visits to Manor Farm House during the 1960s and early 1970s. Stuart knew that music had always formed an important part of the family life and noted that "the great pianist, Arthur Rubinstein," had been among the "many distinguished visitors" who had frequented the McGarvey home back in Vienna. When Stuart came down from his home in Oxford for visits, he would bring Molly stacks of books and learned that her favourites were biographies about talented people, including writers, dancers, actors and so on.

Stuart enjoyed his visits to Manor Farm. "Both the house and gardens were truly lovely. I still recall innumerable happy summer days lazing under the many fine mature trees which once stood where (a housing development) has been built. Christmas was also special, with all the traditional trimmings and many happy evenings spent around the grand piano singing songs and excerpts from opera."

Because of her love of music and her connections to opera and other classics that stretched back to Vienna, Molly developed many friendships in the British theatre. One of them was with the sixth Earl of Harewood, first cousin to the Queen and a grandson of Queen Victoria. Harewood served as director of the Royal Opera House and managing director of the English National Opera and later was president of the BBC.

It was through Harewood's recommendation that Molly ended up hiring his "daily" or house-cleaner. Molly came to enjoy quiet moments after the daily had completed her work, during which they would sit down for a cup of tea. "They loved to share gossip about what the royals were doing," said Carol Chew.

In the early 1970s, shocked by the damage the housing development had done to her property, Molly sold Manor Farm House and bought a home in the northwest London neighbourhood of St. John's Wood. It was just a few streets from where her mother had been raised by John and Clara Bergheim and where Leila herself had been born.

When Ron and Lynda Walsh moved temporarily from the United States to a townhouse next to Molly in St. John's Wood, Molly was one of the first to welcome them to the neighbourhood. "I was heading for a walk down the street and she happened to be in her front garden and hailed to me," Ron Walsh wrote later. "She was so perky and friendly. You couldn't help but fall in love with her immediately."

The Walshes became friends and often shared dinner conversation with Molly. "She regaled us with stories of her grandfather (William) and his brother (James). She told us the story of (James') murder. She must have been a woman of many talents. She showed me some watercolours she did as a young girl which were just beautiful."

In Molly's later years, she became increasingly frail but "she was so vibrant that I didn't think of her as frail really, until the last couple of years of our time in London. She enriched our lives with the fascinating stories she would tell of her life experiences. She was fiercely independent."

On her Christmas trips to friends around England, Molly would be loaded down with gifts of chocolates from the Continent, which she continued to send annually even after her travelling days were over. Other friends were frequently appreciative recipients of Molly's gift-giving. "She was a giving person," said Bea Bushnell, who received frequent packages of Earl Grey tea from England at her California home. In her will, Molly also bequeathed her grandfather's portrait to Bushnell. It has since been lost.

In her later years as she struggled with memory loss, Molly would often fall back onto the German language with which she was very familiar and evidently more comfortable.

Molly was two days short of ninety-six when she died from the effects of cancer. "Her life ended peacefully and without pain about 5 p.m. on April 7, 2002, in bed at her home in St. John's Wood, London," her cousin, David Banting wrote to friends. "Her nurse, Ann, was present, as she has been all day, every day, for some six months."

Banting had visited Molly every two or three weeks for the last four years of her life. "Molly was superbly independent and intensely private," he said. As he began the task of notifying those whom she had kept in touch with, he realized how wide a range of friendships she had kept up.

She had asked Banting, then the vicar at St. Peter's Church in Harold Wood, to conduct the service and asked for the music of Frederick Delius to be played. She adored *Walk To the Paradise Garden*, Banting recalled, and so he chose it as the main piece for her service.

Molly wished to be cremated and buried next to her parents, Fred and Madge, her sister, Leila, aunts Mamie, Kate and Nellie, and grandparents William and Helena McGarvey, back in Headington. After the service, as per Molly's wishes, a brief afternoon tea was held at the nearby Randolph Hotel in Oxford.

David Banting purchased a plaque to commemorate Molly and Leila, and had it placed in a small colonnade where they are buried with their ancestors. Since no funds had been set aside to maintain the other plots in the family burial site, said Banting, "only leaves on a rose bed" remain.

Molly was a great animal-lover. Once she discovered a duck had laid an egg in the garden of her home at St. John's Wood and immediately telephoned her neighbour, insisting that he come over to see it. When she died, Molly left more than 1.5 million British pounds to animal charities. Throughout her life she had regularly donated to such charities.

As the last direct descendant of William and Helena McGarvey, the wealth and possessions Molly distributed through her last will and testament represented the final legacy of the Petroleum King of Austria – the "lucky man" who had learned the science and created the technology of oil, and in creating an empire of oil, transformed himself into the most successful of Canada's Foreign Drillers.

CHAPTER 18

EPILOGUE TO MCGARVEY AND
THE FOREIGN DRILLERS

William Henry McGarvey was a natural leader, born with the kind of charisma and talent that seems to have preordained success – but success that did not come without hard work and perseverance, and a skillful application of his scientifically inclined mind. As a boy, McGarvey honed those innate skills in his father's frontier business before setting off upon his own entrepreneurial path. He could have chosen any number of paths in life – including politics in which he showed an aptitude – but it is hard to imagine any of them would have led him anyplace but to accomplishment.

McGarvey was not unique in the path he took, only in the level of success he enjoyed. He was one of Canada's Foreign Drillers who came primarily from Petrolia, but also from Oil Springs, Sarnia, Bothwell and other area communities in Lambton and Kent counties, Ontario. They left their own country for better opportunities at a time when the domestic industry was flagging. From the 1870s into the 1940s, these pioneers of Canadian oil travelled to eighty-six countries, in Europe, Russia, the Middle East, Southeast Asia, Africa, Mexico, the West Indies, South America, the United States and Australia, where they quickly became recognized and valued for their skills, their tenacity and their innovation. They introduced Canadian drilling methods, know-how and equipment. Their numbers were modest, likely not many more than five hundred, but their impact was enormous. In modern-day parlance, we might say that they "punched above their weight."

They put the small town of Petrolia, Ontario, on the world map. The late Dorothy Stevenson, the daughter of a Foreign Driller, recalled a story told by John Braybrook, a friend of her father's, about the first time he arrived back to the Port of New York from a job he had taken in what Petrolians called the "Foreign Fields."

"The customs officer asked him where he was going and he said he was going to Canada, to Toronto. The customs officer said, 'where's that?' And Mr. Braybrook said, 'I actually come from a little town called Petrolia' and the customs officer said, 'Oh, I know that place. We have someone from there come through about every other month'."

The modern oil industry was built in no small part by McGarvey and the other Canadians who learned their trade the hard way – by the process of trial and error, in the oil fields of Lambton County and Kent County, Ontario. John Henry Fairbank, one of Lambton County's petroleum pioneers and who became known as Petrolia's patriarch, gave testimony to an Ontario provincial Royal Commission studying oil in 1890 about the worldwide demand for, and the accomplishments of the Foreign Drillers. This is part of what he said:

> The cause of the demand is that they have superior tools and possess superior intelligence (knowledge). Our manufacturers of tools have succeeded in getting the greatest possible strength within the smallest limit, and the training here makes the men perfect in their department. When they come in contact with any of the European drillers, they distance (outpace) them completely. The men are largely the sons of settlers and people who drifted into the oil business. The work is very hard, and requires a strong frame and a clear head. Our men become great experts at it. By handling the pole, they can tell what is going on down below one thousand feet as well as if they were there.

The late Arnold Thompson, who spent a year drilling in Cuba in 1904 before returning home to spend the rest of his working life in Lambton's fields, added this thought: "They were ingenious men. There was nothing that came up they wouldn't tackle and be successful."

In McGarvey's case, he succeeded in making the province of Galicia, for one shining moment in time, the third-largest oil producer in the world. No other Foreign Driller proved more successful at creating an oil empire on the world stage. McGarvey's reach went far beyond Galicia, too: he had his own petroleum operations in Russia and Romania, was a speculative investor in the Canadian oil sands and California, owned refineries throughout Europe, built pipelines and sold his own oil drilling equipment – some of which he invented and patented himself – to companies around the world.

McGarvey was one of Canada's early entrepreneurial success stories and its first international petroleum tycoon – a true oil baron. He led the way in the period during which petroleum emerged from its humble beginnings and evolved into what was about to become the primary industry of our society.

While most of the Foreign Drillers spent their careers in the employ of others and made far better wages than they would ever have earned in Canada, McGarvey was one of the handful of them who established overseas companies that became highly successful. A few settled in their new lands, including Poland and the United States. Their descendants can be found there to this day.

Maclean's Magazine published an article in 2012 that identified a handful of Canadians who left Canada and made successful reputations in other countries. Andrew Bonar Law, for example, who was born in Rexton, New Brunswick in 1858, rose to the pinnacle of British politics and served as prime minister. He is still known as the only prime minister of that country who was not born in the British Isles.

The magazine's list was one that was woefully short of businesspeople. Missing from the list are those who made their mark in petroleum, Canada's Foreign Drillers. A few, including William Henry McGarvey, deserve to be there. The experience of the Foreign Drillers is one of a sort of reverse migration. Canada's history has been based upon the arrival of waves of immigration from faraway lands – people who brought with them the culture and language of their diverse homelands and enriched the country they adopted as their new home. The Foreign Drillers travelled in the opposite direction, taking with them the knowledge they learned in Canada, and sharing and adapting it in their new homelands.

While William McGarvey is undoubtedly foremost among Canada's Foreign Drillers, he has remained little known in his homeland. He is better known today in Poland as the founder and creator of that country's petroleum industry than he is in his native Canada. There is a park in Gorlice, Galicia named for him, his work is studied by students of the oil and refining business there, and his first factory, in Glinik Mariampolski, still exists.

Other Canadian Foreign Drillers who created thriving petroleum businesses overseas include brothers Jake and Cyrus Perkins and their brother-in-law, George MacIntosh, who built an important drilling equipment manufacturing firm. Descendants of the Perkinses still live overseas. To this day, one can find Polish-speaking workers named Perkins still employed in Poland's petroleum industry.

Others ended up in the United States and also accomplished a great deal. Among them were the Nicklos family who remained engaged in oil drilling in Texas up until the turn of this century. They are descended from Charles Nicklos, who left Petrolia in 1885 and found himself managing several properties owned by McGarvey, including the Mariampol refinery.

And in Austria, where McGarvey was known as the Petroleum King, it can be argued that the heir to his throne was another Canadian — Keith Van Sickle, who did battle with authorities in the Soviet Union-occupied zone to regain control of the petroleum company he built there. Van Sickle's son, James, finally sold the company in 1996, bringing an end to his family's story in Austrian oil.

Caught Up In Strife

Even though they wanted nothing more than to earn a living – and many achieved that goal in grand style – the Foreign Drillers often found themselves embroiled in politics, in revolution and in world war. McGarvey was one of those brought down by forces far outside his ability to control.

He died at the start of the Great War, a war that was fought with petroleum products, in which the battle for control of petroleum became a crucial goal. As historian Daniel Yergin wrote: "(World War I) was a war that was fought between men and machines. And these machines were powered by oil."

While McGarvey was the highest achiever among those Canadian Foreign Drillers, and on occasion dubbed "the European Rockefeller," he remained the little independent operator – oil driller, refiner, equipment manufacturer, owner of pipelines and storage facilities. His companies never came close to rivalling John D. Rockefeller's Standard Oil. McGarvey's Galician Carpathian Petroleum Company did not survive to challenge Standard Oil or Royal Dutch Shell, and his empire never rivalled that of the Nobels or the Rothschilds.

Those companies, however, were headed by businessmen who were experts in growing their companies and making money. They were not headed by oil technicians, experts in obtaining petroleum. McGarvey was both a businessman and an oil technician.

He was often called upon for his opinions and observations, his expertise respected in the hallowed halls of the oil industry and the British Parliament.

McGarvey was Canadian-born, and throughout his life he remained a proud Canadian and a proud subject of the British Empire. However, he did not consider his European-based enterprise a "Canadian" company. He was an entrepreneur, an international capitalist.

When he introduced his Canadian-learned methods to Europe, McGarvey was ushered into the world of the rich and famous. He socialized with Europe's nobility and enjoyed a privileged lifestyle. There is no telling what he, his two brothers and his son might have achieved had the Great War not interceded, bringing a halt to the business of the company that formed the core of his holdings and even hastening his own death.

McGarvey called himself a lucky man, and for much of his career it would be difficult to argue with that. It took war and revolution to bring an end to his good fortune, to bring down his empire and end his life. Yet the remnants of what McGarvey had achieved survived. After his death, his son put together the pieces of the family company and sold them off, creating a financial bonanza for the family and financing privileged lifestyles and successful careers.

None of them ever returned to live in Canada.

A Final World On The 'Foreign Drillers' Term

In this modern era, some prefer to refer to this crew of Canadian oil experts as the "international drillers," perhaps because the word "foreign" has fallen from favour, or perhaps because it leaves it unclear just exactly who they were. The term "foreign" could beg the question: Were these people Canadians working offshore, or were they people from distant lands who came here to work?

But they were originally, in the streets of Petrolia, called the Foreign Drillers, which is why I believe it is best they remain that way.

APPENDIX 1

The history of drilling

The top layer of soil in Lambton County was about sixty to one hundred feet (eighteen to thirty metres) of clay. Early hunters of oil dug this out by hand but soon afterwards, an auger, originally powered by a horse walking in circles, was used to drill through it. One-inch boards, usually pine, were placed inside the hole to prevent it from collapsing.

Once the hole was dug to bedrock, percussion tool drilling technology used in bringing in salt mines and water wells was used. Originally a spring pole was the favoured method. A "drill bit" was fastened to the end and driven down into the rock. Progress was slow, perhaps two metres a day.

As described by William McGarvey himself in *Oil Fields of the Empire*: "The first method of drilling in Oil Springs was by means of a spring pole. The process of putting down a hole was slow and laborious, and many months were necessarily spent in drilling a well to a depth which at the present time (1910) would occupy only two or three days."

A tripod derrick was built overtop the hole. This consisted of three poles of about six to nine metres in length, placed above the spot to be dug, fastened at the top with an iron ring. A rope, made from manila hemp, was attached to the end of the spring pole and the foot was placed into a loop of the rope. By pulling down on the loop and releasing it back up, the drilling tool was lowered and raised and the bit therefore cut into the rock.

Sometimes instead of the looped rope, a wooden platform and treadle were built on a level with the pole, and a kicker forced down the pole by stepping on it. Then it was released and the pole would resume its normal position.

The percussion drilling process created rock filings that needed to be removed from the hole. When this was necessary, the tools were raised by means of a rope and pulley attached to the tripod derrick. A sand pump was devised, consisting of a long tube with a valve that was opened inwards by use of a pole. The tube would be lowered to the bottom of the hole, the valve would be opened and the tube pulled quickly upwards. The motion drew in the sand and water for removal, and the valve closed.

The Canadian system

As the oilmen became more adept, they looked for easier methods and devised a system for using wooden rods rather than rope. Rods were added as the hole was deepened and their combined weight helped to force the drill bit down to chip into the bedrock. These rods were made of the most common material available, which was black ash. Later, these were replaced with iron rods.

In *Oil Fields of the Empire*, McGarvey described when and where the Canadian or pole-tool method was first used:

> The first well drilled with poles instead of ropes, now known as the Canadian system, was put down in 1866-67 upon the Duncan farm, in the township of Enniskillen, by C.J. Webster of Hartford, Connecticut. … Although primitive in construction, the advantage of the system was recognised, and in a very short time improvements were made and brought it well to the front. That was the start of the Canadian drilling rig.

A Driller's Sixth Sense

A good driller needed to be intelligent, perceptive and physically strong. They also needed to be able to read the signs as a hole was drilled down. Much of the operation was taking place out of sight, many metres below the ground, and as a result it was often said a skilled driller needed to develop a "sixth sense."

"A competent and successful driller must be able to understand the language of his tools, as when drilling is in progress, the tools are addressing him constantly and telling him many things he should be able to interpret readily," Andrew M. Rowley wrote in an article for the *Oil and Gas Journal* in 1923.

Listening to the "choo (pause), choo (pause), cho-choo-choo-choo" of the steam engine conveyed the lifting and dropping of the drilling tools within the hole, Rowley said. Then there was the spring in the cable when the walking beam "picks up" the tools and the vibration in the cable indicating whether the hole is adequately sized and drilled in a true line. Each sign is crucially important if the driller is to complete his job – to drill a well in the least time and with the least possible mishaps.

Drillers kept records of the formation passed through and, when inevitably something went wrong, they were responsible for figuring out how to fix it. For example, through no fault of his own, a driller could "jump a pin"– meaning the threads on the pin might slip – letting the tools fall into the hole.

"The successful driller possesses good judgement, bold initiative and considerable mechanical ability," wrote Rowley. "He must be able not only to sense and avoid dangers, exercise patience and constant vigilance, but also solve numerous puzzling problems."

APPENDIX II

Glinik Factory

The private company, Bergheim & McGarvey, established its first oil refinery and tool repair workshop in 1885, two years after the partners began drilling in Galicia. When the company became publicly traded in 1895, the workshop and factory was renamed Fabryka Maszyn I Narzedzi Wiertniczych (Machinery and Drilling Tools Factory). It was known as the finest in Europe, exporting drilling rigs, pumps, steam engines, impact drills and tools for shaft drilling around the world.

During the Second World War, it became Karpathen Oil AG, a German national company. After the war, it became the Centralne Warsztaty Naftowe (Central Oil Workshops) and added rotary tools and deep-drilling tools to its catalogue.

In 1962, the factory was again renamed, this time Fabryka Maszyn I Sprzetu Wiertniczego Glinik (Glinik Machine and Drilling Equipment Factory).

Six years later, the factory began putting out mechanized mining machines and equipment, as well as hydraulic roof supports for coal mines. A new forge and power plant were built and production grew significantly as a result of its unique designs and technology. In 1973, it was renamed Fabryka Maszyn Wiertniczych I Gorniczych Glinik (Glinik Drilling and Mining Equipment Factory).

Growth continued in the 1980s with the addition of roof supports for mining applications and expansion into coal mining equipment with ploughs, conveyors and longwall systems. Now wholly owned by the state, Fabryka Maszyn Glinik S.A. (Glinik Machine Factory Corporation) was restructured and land and buildings were sold. Separate factories were created, including Kuznia Glinik (Glinik Forge Ltd.), Narzedzia I Urzadzenia Wiertnicze Glinik (Glinik Drilling Tools and Equipment), and Zaklad Maszyn Gorniczych Glinik (Glinik Mining Machinery).

In 2001, a decade after the fall of the Soviet Union, a company was created by management and employees named Inwest Glinik (Invest Glinik). The company purchased an eighty-eight percent interest in Fabryka Maszyn Glinik.

A decade later, the Polish investment company TDJ S.A. acquired the Glinik Group of Companies of Gorlice. TDJ Corporation acquired a block of shares in Fabryka Maszyn Glinik and took control of its subsidiaries.

After further intense restructuring, in 2013, Kuznia Glinik joined Polska Grupa Odlwenicza (Polish Foundry Group) under a share purchase arrangement.

Today, the successor to William McGarvey's original machine shop operates under the name Narzedzia I Urzadzenia Wiertnicze (NiUW Glinik).

Glimar Refinery

The world-class refinery constructed by William McGarvey was largely destroyed during the First World War. Afterwards, Fred McGarvey and other large shareholders from the Galician Carpathian Petroleum Company sold their shares and Pétroles-Premier-Malopolska was created to operate the refinery.

A German company, Wolff, experimented with a cutting-edge cracking system in the 1930s, but the start of the Second World War prevented its full installation. During the war, the refinery produced much-needed products for the Nazi war machine. When the Soviets neared the plant's gates, the Germans disassembled much of the plant and moved it to various other locations.

By 1949, the plant had been restructured and rebuilt. Modernizations continued and by the early 1960s, the plant was processing 1.1 million barrels of crude a year.

The refinery's old Glimar name was reestablished in 1984. The plant continued its modernization program and after Poland gained autonomy from the Soviet Bloc, Glimar was reorganized into a privately managed corporation. Refining capacity reached 3.65 million barrels a year. Various fuel fractions were produced.

In 1997, Glimar was fully privatized. In some cases, workers established their own outsourced services to sell back to the company.

The refinery diversified, expanding into bio-ethanol fuel, a small chain of gas stations and renovation of an existing hotel and conference centre. These were then spun off as independent companies.

However, difficult economic times hit the company hard in the early 2000s and Glimar Oil Refinery was sold to Grupa Lotos S.A. and later to Hydronaft. In 2011, the Toronto-based Hudson Oil Corporation Ltd. acquired Hydronaft and with it the Glimar refinery.

While Hudson announced exciting new plans for Glimar, costs became prohibitive and the facility was permanently shut down.

NOTES ON SOURCES

General Sources

Reverend David Banting of Harold Woods, Essex, UK, a cousin of Molly and Leila McGarvey, provided Molly's painstakingly produced family tree, as well as family guestbooks and diary entries, photographs and insights into the family, as well as his own detailed recollections. His work in aid of the author was tireless and he always had time to answer "just one more question." The genealogical research was commenced by Fred McGarvey and passed on to Molly who became the keeper of the family story. Banting also provided materials about John Bergheim and his family. Guestbooks kept by Madge McGarvey and Mamie von Zeppelin provided names of visitors, home addresses and remarks and observations.

Carol and Dan Chew of Silver Spring, MD, conveyed their recollections of the McGarveys as well as passing on those of Dan's mother, Beth Chew. Mamie, the Countess von Zeppelin, chronicled details of her experiences during wartime in letters to Beth Chew, as well as to Fred McGarvey and other friends. Carol Chew also provided photographs of Schloss Graschnitz and McGarvey family members from Beth's collection.

Additional details of Molly's and Leila's lives were compiled from information provided by George Stuart (from the online source headington. org), and in letters from Patricia and Sonia Lindsay, Ron and Lynda Walsh of Houston, and Bea Bushnell of California. The author corresponded with the Lindsay sisters.

Charles Fairbank III helped provide funding for the author's research trip to Poland and Austria. Charlie and his wife, Pat McGee, offered immeasurable help, guidance and encouragement throughout this project. Pat is the author of *The Story of Fairbank Oil* (Petrolia: 2004, Words Unlimited Ink).

David Ingleby of Utrecht, Netherlands provided information about James McGarvey's branch of the family from which he is descended, including his own recollections and a letter James's wife, Julia, wrote to a friend in England describing her experiences in Russia.

Joan Darby of Pittsburgh, PA shared information about the Perkins and Nicklos families and their work with McGarvey.

The author commissioned genealogist Tessa Szczepanik of Kent, England, to collect research material from the National Archives on the British Royal Commission on Fuel and Engines.

Nicole Aszalos, archivist/supervisor of the Lambton County Archives, Erin Dee-Richard, curator/supervisor of the Oil Museum of Canada and their staff members helped locate materials at their respective institutions. Earlier assistance was offered by former archivist Dana Thorne and former museum curator Connie Bell. Special thanks to Liz Welsh of Petrolia, manager of Petrolia Discovery, whose enthusiasm for this project was limitless.

Slawomir Duran of Jaslo, Poland provided information about Eleanor Hamilton, Helena McGarvey's death, the Wesolowski family history, Beata Obertynska and her family, McGarvey colleagues such as Wladyslaw Dlugosz and August Gorayski, helped the author with translations of Polish documents into English, and offered advice on spelling the names of Eastern European communities. Any errors are those of the author.

Krakow, Poland-based guide/lecturer Tomasz Cebulski took the author through the historic Galician oil lands and museums and introduced him to Glimar chemist Maria Mockal, Marek Klara, Michal Gorecki and other officials of the Lukasiewicz Oil and Gas Museum in Bobyrka, and officials of the Glinik factory. Cebulski also located documents and helped with translations.

Maria Mockal worked for the Glimar refinery for forty-five years and retired as its manager of paraffin and asphalt production. She lived in the original McGarvey home in Mariampol. Her dream has always been to open the home as a McGarvey museum.

Vienna researcher Andrzej Selerowicz helped the author with his Vienna research, including translation of German-language records from the Austrian National Archives and other sources. Selerowicz also conveyed Christian Ducker-Plettenberg's childhood recollections of playing at Schloss Graschnitz. Also in Vienna, the late Dr. Hermann F. Sporker helped locate McGarvey burial and disinterment information.

Mary-Jane Selwood of Helensburgh, Scotland offered details of, and diaries from the Keith family, including Willie Keith's recollection of family members drilling with McGarvey. Her cousin, James Van Sickle of Vienna added records and recollections related to the Van Sickle family.

Details of the death at Schloss Graschnitz of Countess Mamie McGarvey come from the Archives of the Office of the Styrian Provincial Government in Graz, courtesy Dr. Peter Wiesflecker. The archives also provided information about the death of Helena McGarvey.

Additional McGarvey family genealogy — including birth notices, marriage and death certificates and addresses — is from census records and directories obtained through ancestry.ca.

A number of websites were used to discover additional source material, including "Poland's Petroleum Trail"; the history of Galician oil; the history of Gorlice; and "Petroleum in Galicia from the Drohobycz Administrative District, by Valerie Schatzker, Claudia Erdheim and Alexander Sharontitle.

Books and articles

The early history of Galicia's oil industry is detailed in a two-volume set, *Historia Polskiego Przemyseu Naftowego* (*History of the Polish Petroleum Industry*), edited by Ryszrda Wolwowicza (Brzozow-Krakow: 1994, Muzeum Regionalne). Other sources of early Galician oil history are from the Science Conference of Polish History, Bobrka, 1993; websites for The Petroleum Trail and the City of Gorlice; and "The Chaotic Saga of Oil in Galicia", by Jérôme Segal and Renaud Lavergne, translated by Janice M. Sellers.

Oil Empire: Visions of Prosperity in Austrian Galicia, by Alison Fleig Frank (Cambridge, MA: 2005, Harvard University Press) discusses the Galician industry of the era through the perspective of the social, economic and political conditions.

Titan: The Life of John D. Rockefeller Sr., by Ron Chernow (New York: 1998, Vintage Books) records the life of America's first billionaire and petroleum entrepreneur.

Oil Field Development and Petroleum Mining, by Arthur Beeby Thompson, (London: 1916, C. Lockwood and Son) is a good general description of early history and technology of the industry.

Further early history of Polish oil is discussed in Tomasz Sliwa, Marc A. Rosen and Zbigniew Jezuit, in "Use of Oil Boreholes in the Carpathians in Geoenergetic Systems From a Historical and Conceptual Review," *Research Journal of Environmental Sciences*, 2014, 8: 231-242.

Various editions of the *Imperial Oil Review* contained articles about McGarvey and the other Foreign Drillers. The magazine was published 1917-2014. Many copies are available at the Oil Museum of Canada in Oil Springs. In digital form, it is available on the Glenbow Museum of Calgary website (glenbow.org).

Specific Source Materials

Introduction

William Henry McGarvey's words on the oil industry's first half-century are from the preface to *Oil Fields of the Empire*, by J.D. Henry (London: 1910, Bradbury, Agnew & Co. Ltd.)

Chapter 1

McGarvey's recollection of the cow incident is translated from Beata Obertynska's "Quodlibecik" in *Memories* (Warsaw: 1974, State Publishing Institute). McGarvey recounted his story to Mrs. Obertynska and her family when she was a child.

Details of early Huntingdon are from *The History of the County of Huntingdon and the Seigniories of Chateaugay and Beauharnois*, by Robert Sellar (Huntingdon, QU: 1888, *The Canadian Gleaner*). A description of the Huntingdon region's natural vegetation is from "The landscape history of Godmanchester," by Gerald Domon and André Bouchard, published in Springer Science + Business Media, 2007; and from Gordon Hope's pamphlet, "A Brief History of Huntingdon," published 2006.

McGarvey family birth, christening, marriage and death records are from the Episcopal Church, and the Wesleyan Methodist Church, Huntingdon, QU., and the Wesleyan Methodist Baptismal Register from 1828-1910.

Edward McGarvey's sawmill is mentioned in his obituary carried in the *Huntingdon Gleaner*, 23 June 1900; the sawmill is listed and located in John Lovell's *Canada Directory*, (Montreal: 1851).

The Huntingdon Academy is mentioned in the article, "Romantic Career," in *Toronto Saturday Night Magazine,* 29 October 1931.

Victor Lauriston wrote about McGarvey's early career in "Oil In the Splendid Sixties," *Maclean's Magazine*, 15 April 1921.

The Tripp brothers' International Mining and Manufacturing Co. is referenced in *The County of Lambton Gazetteer and Business Directory for 1864-5*, Sutherland Bros., Ingersoll, Canada West: 1864, p. 100. The description of Wyoming is from p. 19.

The *Sarnia Observer* and its various other titles recorded pertinent historical events, including the opening of the Great Western Railway branch from London to Sarnia in 1856. *The London Free Press* frequently carried news from the oil lands and is used extensively.

Facts about Petrolia's early history are as reported by the *Advertiser* (under its various names), the *Topic* and, after amalgamation the *Advertiser-Topic*.

Messers E. McGarvey & Co. of Wyoming is referenced in *Counties of Lambton, Kent and Essex Gazette*, 1867.

William McGarvey described his own early experiences in oil in the preface he wrote for *Oil Fields of the Empire* by James Dodds Henry (London: 1910; Bradbury, Agnew & Co. Ltd.)

The location where McGarvey established and first used the Canadian pole-tool drilling system was identified with the help of researcher Colleen Inglis.

J.E. Brantly reflected on the development of the Canadian pole tool drilling system, and McGarvey's contribution to it, in *The History of Oil Well Drilling*, (Houston: 1971, Gulf Publishing Company).

The building of the Petrolia spur rail line is explained by R.B. Harkness in "Ontario's Part in the Petroleum Industry," an unpublished manuscript; and Report of the Directors, No. 26, Great Western Railway of Canada for 1866-67.

The McGarveys' marriage is recorded in Michigan County Marriages, 1820-1935 for Macomb County, Marriage indexes 1861-1867, v. E, p. 329.

Details of McGarvey's life and career, as well as physical descriptions, are compiled from obituaries and tributes published in various Canadian, Austrian, German and Polish newspapers and periodicals of the era.

Charles Whipp and Edward Phelps published an excellent description of early Petrolia, its buildings, its people and events, in *Petrolia 1866-1966*, (Petrolia: 1967, Advertiser-Topic Press).

Wilfred Durham "Willie" Keith's recollections date from January 1950 and were compiled at the request of his nephew, Keith van Sickle, a Vienna oilman who sought the background for a speech he gave in the United States about early oil exploration.

John Henry Fairbank discussed the early oil industry in testimony to the Royal Commission on the Mineral Resources of Ontario (Toronto: 1890, Warwick & Sons). It is available online.

Whipp and Phelps concluded that McGarvey quit village council because with the influx of oil workers, the Mammoth Store required his full attention.

Chapter 2

Details of Ludwik Wesolowski's life and career, and his daughter, Helena Idwega Wesolowski, are from "Local History Sketches" at the Mount Clemens Public

Library, by Betty Lou Morris; from *Enduring Poles*, by Harry Milostan, Mount Clemens, MI: 1977; from *The Ill-Fated Clinton-Kalamazoo Canal*, by the Rochester, MI Historical Commission and Avon Township Public Library: 1983; and from ancestry.ca.

In an account of a speech given at a testimonial in Glinik Mariampolski to honour company official August Gorayski, McGarvey joked about why he spoke German rather than the local Polish language which he admitted he could never master. The account is from the McGarvey file at the Gorlice, Poland public library.

Articles of partnership for McGarvey's refinery, and a company invoice, are from the Lambton County Archives at Wyoming, ON.

John Scott's account of the 1873 gusher at the Deluge well is from *Imperial Oil Review*, Vol. XIV, No. 4, August/September 1930: Toronto.

Walter Sheldon Tower's *The Story of Oil* (New York: 1909, D. Appleton and Co.) explains the American standard drilling system.

Historical events are from local newspaper accounts, including the *Sarnia Observer* and the *Petrolia Advertiser*. Census records and municipal directories were helpful in locating residences and business addresses. Directories and newspapers were used to locate advertisements.

Canada's National Archives online service was used to locate Revenue Department records of Edward McGarvey's legal problems and fine.

James Dibb's recollection of encountering McGarvey and friends on the train is from the *Petrolia Topic*, 13 March 1947.

Chapter 3

A description of Petrolia is from the *Illustrated Atlas of the Dominion of Canada*. (Toronto: 1880, H. Belden and Co.)

John Sinclair wrote about the Foreign Drillers in an article for the *Petrolia Advertiser-Topic*, 28 February 1924. Helen Corey recounted the story of the farewell to the first Foreign Drillers at the Petrolia train station in a 17 September 1992 interview with Hope Morritt, author of *Rivers of Oil* (Kingston: 1993, Quarry Press); *Maclean's Magazine*, 1 May 1924, contained an account of the first Foreign Drillers who went to Southeast Asia.

The author used Mal Scott's 1874 letters published in the Petrolia *Advertiser* to approximate the departure date of the first Foreign Drillers.

Experiences of the early Foreign Drillers are from *Hard Oiler! The Story of Early Canadians' Quest for Petroleum at Home and Abroad*, by Gary May.

(Toronto: 1998, Dundurn Press), and from *The Scent of Oil*, by Gary May (Windsor: 2014: Your Story Publishing).

McGarvey's letters to Sir John A. Macdonald were obtained from the National Archives of Canada, Sir John A. Macdonald papers, vol. 3354.

Facts about Bergheim's early life are from *Finding The Bergheims Of Belsize Court*, by Mary Shenai (London: 2007, Belsize Conservation Area Advisory Committee); Bergheim family genealogy is from ancestry.ca; A. Raymond Mullens mentions Bergheim's 1879 visit to Petrolia in "Liquid Gold," *Maclean's Magazine*, 15 April 1931; a copy of the official portrait of McGarvey and Bergheim in Petrolia published in the *Imperial Oil Review*, vol. XIV, no. 4, August/September 1930 also dates the visit to 1879.

Speculation over John Bergheim's father's religion and conversion from Judaism to Christianity is from both Mary Shenai's work and an article by Bert M. Zuckerman, "Peter Bergheim's Holy Land Stereoviews," in *Stereo World* magazine, Vol. 26, No. 6, January/February 2000, pages 10-17.

McGarvey's use of the Canadian or pole-tool drilling system is referenced in *Petroleum* magazine, Volume 4. Vienna: 1914, p. 170. The Canadian system's impact on petroleum in Europe is described in the author's interview with Stanislaw Szafran in Krakow, 11 June 2007.

Chapter 4

A family memorandum prepared by Fred McGarvey in 1959 follows the family's treks back and forth across the Atlantic from Petrolia to Hanover and then on to Mariampolski. It is this account that clears up contradictory accounts of when McGarvey went to Galicia and founded his company there.

The progress of McGarvey's business is taken from various newspaper accounts and census reports.

Oil discoveries in Celle and Oelheim, Germany are outlined in *Studies In Early Petroleum History* by R.J. Forbes, Vol. 1 (Leiden, Netherlands: 1958, E.J. Brill).

A description of Nellie McGarvey, and her friends, is from *Charlotte and Jake: A Love Story*, by Judith Keightley.

Chapter 5

The Canadian pole tool drilling system is described in *Early Development of Oil Technology*, by Wanda Pratt and Phil Morningstar (Oil Springs: 1987, Oil Museum of Canada.) The pamphlet describes early drilling practices in Canada.

Dorothy Stevenson's remarks are from an interview with the author in 1997.

Some family developments are from Fred McGarvey's ancestral memo written in 1959.

The description of early oil collection methods in Galicia appeared in "The Chaotic Saga of Oil in Galicia," by Segal and Lavergne, December 2012. The system of leases and drilling rights in Galicia is explained in *Chemiker und Techniker Zeitung* (*The Chemist and Technician* newspaper), 1914; volume 8, p. 61. The same volume of *Chemiker und Techniker Zeitung* described ownership of petroleum resources in Galicia before the time of McGarvey.

Szczepanowski's approach to McGarvey is from the author's June 2007 interview with Stanislaw Szafran in Krakow. Szafran also detailed the carnival atmosphere that surrounded the arrival of McGarvey's drilling teams.

The part played by Jewish workers in the Galician fields is discussed in "A History of the Jews of Boryslaw," translated by D. Shimon Barak and edited by Valerie Schatzker.

A description of transportation in late nineteenth-century Galicia is from *The Jewish Oil Magnates of Galicia*, Valerie Schatzker (Montreal: 2015, McGill-Queen's University Press); details of McGarvey and Bergheim's first trip to Galicia are translated from *Pioneers of the Polish Refining Industry*, a paper produced for the Lukasiewicz Oil and Gas Museum, Bobrka, Poland.

Sir Thomas Boverton Redwood discussed McGarvey's seminal contributions to the oil industry in Eastern Europe in *The Petroleum Technologist's Pocket-Book* (London: 1915, Charles Griffin & Co. Ltd.)

Ignacy Lukasiewicz's work on the development of kerosene and oil-burning lamps is from Dr. Stanislaw Szfran, from William McGarvey's tribute to August Gorayski, and from the Lukasiewicz Museum of the Petroleum Industry in Bobrka.

Driller's intuition is discussed in "Sixth Sense Acquired By the Driller," by Andrew M. Rowley, from *The Oil and Gas Journal*, 1 February 1923, p. 11, obtained from the Oil Museum of Canada, Box 5910. Further details from this article can be found in the Appendixes section of this book. John Henry Fairbank described the skills of a Canadian driller, as well as the jerker-line system he invented, to the Royal Commission on Mineral Resources in Ontario, 1890.

Wilfred "Willie" Keith's remarks and descriptions of the McGarvey drilling site are courtesy of his daughter, Mary-Jane Selwood of Scotland.

The establishment of McGarvey's first refinery is chronicled in "The History of The Hudson Oil Corporation," by Hudson Oil of Toronto. Hudson Oil purchased the old Glimar refinery in 2011 and re-opened as Glimar Hudson Oil. It has since been permanently closed. Further details of the refinery's history are in Appendix II.

Details of the Galician drilling rigs and winter protection are compiled from the author's interviews with Marek Klara, Michal Gorecki and others at the Lukesiewicz Museum of the Oil and Gas Industry, Bobrka, Poland, June 2007.

Chapter 6

Evidence McGarvey did not sell his home is from an advertisement for the same property on 1 October 1888, and from McGarvey's last will and testament dated November 1914.

The site of the McGarvey home was located by former Glimar refinery employee, chemist Maria Mockal of Gorlice, Poland. Fred McGarvey established the year the family moved to Mariampol. Details of the first Bergheim & McGarvey administrative office and refinery are from the state archives in Rzeszow, Poland.

The history of early Galician railways is from *Historia Polskiego Przemyseu Naftowego.*

The Perkins family's observations of their early experiences in Galicia are provided by Joan Darby of Pittsburgh, PA.

General descriptions of the Galician countryside are compiled from *Here Lies A Most Beautiful Lady*, by Richard Blaker (New York: 1935, the Bobbs-Merrill Company); the Perkins family accounts; and translations from *Geographic Dictionary of the Polish Kingdom and Other Slavic Countries* (Slownik Geograficzny Krolestwa Polskiego I Innych Krajow Slowianskich), Wydany pod redakcja Bronislawa Chlebowskiego. (Warsaw: 1892).

Maria Mockal described McGarvey's "plantation" and home during an interview with the author in June 2007. Further insight into the local Polish people's philosophy and outlook is furnished by Krakow guide/lecturer Tomasz Cebulski.

Chapter 7

The reports of the train crash that killed Thomas McGarvey are from the *New York Times*, with further details of his fate from the *Aspen Weekly Times*, 21 October 1893.

Edward Wesley McGarvey's death was reported in the *Advertiser-Topic* on 13 February 1896.

The purchase of Schloss Graschnitz was described in a letter dated 6 March 1897 from Edward McGarvey to his brother, James, in Saskatchewan. Provided by the late James A. "Pete" McGarvey, of Orillia, Ontario. The description and some of the castle's history is from the website burgen-austria.com. Edward also wrote of his daughter-in-law, Annie, widow of Edward Wesley McGarvey.

Recollections of Schloss Graschnitz, Mamie von Zeppelin and the family of Fred McGarvey are from the author's correspondence with their cousins, Patricia and Sonia Lindsay, 2 November 2008, who lived at Holmes Farm, Hatherleigh, Okehampton, Devon. Sonia had further recollections of her father's visit to cousin Fred in Galicia.

Helena McGarvey's correspondence to Ann Reese, dated 27 December 1895, provided by Delores Broad (nee Reese) of Petrolia, granddaughter of Ann.

Fred McGarvey outlined his own education and work history in his ancestral memo of 1959. His discussion of Heidelberg University with Dan Chew is provided by Dan Chew. Fred also described his "gap year" trip to the Middle East and North America.

Early Austrian divorce law is explained in the article, "Austrian Divorce Law," *Journal of the Society of Comparative Legislation*, Vol. 12, No. 1 (1911), pp. 44-51.

Details of the Zeppelin family are from the Zeppelin Museum in Friedrichshafen, with the help of the late Dr. Hermann Sporker of Vienna.

Chapter 8

Austria-Hungary Kaiser Franz-Josef's life and accomplishments are obtained from *Emperor Franz Joseph: Life, Death and the Fall of the Habsburg Empire*, by John Van der Kiste (London: 2005, Sutton Publishing); *Franz Joseph and Elisabeth: The Last Great Monarchs of Austria-Hungary*, by Karen Owens (Jefferson, NC: 2013, McFarland Publishing); and the Kaiser Franz Josef Museum, Baden, Germany.

Descriptions of turn-of-the-century Vienna are from "How Vienna produced ideas that shaped the West," *The Economist*, 24 December 2016; and from various official Vienna websites.

The records of McGarvey's residential and commercial properties in Vienna are obtained from the Austrian National Archives. They are also mentioned in a history of Viennese buildings, Paul Harrer, *Wien Seine Hauser, Menschen und Kultur* (Vienna Houses, People and Culture: 1951), Vol. I, p. 135.

Details of the life of Erik Jurié von Lavandal are from *Neue Freie Presse*, Vienna, 3 May 1904; *Wiener Zeitung*, Vienna, 22 October 1914; and "News of Canadian fields" in the *Oil and Gas Journal*, 17 December 1914

Beata Wolsk Obertynska describes some of the over-the-top details of McGarvey's gift-giving in *Memories* (Warsaw: 1974, State Publishing Institute).

Chapter 9

Details of Wladyslaw Dlugosz's life and career are from biographical material provided by the Malopolski Instytut Kultury (the Malopolski cultural institution) in Krakow. Dlugosz's own recollections are included in *Boryslaw in okruchach wspomnień* (*Fragments of memories from Boryslaw*), by Adam Krupa and Boguslawa Krupa, published in 2000 by the Association of Friends of the Drohobycz Region.

Company business, including new oil strikes, was frequently recorded in the industry journals, primarily *Nafta*, as well as Austrian newspapers of the day, including *Kuryer Lwowski, Neuigkeits Welt Blat, Neue Freie Presse, Neues Wiener Journal, Die Arbeit, Wiener Montags-Journal*, and *Neues Wiener Tagblatt*, from 1888 to 1914. Profits and stock prices for the Karpath are from *Neues Wiener Journal*, 19 November 1899.

A copy of a typical Bergheim & McGarvey contract is from the Oil Museum of Canada, Document No. FD.001.003.001.d.

Training schools were discussed during the author's interview with Slavomir Duran; further details are translated from *Swiatlo z Ziem* (*Light from the Earth*), (Gorlice: 2002, Text Publishing House). The skills brought by Canadian oil workers are further discussed in Alison Fleig Frank's *Oil Empire*, p. 127.

The estimate of Boryslaw/Tustanowice oil production for 1909 is from *Wiek Nafty* (*The Oil Age*) by the Society of Oil and Gas Engineers and published by the Lukasiewicz Museum of Oil and Gas in Bobrka, December 1998; some other Galician oil production numbers are from Alison Fleig Frank in *Oil Empire, p. 92*.

A detailed description of the establishment of Galicia's oil fields is contained in *The Petroleum Technologist's Pocket-Book*, by I.H. Thomson and Sir Boverton Redwood, (London: 1915, C. Griffin & Co.)

Austria's Rough Industry (Die Gross Industrie Osterreichs) by Leopold Weiss (Vienna: 1898) follows the Bergheim & McGarvey company's early progress.

Details of McGarvey's progress are from a paper prepared for the scientific conference marking "140 Years of Polish Oil", delivered in Bobrka, 20 August 1993, and *The Polish Biographical Dictionary*, Vol. 13.

The creation of the limited stock company in 1895 is outlined in the articles of incorporation on file at the Austrian National Archive, Vienna, Register fur Gesellschafts-Firmen, Band LII, company records Vol. 52. The incorporation was reported in the journal *Nafta*, 15 August 1895, p. 139.

Fred McGarvey described his positions and duties with the Karpath in an ancestral memorandum he drew up in 1959. Provided by David Banting.

Details of McGarveys progress and information about his patents are from *Poland Oil History*, Vol. 1. The oil cartel, Petrolea, is described in Volume 2.

An article written by Dr. Stefan Bartoszewicz, "Memories from the Oil Industry," published in the publication *Oil Industry*, 25 February 1934, recounts McGarvey's close association and friendship with August Gorayski. Details of the creation of OLEX are reported 4 December 1910 in *Neues Wiener Journal* and 16 December 1910 in *Neues Wiener Tagblatt*.

Accounts of the 1911 fire at Glinik Mariampolski are from *Neues Wiener Tagblatt*, 28 June 1911 and *Illustrierte Kronen Zeitung*, 29 June 1911.

Hugh Nixon Shaw was overcome by fumes from his Lambton County well and fell to his death inside it. Confusion existed for many years between the unfortunate Hugh Shaw, and an unrelated man named John Shaw who brought in Oil Springs' first gusher in 1862. The confusion was ultimately sorted out by a then-M.A. student, Dana Johnson, in 2010, titled *The Shaw Investigation: A Review of Sources To Discover Who Drilled Canada's First Oil Gusher*.

The McGarvey company's employment numbers are mentioned in *The Canadian Men and Women of the Time*, first edition edited by Henry James Morgan, entry for William Henry McGarvey, (Toronto: 1898, William Briggs).

Charles Wallen's career in the Foreign Fields is from the author's interview with the late Mary Wallen of Grand Bend, Ontario, in 1998, and from an interview Charles Wallen conducted with the *London Free Press*, 15 February 1919.

Some details of McGarvey's charitable acts and contributions to his community are from a translation of *The Polish Biographical Dictionary*, Vol. 18, 1973. Various Viennese newspapers reported on McGarvey's charitable contributions.

McGarvey's links to California are noted in *Nafta*, 22 March 1906, XIV-6, and in the web-based history of the Union Oil Company of Avila Beach, California.

McGarvey's patent setback is from *Historia Polskiego Przemyseu Naftowego*.

Enquete uber die Krise in der Mineralolindustriem (Inquiry into the crisis in the oil industry), quoted by Alison Fleig Frank in "The Petroleum War of 1910," and obtained from Harvard digital library, contains information about McGarvey's thoughts on Standard Oil and the dispute that ensued. McGarvey's remarks are further reported 29 November 1910 in *Wiener Zeitung*.

Early discussions of a petroleum co-operative were reported in *Die Arbeit* newspaper, Vienna, 5 January 1902. The Karpath's annual general meeting discussions of tariffs, expanding storage facilities and building its own refinery are reported in *Kuryer Lwowski*, 7 June 1903.

For labour relations in Galicia, see "The Chaotic Saga of Oil in Galicia," by Jérome Segal and Renaud Lavergne, translated by Janice M. Sellers, first published in "L'épopée oubliée du pétrole de Galicie in *Geo-Histoire*, October/November 2012, pp. 116-127. Work stoppages are discussed in the Central State Historical Archives of Ukraine in Lviv (f. 146.4.3773: 18-20).

An explanation of the philosophy behind labour training and management techniques, including the provision of health care and establishment of common wage rates, is taken from a series of articles in the Oil Workers files of the Gorlice Public Library.

The story of the Apollo refineries and McGarvey's leading role in modernizing and centralizing refinery operations is compiled from: "Death of W.H. McGarvey," *The Oil and Gas Journal*, 17 December 1914; *Petroleum* magazine, No. 4, 1914, p. 170; the internet-based "Slovnaft: Establishment of the Refinery Apollo;" *Polish Biographical Dictionary*, 1973; *Oil History*, Vol. 2, p. 411; and the internet-based history of the Deutsche BP Aktiengesellschaft. McGarvey was among a group of Viennese industrialists who founded the Austrian and Hungarian Mineral Oil Products Corporation (Aktiengesellschaft für österreichische und ungarische Mineralölprodukte) which replaced an earlier cartel of refiners. The first president was the Karpath's Robert Biedermann, a close McGarvey friend.

Chapter 10

Baku: An Eventful History, by J. Henry (London: 1905, Archibald Constable & Co. Ltd.). With an introduction by Boverton Redwood, the book describes the early petroleum business in Russia.

The history of the Nobels in Russia is recounted by Robert Tolf in *The Russian Rockefellers*, (Stanford, CA: 1976, Hoover Institute Press). The book also traces the rise of the Maikop oil district after 1905.

The history of Anglo-Terek was short. Created in 1901, it was liquidated at the end of the First World War. A final meeting of the board was held November

19, 1924, in London, with Fred and Albert McGarvey presiding, according to the *Register of Defunct Companies*, (Basingstoke, UK: 1990, Macmillan Publishers).

George Tweedy's papers, housed in the London Metropolitan Archives, include a report on the Anglo-Maikop Group and are available online.

A description of the Grosny countryside comes from *Here Lies A Most Beautiful Lady*; and from Julia McGarvey's letter to friends in England. Details of the attack on the McGarveys are from an account told by James and Julia McGarvey's daughter, Mamie, and published in *The Flower of Battle: British Fiction Writers of the First World War*, (London: 1995, Hugh Cecil, Secker and Warburg). Newspaper accounts provide further details of the incident: the Toronto *Evening Telegram*, the *London Free Press* and the London *Advertiser*. Finally, more information was obtained from this author's correspondence with David Ingleby, great-grandson of James and Julia McGarvey and grandson of Julia and James's daughter, Helena "Mamie" Blaker.

Neues Wiener Tagblatt of Vienna reported on 3 July 1909 that Fred McGarvey was leaving the board of the Galician Carpathian company to take up duties in Russia. This occurred eighteen months before the assassination of his Uncle James McGarvey, leading to speculation the younger McGarvey was headed off to learn more about the Russian arm of the company he was to eventually manage.

Chapter 11

The preface McGarvey wrote is from *Oil Fields of the Empire*, by J.D. Henry. (London: 1910. Bradbury, Agnew & Co. Ltd., p. vii.)

References to McGarvey being "decorated" by Emperor Franz Josef for introducing improved oil-drilling methods can be found contemporaneous to his death in the *Fuel Oil Journal*, December 1914, and *London Free Press*, 8 December 1914, as well as in "Petrolia Boy Who Became Oil King," *Petrolia Advertiser*, 16 June 1921. Further confirmation of McGarvey's knighthood, and details of the Order of the Iron Crown, are from the Emperor Franz Josef Museum in Baden.

Bergheim's obituaries are from the periodical *Ropa*, No. 17, December 1912, p. 104, and from *Petroleum*, No. 1, 1912, p. 24. Together, they contain details of his holdings and positions as well as excellent descriptions of his other life accomplishments.

Arthur Rubinstein wrote about his experiences with the Bergheims and the McGarveys in *My Young Years*, (New York: 1973, Alfred A. Knopf); and *My Many Years*, (New York: 1980, Alfred A. Knopf).

Details of Bergheim's work in Nigeria come from research compiled by N. K. Obasi and published on onlinenigeria.com in the article "Foreign Participation in the Nigerian Oil and Gas Industry;" and from "Oil Exploration in Colonial Nigeria," presented at XIV International Economic History Congress, Helsinki, 2006, Session 11.

The story of Bergheim and the tea tannins is from the author's correspondence with Sonia Lindsay of Holmes Farm, Hatherleigh, Okehampton, Devon, UK, 2 November 2008.

Chapter 12

McGarvey outlined his views on oil and security in the preface to *Oil Fields of the Empire*, by J.D. Henry. (London, 1910. Bradbury, Agnew & Co. Ltd.)

Reports, memoranda, evidence and proceedings of the Royal Commission on Fuel and Engines, 1912-14, are maintained at the Public Record Office of the UK, ADM 116/1208-09 and ADM 265/32-38. Besides the testimony, these records also confirm that the McGarveys were in London for Bergheim's funeral and that they agreed to present their opinions prior to the date of the commission opening its proceedings. The intention of the commission managers to utilize Bergheim's expertise in a key role is from his obituary published in *Petroleum* (No. 1, 1912, p. 24).

Churchill's correspondence with Lord Fisher and their opinions of the political situation are from *Winston S. Churchill*, by Randolph S. Churchill, companion vol. ii, Part 3, 1911-1914.

Germany and the Next War is translated by Allen H. Powles (New York: Longmans, Greens, and Co., 1914.)

The report of the coal fire's part in the sinking of the *Titanic* is from research conducted by engineers for the Imperial College of London report, *What Really Sank the Titanic?* and reported on in the BBC film, *Titanic: The New Evidence*, broadcast on UK Channel 4 on 1 January 2017.

A biographical sketch of McGarvey from *The Canadian Men and Women of the Time*, second edition, 1912, mentions the size of McGarvey's workforce. Further numbers for Russia were mentioned by his brother, Albert, in an article written while he was visiting London, Ontario in 1915.

Details of early work in the Athabaska oil sands come from the author's correspondence with Calgary author Joyce Hunt, as well as from her book, *Local Push — Global Pull: The Untold Story of the Athabaska Oil Sands* (Calgary: 2012, Pushpull Limited).

Chapter 13

A report about McGarvey's seventieth birthday party at Hotel Metropole is translated from the journal *Nafta*, Lviv , 30 November 1913, Notebook No. 22.

The purchase of William and Fred McGarvey's Rolls-Royce cars is chronicled in *Allgemeine Automobil-Zeitung (Automobile Newspaper)* in issues from October 1913 to May 1914. Fred's car crash was reported in *Weiner Zeitung* and *Fremden-Blatt (Foreign Leaf*, Vienna), 31 May 1914.

Boverton Redwood's observations are from *The Petroleum Technologist's Pocket-book*.

The part oil played in early twentieth-century political and military decisions is discussed in *Moguls and Mandarins: Oil, Imperialism and the Middle East in British Foreign Policy, 1900-1940*, by Marian Kent, (London: 2013, Routledge.)

The causes of the First World War are expertly discussed in "The Great War's Ominous Echoes," by Margaret MacMillan, *New York Times*, 13 December 2013.

The text of McGarvey's letter to Sir Edward Grey and the British government is reported in *Wiener Zeitung*, 3 August 1914.

Edward Grey's part in precipitating the First World War is from *Sir Edward Grey: A Biography of Lord Grey of Fallodon*, by Keith Robbins (London: 1971, Cassell & Co. Publishers).

Moguls and Mandarins: Oil, Imperialism and the Middle East in British Foreign Policy 1900-1940, by Marian Kent (London: 2011, Routledge Publishers) explains how the need to secure oil supplies, and the ensuing search, influence British foreign policy around the Great War.

Oil production figures are from multiple newspaper accounts as well as from Boverton Redwood's research (*The Petroleum Technlogist's Pocket-Book*) and *Historia Polskiego Przemyseu Naftowego*.

McGarvey's Glinik Mariampolski (Glimar) refinery and equipment plant were taken over by Hudson Oil of Toronto which compiled details of the company history. This is contained in the company's "The History of Hudson Oil" which was available on its (now-defunct) website. The Lukasiewecz Oil and Gas Museum at Bobrka provides a history of McGarvey's Glinik Mariampolski installations in "Pioneers of the Polish Refining Industry." Further historical details are from the author's 2007 interview with Piotr Dziadzio, president of Glinik Drilling Tools and Equipment Ltd. See Appendix II for more information.

The Perkins and Nicklos families' wartime experiences, including their house arrest and the internment of son Eddie, are from materials provided by Joan Darby of Pittsburgh, PA.

Fred McGarvey recounted the party held for William's seventy-first birthday in a 5 December 1914 letter to Canadian relatives provided by the late Pete McGarvey of Orillia; further details of his death are from various published obituaries, including *Oil News* (December 1914), *Zeitschrift des Internationalen Vereines der Bohrigenieure und Bohrtechniker* (No. 24, 1914), *Petroleum* magazine (No. 4, 1914), *Neue Freie Presse* (29 November 1914), *Neues Wiener Tagblatt* (29 November 1914), *Der Morgen Wiener Montagblatt* (30 November 1914), and Wiener Zeigung (29 November 1914).

McGarvey's last will and testament was preserved by his granddaughter, Molly, and provided by David Banting.

McGarvey's funeral was reported, and some attendees listed, in *Neues Wiener Journal* on 1 December 1914.

In its McGarvey obituary obtained from the Austrian National Library, *Wiener Zeitung* newspaper reported on 28 November 1914 that he established a fund for injured Austrian soldiers. McGarvey's charitable donations, and those of his son, Fred, were earlier reported in *Neues Wiener Tagblatt* (26 August 1914) and *Neue Freie Presse* (15 September 1914).

The Austrian military authorities' treatment of suspect Galician residents, including courts-martial, executions and house arrests, is discussed in Elisabeth Haid's article, "Galicia: A Bulwark against Russia? Propaganda and Violence in a Border Region during the First World War," European Review of History, Vol. 14, 2017, Issue 2.

Chapter 14

Descriptions of the fighting in and around Glinik Mariampolski come from the mayor at the time, Father Bronislaw Swieykowski, as well as from the Malopolski Instytut Kultury.

The wartime experiences of the MacIntosh family are from diaries maintained by Frieda Erika von Espenhan MacIntosh and provided by Lorna Mays of Mississauga, ON.

A civilian's report on life in Boryslaw, Galicia, is titled "A British Eyewitness in Galicia," catalogue reference CAB 37/126/32 of the National Archives of the UK.

The Perkins family's wartime experiences are from letters and family stories provided by Joan Darby.

The selling off and closing of the Galician Carpathian Petroleum Company is described by Fred McGarvey in his ancestoral memorandum of 1959. The sale of the company and the wrapup meeting is translated from Handelsgericht Wien B75, "Gesellschafts-Register 1863-1906," Vol. 63, on file at the Wein-Archiv (Vienna Archive).

Dabrowa's relationship with the Glimar refinery is from the history of the Hudson Oil Corporation and *The History of Polish Oil*, Vol. 2.

Albert McGarvey's recruitment of workers is described in the *Petrolia Advertiser*, 13 November 1885, and 16 July 1886. The *Petrolia Topic* and the *Advertiser* frequently carried stories about trips back home by former residents living in the oil lands of Europe.

Albert McGarvey spoke to the *Chatham News* about the impact war was having on the oil business for a story published 17 July 1915.

The story of Charles Wallen and family is compiled from articles in *The London Free Press*, 15 February 1919, an interview by the author with Mrs. Mary Wallen of Grand Bend, Ontario in 1998, and details from the diaries of Frieda Erika Von Espenhan, provided by Lorna Mays of Mississauga, Ontario. Further details of Wallen's experiences are from his obituary in the *Advertiser-Topic* on 13 October 1921.

The London *Advertiser*, 12 January 1925, p. 11, and *London Free Press*, 12 January 1925, p. 3, reported on Albert McGarvey's death.

Further details of the MacIntosh family's experiences are from R. H. MacIntosh's diary, "Memories of 70-odd years," provided by Jane Day of Bury St. Edmunds, Suffolk, UK.

Chapters 15 - 17

The guestbooks kept by Fred and Madge McGarvey at Mariampol and Vienna, and by Mamie von Zeppelin at Schloss Graschnitz in Graz, Austria contain not only details of visitors and when they came and went, but also in many cases remarks about their visits. This enabled this author to track visitors, as well as dates that Fred, Madge and Mamie travelled. Family gatherings were thus recorded as were observations about what they did. Further events were recorded and observations made by relatives and friends of the McGarveys, including Fred's daughters, Leila and Molly.

Molly McGarvey kept pamphlets and reviews of her singing career in Vienna. Provided by David Banting.

Additional family details were gleaned from Sonia and Patricia Lindsay, David Banting and George Stuart.

Fred McGarvey's interactions with the Stokes & Cox agency for genealogical study is from "Pioneering Women Archivists in England"; from conversations with Slawomir Duran of Jaslo, Poland; and from documents and correspondence preserved by Fred and Molly McGarvey.

Fred McGarvey described his and Madge's 1939 trip through North Africa and Europe in his ancestral memorandum.

Fred McGarvey's participation in the Home Guard was recognized with a certificate from the British military.

Mamie von Zeppelin detailed her wartime and post-war experiences in a series of letters to Fred and Madge McGarvey and a cousin in Canada.

Beth, Dan and Carol Chew shared memories and other information about Molly and Leila McGarvey.

Mamie von Zeppelin's agreement to sell Schloss Graschnitz is contained in a letter in brother Fred McGarvey's files. That and her last will and testament were preserved by Molly.

Death certificates were used to discover causes of death.

Ron Walsh of Houston, TX wrote a letter describing his and wife Lynda's years as Molly McGarvey's neighbour in England. Provided by David Banting.

Chapter 18

Details of the experiences of the Keith and Van Sickle families are from correspondence with Mary-Jane (Keith) Selwood of Scotland; *Maclean's Magazine*, 1 June 1950; the James Van Sickle Collection from the Austrian National Archive; the Oil Museum of Canada publication, "The Sampler", Spring 2013 edition; and correspondence with James Van Sickle of Vienna.

Arnold Thompson's remarks are from an interview conducted by Sheila Rose for the Oil Museum of Canada, 16 April 1984.

Daniel Yergin's remarks about oil and history are from *The Prize*. (New York: Free Press, 1991, reprinted 2009, p. 151.)

Appendix I

The early technology of oil drilling is compiled from remarks by William McGarvey as well as from *Early Development of Oil Technology*, by Wanda

Pratt and Phil Morningstar (Oil Springs: 1987, Oil Museum of Canada), and by Willie Keith in notes provided by his daughter, Mary-Jane Selwood. "A Driller's Sixth Sense" is taken from *Oil and Gas Review* of 1923.

Appendix II

Hudson Oil Ltd. of Toronto detailed the later history of the McGarvey refinery and factory. Other details are from the Glinik manufacturing plant Narzedzia I Urzadzenia Wiertnicze (NiUW Glinik), and the factory's president, Piotr Dziadzio.

INDEX

Note that communities in Galicia are designated in parentheses with their current country, either Poland or Ukraine